Intermediate Accounting
DeMYSTiFieD®

DeMYSTiFieD® Series

The Demystified Series publishes over 125 titles in all areas of academic study. For a complete list of titles, please visit www.mhprofessional.com.

Intermediate
Accounting
DeMYSTiFieD®

Geri B. Wink
Laurie Corradino

New York   Chicago   San Francisco   Lisbon   London   Madrid   Mexico City
New Delhi   San Juan   Seoul   Singapore   Sydney   Toronto

The McGraw·Hill Companies

Copyright © 2011 by The McGraw-Hill Companies, Inc. All rights reserved. Printed in the
United States of America. Except as permitted under the United States Copyright Act of
1976, no part of this publication may be reproduced or distributed in any form or by any
means, or stored in a database or retrieval system, without the prior written permission of
the publisher.

1 2 3 4 5 6 7 8 9 10   QFR/QFR   1 9 8 7 6 5 4 3 2 1 0

ISBN   978-0-07-173885-9
MHID   0-07-173885-1

This publication is designed to provide accurate and authoritative information in regard to
the subject matter covered. It is sold with the understanding that neither the author nor the
publisher is engaged in rendering legal, accounting, securities trading, or other professional
services. If legal advice or other expert assistance is required, the services of a competent
professional person should be sought.

*—From a Declaration of Principles Jointly Adopted by a Committee of the American Bar
Association and a Committee of Publishers and Associations*

Library of Congress Cataloging-in-Publication Data

Wink, Geri B.
    Intermediate accounting demystified / by Geri B. Wink, Laurie Corradino.
       p.   cm.
    Includes index.
    ISBN 978-0-07-173885-9 (alk. paper)
    1. Accounting. I. Corradino, Laurie. II. Title.
    HF5636.W74   2011
    657'.044—dc22   2010029854

Trademarks: McGraw-Hill, the McGraw-Hill Publishing logo, DeMystified®, and related
trade dress are trademarks or registered trademarks of The McGraw-Hill Companies and/
or its affiliates in the United States and other countries and may not be used without
written permission. All other trademarks are the property of their respective owners.
The McGraw-Hill Companies is not associated with any product or vendor mentioned
in this book.

McGraw-Hill books are available at special quantity discounts to use as premiums and sales
promotions or for use in corporate training programs. To contact a representative, please
e-mail us at bulksales@mcgraw-hill.com.

This book is printed on acid-free paper.

Geri:
To my parents, Bess C. and Marvin J. Bridges,
I wish you were here to celebrate this accomplishment with me.
I love you and miss you.

Laurie:
To my grandfather, Tony Burrescia. Who would have thought
I would ever coauthor a book? I wish you were here to read it and
celebrate this feat with me. Thanks Papa Tony for everything.
I am sure you are looking down from heaven and smiling. Love you always.

About the Authors

Geri B. Wink is a lecturer in accounting at the Hasan School of Business, Colorado State University–Pueblo. She is a Certified Public Accountant in both Colorado and Texas. She has previously been a lecturer at the University of Texas at Tyler and has worked professionally as a financial analyst, auditor, and tax preparer. She has taught intermediate accounting for most of her teaching career. Her work has been published in *Oil and Gas Quarterly* and *The Management Accountant*, and *Allied Academies' Journal of the International Academy for Case Studies*, and she has received a Distinguished Research Award. She has held officer positions in the Southeast Chapter of the Colorado Society of Certified Public Accountants (CSCPA) and is currently a trustee on the Educational Foundation of the CSCPA.

Laurie Corradino is in her last semester of the MBA program at Colorado State University–Pueblo. She has sat for and passed all four sections of the Uniform CPA Exam and is currently teaching an advanced financial accounting course and an accounting information systems class at the university. Her work has been published in *Allied Academies' Journal of the International Academy for Case Studies*, and she has received a Distinguished Research Award. Currently, she is a student member of the American Institute of Certified Public Accountants, the Colorado Society of Certified Public Accountants, and the Public Accountants Society of Colorado.

Contents

Part V   The Statement of Cash Flows—Where's the Cash?   297

Acknowledgments

From Geri

The very first person for me to thank for this book is Marc Petros. Without his idea for this book, it never would have been started, much less completed. Thank you, Marc, for your wonderful recognition of a need in this area of accounting.

The next person I would like to thank is my coauthor, Laurie. Your creative writing skills are amazing! I appreciate your patience and perseverance throughout this project. Without you, this book would not exist. I value the friendship we have cultivated.

There were many former students who have asked, "Why don't you write a book? You make the material so much simpler than the other authors." To all of you, thanks for the encouragement, and here it is.

Thank you to my sons, Benton and Prentice, for all the encouraging comments you have given me, such as "What do you mean you haven't been working on the book?" and "Have you worked on the book this week?" as well as "Good job, glad to hear you have been working on the book." A big thank you to my friend, Michael, who provided encouragement and a peaceful place to work on the book while watching the deer roam or the snow fall in his backyard.

The thanks would not be complete without thanking our editor, Brian Foster. It has been a pleasure working with you and McGraw-Hill.

And last, but certainly not least, is a big thanks to God for combining our technical knowledge, teaching skills, and creative writing abilities to make this book a reality.

From Laurie

There are so many to thank. First, Marc. As Geri said, without your suggestion, we never would have written this book. Thanks for proposing the idea and helping us get started.

To my parents, Larry and Pam, thank you for being so supportive throughout the writing of this book. I'm sorry I had to ditch you again for one of my "projects." Thanks for offering calming words when I needed them most and for being among my first problem solvers; you both did a great job! By the way, I do appreciate you lifting the heavy snow that week when I was focused on words and numbers. To my grandparents, thank you for all the support and encouragement. It was a crazy year in so many ways, and I am so thankful for you all!

To my coauthor, Geri, thank you so much for providing me with this wonderful opportunity and always believing in my abilities. Sitting in your intermediate class just a few years ago, never would have I dreamed that we would again delve into this material together. Thanks for putting up with my need to stay on schedule even when we missed some great kayaking and biking weather. I appreciate your friendship, kind words, and constant encouragement, even though you don't want to be one of my students. I am amazed at what we have accomplished. I hope that you had as much fun as I did!

To the handful of other teachers who have provided me with the knowledge to understand this material, the means to relay it effectively to others, and the encouragement to, yes, enjoy accounting. I appreciate all of your hard work, and hopefully this book is a testament to the efforts you have exerted. Some have told me that I should write, and yet, accounting is my passion; this book represents a happy middle between the two.

To my friends, both accounting fans and those who, after reading this book, soon will be, thanks for expressing an interest in this book and constantly inquiring about it. To the rest of you who are reading this, thanks for purchasing the book and letting us help you to understand and enjoy accounting on a new level. To Brian Foster and McGraw-Hill, thank you for offering us the chance to write this book and making it a joy to work with you. Finally, thank you Lord for orchestrating the sequence of events that allowed the people involved in this publication to come together and for giving us the strength to complete it successfully.

Introduction

We are extremely glad that you have chosen to accompany us on this journey through intermediate accounting. Whether intermediate accounting is currently part of your college curriculum or is somehow a piece of your past or you are hoping that the subject matter can be a part of your future in terms of a job or schooling, this book is certainly for you.

Intermediate accounting has and probably always will be known as the "weed out" class for accounting majors. In both a student and instructor or tutoring capacity, we have seen the intermediate accounting "monster" scare off more students than we care to mention. If accounting is something you really want to do, though, we do not want that to be you. This is one of the reasons that we have created this book.

We both fondly remember our intermediate classes. The oodles of homework, the long hours of reading, the punching of calculators or pressing down on pencils so hard that they almost broke, and even the dreadful exams all represented some of the best days of our college careers. Why, you ask? Because it was in this class that we knew for sure that accounting was our thing, our forte and passion, if you will. At the end, those A's really meant something to us, and we were proud to have survived the "beast." We were from that moment on truly accounting majors. We want you to have just as positive and memorable experiences as we did.

Of course, we also remember sitting in a classroom listening to what sometimes seemed like a talking head telling us how important everything was to know. In this book, we hope to perform a similar feat but also explain *why* everything is so important while providing instructions in a simpler manner than is found in a regular textbook. This is our first attempt at this, so let us know how well we did!

How to Use This Book

Accounting, just the name is intimidating, right? Well, at least we don't have to work at scaring you; that task is likely already accomplished. Don't be frightened, though. With a little help from this book and a moderate level of effort on your part, you will be just fine! Of course, you may need to brush up on some math skills and jog your memory a bit regarding the information about debits, credits, and normal balances that you gleaned from your principles class. We would say that those two items are key to being successful in learning intermediate accounting; everything else just requires a little bit of time and a willingness to learn.

So what exactly besides our lecture content can you find in this book? Well, the book contains over 150 multiple-choice quiz questions very similar in nature to what can be found on a standardized test or a chapter quiz in an accounting textbook. The quizzes are designed to test your understanding of the material presented in each chapter. We have tried to include an even mix of both conceptual and mathematical-based questions because without the theory, the math makes no sense, and without the math, the theory cannot be applied properly. Additionally, while most of the questions are not nearly as in-depth as those presented on the CPA exam, this book still is a good prep for understanding the financial accounting concepts that are heavily tested. At the end of the book, 100 of those multiple-choice questions again appear randomly as part of the final exam. The final exam is a true test of how much you have learned and, more important, retained as a result of reading and working with us from cover to cover.

How should you approach the quiz questions? After reading a chapter, look over the quiz questions, and try to answer as many as you can from memory. If you are unable to remember a concept, journal entry, or mathematical technique needed to complete a quiz question, we encourage you to review the appropriate chapter sections as many times as necessary and to work some or all of the examples provided throughout the chapters. All the quiz questions cover topics and procedures presented in the book, so you should be able to easily find something to help you. Once you have answered all the questions to your satisfaction, check the answers in the back of the book to see how well you have done. Look over the questions you missed, and make sure that you understand why you missed those particular problems. Reread the chapter if necessary, and continue to work both the example and quiz problems. Remember, practice makes perfect. Once you feel confident that you can answer all the questions correctly and know why you are choosing a particular answer, it is likely time to move on to the next chapter.

What about the final exam? Well, the final exam is a different type of beast. First, it is should be taken closed-book. Second, it is comprehensive.

What most people do not realize is that every topic in accounting builds on a previous topic. Therefore, a comprehensive test, to the dread of most students, is only appropriate. It is simply not enough to know just a few chapters; to really say that you have studied and understand intermediate accounting, you need to be able to do it all. For the final exam, we suggest that you take a blank sheet of paper (scratch paper will do) and write down your answers on that sheet. You can work the questions in sections or all at once; it doesn't matter. Sometimes, though, it may boost your self-esteem to know that you have gotten seven or eight of those ten problems you worked correct. At the end of your self-designated section or on completion of all the questions, check your answers with those in the back of the book. How well did you do? Similar to a school grading system, if you manage to get 90 or more questions correct, you have done excellent work and really know the material; 80 to 89 correct answers is above average, so you may need only a little bit more work; 70 to 79 correct answers is simply average, so work at it some more; and anything below 70 correct answers is poor, and we suggest that you revisit many of the chapters that appear to be troubling you. Really, our goal is to see at least 75 correct answers from each one of you on your first try! Remember, practice makes perfect. While we don't want you to just memorize answers, we do want you to be able to learn from your mistakes, so after you finish the exam, go back and look at the questions you missed, and revisit the corresponding chapters. Hopefully, this will help, and you will be less inclined to make the same mistakes again.

As for the time necessary to complete this book, that likely will depend on you and the level of previous training you have had in this area. If you are using the book as a supplement to an intermediate text that you are currently using for a class, we suggest that you complete the chapters in this book concurrently with the related chapters in your text. If you have completed an intermediate class and are just using this book as a quick brush-up, a day or two per chapter, depending on your available time, should be sufficient. Of course, if you have never before been immersed in intermediate accounting, you will need to take a bit more time with each chapter. A week should do it, but again, this depends on how much time you have available. The key to remember is that you do not want to speed through any of the material, but you also want to ensure completion within a few months; if you spread it out too long, you likely will never complete it! Finally, we cannot stress enough the importance of good study habits. Your study habits can either make or break you when it comes to accounting!

We hope that these tips have been helpful and are excited that you have chosen to join us on this journey.

Part I

The Balance Sheet: Assets—What Do I Own?

chapter 1

Cash and Accounts Receivable

CHAPTER OBJECTIVES

After completing this chapter, the student should

- Understand the financial statement presentation for cash and accounts receivable
- Know what is included in and excluded from cash
- Account for petty cash transactions
- Complete a bank reconciliation
- Account for the direct write-off method
- Account for the allowance method using both the balance sheet and the income statement approaches
- Understand internal controls over cash and accounts receivable transactions

Overview

BLP, Inc., a newly established local wholesaler of clothing, has just opened a bank account. The funds received by the company from sales and other revenue sources will be placed into that depository. Those funds, along with money that

3

is on hand at any given point in time, comprise BLP's *cash*. Because the company plans on offering its customers the option of making their purchases on account, some goods will be sold without any immediate inflow of cash. To recognize that sale, however, an asset still will be recorded on BLP's books. That asset, known as *accounts receivable*, will reflect the sales price of inventory that has been sold and that is expected to be realized in a short period of time, usually within a month.

And with this foundation, welcome to the exciting world of intermediate accounting. Yes, we know that the name and subject matter may seem frightening, but we also remember being in your shoes once, so do not fret. Whether you are taking an intermediate class and are using this book as a supplement, are just trying to learn a bit more about accounting, or are one of those crazy people like us who really do enjoy playing with all these numbers, this book is sure to help you to understand accounting beyond the principles level. Intermediate accounting is all about new accounts and rules, so do not expect it to be as simple as cash and accounts receivable. Like life, there are always complications and exceptions to the rules, and with those exceptions come new accounts, so be prepared throughout this book to become friends with a whole new crew (of accounts, that is—we can help you with numbers; as for your social life, that is entirely up to you).

To help you better understand all those accounts and their relationships, we will begin each chapter with a discussion of financial statement presentation. You would not set out on a trip to a new location without some specific directions, so why do that with accounting? Consider the financial statements to be your road map. Once you know where you are going, you can plan your trip much better.

What will make your journey easier? Remember, we said *easier*, not easy. Undoubtedly, the best advice we can provide is that you need to understand the ins and outs of every account. What exactly do we mean? You need to know an account's normal balance as well as the ways to increase or decrease its balance. In order to make this a bit easier and to refresh your memory from principles, we have prepared a chart in Appendix A that we hope you will find helpful. Appendix A lists each account discussed in this book by chapter along with its normal balance and financial statement classification. Remember that you always increase an account with its normal balance and decrease with the opposite balance. For example, cash has a normal debit balance, so to increase cash, you debit the account, and to decrease cash, you credit the account.

Financial Statement Presentation

Cash and accounts receivable are presented on the balance sheet in current assets. Both accounts have normal debit balances. Remember that current assets are listed in their order of liquidity. This therefore reserves the top seat for cash. Because there are some short-term investments (cash equivalents) that can be converted into cash within a very short period of time, usually three months or less, cash and cash equivalents are often listed together as one account. Immediately following cash is the next most liquid asset, accounts receivable.

So what are the "personalities" of cash and accounts receivable? In other words, what do you need to specifically know about them? First, there are four items you need to understand about cash: what can be considered cash, what *cannot* be considered cash, how a petty-cash system works, and how to reconcile the cash account with the bank account to arrive at the true cash balance presented on the balance sheet.

Cash

Cash Includes

Cash usually consists of

- Coins
- Currency
- Traveler's checks
- Negotiable checks
- Bank drafts
- Any unrestricted funds that are on deposit in the bank

Cash Exclusions

While they may seem like cash, the following items are not included as cash (and their proper classification is noted in parentheses):

- Certificates of deposit (short-term receivables)
- Bank overdrafts (current liabilities)
- Postdated checks (accounts receivable)
- Travel advances (prepaid expenses)
- IOUs (accounts receivable)
- Postage stamps (prepaid expenses)

Petty Cash

A petty cash account is used for small, frequent expenditures. It is likely that most of you have used a petty cash system at some point during your lives in the various companies for which you have worked. Use of a petty cash system is not restricted to any size or type of firm. In fact, it is more uncommon for a company not to have a petty cash reserve than it is for it to have one. The money that your boss hands you to go pick up an ink cartridge at the local office supply store and the cash that you use to buy a package of postage stamps for the office both traditionally come from a petty cash fund. So what is the main distinction between petty cash and cash? Well, petty cash is a minimal amount of money that is kept on hand and used usually for small miscellaneous purchases. There are only three journal entries that affect the actual petty cash account:

- When it is *established*, debit *petty cash* and credit cash,
- When it is *increased*, debit *petty cash* and credit cash.
- When it is *decreased*, debit cash and credit *petty cash*.

So how does this whole system work? First, take a check to your local bank and obtain the funds to place in the petty cash drawer. As money is removed from the drawer to pay for small expenditures, place the receipts for such expenditures in the drawer. At all times, the receipts plus the cash in the drawer should equal the amount in the petty cash account. Again, life is not perfect, and for whatever reason, sometimes the two do not balance. When the drawer is replenished and that occurs, an additional account, cash short and over, needs to be used. But a little bit more about that later.

Replenishment

At the time of replenishment, another journal entry is required. You must determine the total cash in the drawer and subtract that amount from the total in the petty cash account. The difference will be the credit to cash and the amount of cash you will obtain from the bank to replenish petty cash. You will create a debit entry to correspond to each of the receipts in the drawer, and book the uses of the funds to the appropriate expense accounts. Remember that cash short and over account we mentioned a while ago? If the debits do not equal the credits, then that account is used to achieve the balance. At the end of the year, if cash short and over has a net debit balance, it is reflected as a miscellaneous expense on the income statement. Alternatively, if cash short and over has a net credit balance, it is reflected as a miscellaneous revenue on the income statement.

 EXAMPLE 1-1

BLP, Inc., established a petty cash account on February 1 with $200. During the month of February, the following expenditures were paid out of the petty cash drawer:

Postage	$55
Coffee supplies	$23
Office supplies	$48

When the time came to replenish the drawer at the end of February, a count of cash indicated that there was $75 in the drawer. Because the full $200 was not used during February, the company decided to decrease the petty cash fund to $175 on February 28. The following journal entries should be made:

February 1:

Petty cash	200	
Cash		200

February 28:

Postage expense	55	
Coffee supplies expense	23	
Office supplies expense	48	
Cash		125
Cash short and over		1

February 28:

Cash	25	
Petty cash		25

Bank Reconciliations

Bank reconciliations are extremely important. We are always amazed at the number of people who readily admit to not reconciling their bank accounts, especially today, when online banking is so easily accessible. You might even be one of those people. Hopefully, you are not, but if you are, we hope that after reading this section, you will realize how easy the process really is and next time actually match up your bank statement with your checkbook rather than throwing the statement in the junk pile for perusal months later.

Bank reconciliations are an essential piece of the internal control over cash, both personally and professionally. The objective of the bank reconciliation is to compute the true cash balance that will be reflected on the balance sheet as of a particular date. The balance in the general ledger for the cash account will seldom equal the bank's balance. There can be many reasons for this difference. Sometimes the bank is aware of items that the company is not yet aware of. Examples include

- A service charge on the bank account
- A note receivable the bank collected for the company
- Interest earned on the bank account
- An error made by the bank

When such items are present, the company will need to make a journal entry to record those items in the company's books. For example, banks often charge various fees related to checking accounts. While some fees are explicit and regular, others, such as charges for overdrafts on an account, may be a complete surprise to you because you may not have realized that you have overdrawn your account. Additionally, suppose that you enlist your bank's help to collect a note receivable from a stubborn customer. The bank will know about the collection before you do. As a result, the amount of the note receivable must be added to the balance in the business's checking account records. If the checking account bears interest, you may find that the money on deposit has earned some interest that also must be added to the company's balance.

Other times the company is aware of items that the bank is not yet aware of. Examples include

- Deposits in transit that have been recorded in the books but have not yet cleared the bank

- Outstanding checks that have been recorded in the books but have not yet cleared the bank

- Errors made in the company's books

For example, you may make a deposit on February 28, but the deposit may not be fully processed by the bank until March. February's bank statement would omit the deposit, even though you know those funds are in the bank. The amount of the deposit, therefore, must be added to the bank's balance. Alternatively, you may write a check to a vendor for some supplies purchased during the month. However the vendor is not as business wise as you and tends to wait a long time before cashing the check. In this case, the deductions from your cash balance are not reflected on the bank statement even though you know that they will be taken out of your account at some point soon. The amount of all such outstanding checks must be subtracted from the bank's balance.

Again, all these items will appear on the bank reconciliation. The bank will not let the company adjust the bank's books! After the true cash balance has been determined by the bank reconciliation, remember to make an adjusting entry to get the general ledger cash account to equal the true cash balance. This figure will be reported on the balance sheet.

EXAMPLE 1-2

BLP, Inc., has the following information available on March 31:

- Balance per books is $100,299.

- Balance per bank is $98,428.

- The deposits in transit are $3,058.

- **The monthly service charge is $50.**
- **The outstanding checks total $1,237.**

The bank reconciliation would appear as in Table 1-1.

TABLE 1-1 March Bank Reconciliation for BLP, Inc.	
Balance per books	100,299
Less: Service charge	(50)
True cash balance	100,249
Balance per bank	98,428
Add: Deposit in transit	3,058
Less: Outstanding checks	(1,237)
True cash balance	100,249

Now that cash has stolen the spotlight, it is time to move on to accounts receivable. Similar to cash, we will discuss some general information regarding accounts receivable, the financial statement presentation for accounts receivable, the direct write-off method for bad debts, and the allowance method for writing off bad debts.

Accounts Receivable

General Information

Historical cost is the generally accepted accounting principle (GAAP) used to record assets and liabilities on the balance sheet; however, the accounting for accounts receivable is an exception to the general rule. Accounts receivable are reported at net realizable value (NRV), which is more conservative than reporting accounts receivable at gross.

For example, you might sell $1,500 worth of merchandise on account. While you would like to collect that full amount, there is a chance that you will not. Because you cannot guarantee to actually have the full $1,500 flow into your business, you need to reduce that amount through the use of a bad debt account. The bad debt account allows you to not overstate your assets and thus be more conservative. Therefore, rather than $1,500, the actual accounts receivable may be recorded at $1,200 ($1,500 × 0.8), which assumes that 20 percent of the outstanding amount will not be collected. The $1,500 is the gross amount and the $1,200 is the NRV.

Several new accounts are presented in this section. The new accounts are

Account	Normal Balance	Financial Statement Classification
Allowance for bad debts	Credit	Contra to accounts receivable in current assets on the balance sheet
Bad debt expense	Debit	Operating expense on the income statement
Sales	Credit	Revenue on the income statement

Financial Statement Presentation

The GAAP financial statement presentation of accounts receivable appears as follows:

> Accounts receivable, gross
> Less: Allowance for bad debts
> Accounts receivable, NRV

So, based on our preceding example with gross accounts receivable of $1,500 and an allowance for bad debts of $300, the balance sheet presentation would appear as follows:

Accounts receivable	$1,500
Less: Allowance for bad debts	(300)
Accounts receivable, net	$1,200

Direct Write-Off Method

Two methods are used to account for the bad debts a company will experience. The first method is called the *direct write-off method*. It is not GAAP because it provides for matching of current year sales with prior year bad debt expenses. The direct write-off method can be used only when the bad debt expense of a company is immaterial. It is often used by companies because it is the only method allowed by the Internal Revenue Service (IRS).

There are three journal entries associated with the direct write-off method:

- *Record the initial sale:* Debit accounts receivable, and credit sales.

- *Write off an account that is not expected to be paid:* Debit bad debt expense, and credit accounts receivable.

- *Record the collection of an account that was previously written off by making two entries:* First, the account must be put back on the books by debiting accounts receivable and crediting bad debt expense. Second, the receipt of cash is recorded by debiting cash and crediting accounts receivable. This provides a complete audit trail of the transaction.

EXAMPLE 1-3

During the current year, BLP, Inc., had total sales of $1 million. The company also determined that three former customers were not able to pay their bills because they had each entered bankruptcy proceedings. The total of the three bad debt accounts was $1,500; however, in December of the current year, one of the three did pay its $400 bill. The journal entries that would be made are as follows:

During the year:

Accounts receivable	1,000,000	
Sales		1,000,000

December 31:

Bad debt expense	1,500	
Accounts receivable		1,500

December 31:

Accounts receivable	400	
Bad debt expense		400
Cash	400	
Accounts receivable		400

Allowance Method

The second method is called the *allowance* (or *estimation*) *method*. Because it provides for matching of current year sales with current year bad debt expenses, it is considered GAAP.

There are four journal entries associated with the allowance method:

- *Record the initial sale:* Debit accounts receivable, and credit sales.

- *Record the estimate of bad debts at year end:* Debit bad debt expense, and credit allowance for bad debts (or allowance for doubtful accounts).

- *Write off an account that is not expected to be paid:* Debit allowance for bad debts, and credit accounts receivable.

- *Record the collection of an account that was previously written off by making two entries:* First, the account must be put back on the books by debiting accounts receivable and crediting allowance for bad debts. Second, the receipt of cash is recorded by debiting cash and crediting accounts receivable.

For the allowance method, the focus is computing the dollar amount for the estimate of bad debts in the second journal entry. There are two approaches for this computation: an income statement approach and a balance sheet approach.

Allowance Method Income Statement Approach

The first method is the *income statement approach*. If you are presented with information regarding bad debts as a percentage of either total sales or net credit sales, you are using the income statement approach. Performing the computation will allow you to determine the journal entry amount. Do not be fooled! Whatever your result, this will be the amount of the entry. No adjustments are made for the previous balance in the allowance for bad debt account.

 EXAMPLE 1-4

During the current year, BLP, Inc., had total sales of $1 million, of which net credit sales were $825,000. As of December 31, the gross amount of accounts receivable was $130,000, and the allowance for bad debts had a credit balance of $1,300. The company estimates its bad debt expense at 3 percent of net credit sales. The journal entry to record the bad debt expense would appear as follows:

December 31:

Bad debt expense (825,000 × 0.03)	24,750	
Allowance for bad debts		24,750

Note: The number you computed was the journal entry amount, and you did not take into account the previous balance in the allowance account.

Allowance Method Balance Sheet Approach

The balance sheet approach works almost the same. You will be given information that the bad debt expense is expected to be a percentage of outstanding accounts receivable, or you will be asked to complete an aging schedule of accounts receivable. Either way, the number computed is the *required credit balance* in the allowance for bad debt account. To compute the journal entry amount, you must take into consideration the previous balance in the allowance for bad debt account.

 **EXAMPLE 1-5**

During the current year, BLP, Inc., had total sales of $1 million, of which net credit sales were $825,000. As of December 31, the gross amount of accounts receivable was $130,000, and the allowance for bad debts had a credit balance of $1,300. The company estimates its bad debt expense at

3 percent of outstanding gross accounts receivable. The journal entry to record the bad debt expense would be as follows:

December 31:

Bad debt expense (130,000 × 0.03 – 1,300)   2,600

                Allowance for bad debts   2,600

Note: **The number you computed was the required credit balance in the allowance account, and you did take into account the previous balance in the allowance account.**

Internal Controls

In general, the purposes of internal controls are to safeguard the company's assets, provide for accurate and reliable accounting records, provide for operational efficiency, and enhance adherence to managerial policies. Controls help to protect a company from risks and ensure that the objectives of the company can be achieved.

No company wants to be the victim of fraud or other misappropriation of assets. In recent years, internal control has become an even more important issue as a result of scandals plaguing the news. As society becomes less and less ethical, the need for better controls increases.

Some categories of internal controls include:

- Establishment of responsibility
- Segregation of duties (authorization, custody, and recordkeeping)
- Documentation procedures
- Physical, mechanical, and electronic controls
- Independent internal verification
- Other controls

Establishment of Responsibility and Segregation of Duties

The credit department should approve credit policies and determine customers' eligibility to charge on company credit. Unfortunately, not everyone and not all companies are creditworthy. Therefore, the credit department must be responsible for approving customer credit before a sale on account can occur. The individual representing the credit department must be distinct from the salesperson as well as the individual who records the sale in the company's books.

Additionally, checks cannot be issued randomly. If they were, anyone could pay for personal purchases using company funds. Therefore, the treasurer normally has the responsibility for signing outgoing checks, and he or she signs the checks only after they have been approved and verified with related documents. All authorizations should be completed by someone who does not have recordkeeping or custody duties.

Documentation Procedures and Physical, Mechanical, and Electronic Controls

As part of documentation procedures, a company should ensure that all check numbers are accounted for. Along these same lines, for all expenditures other than petty cash transactions, checks should be used so that a proper audit trail can be maintained. For further control, when opening the mail, cash receipts should be counted, any checks received should be restrictively endorsed, and a list of payments received should be provided to the cashier and to the accounts receivable department. Deposits should be made daily with prenumbered deposit slips. All such deposit slips must be accounted for. Unused checks should be kept in a locked facility, with access given only to those authorized to write checks. In order to reduce the handling of cash by company personnel, a company may use lockboxes in which customers remit payments directly to a bank, and the bank then records the payments by customers and notifies the company of the receipts. A final control involves ensuring that an invoice is not paid twice. After an invoice has been paid, it should be canceled by marking it "PAID" or punching a hole in the invoice to designate that the payment has already been remitted.

Independent Internal Verification

Independent internal verification requires that an unrelated internal party ensures that activities are carried out properly and transactions are recorded accurately. As one internal measure, bank reconciliations should be prepared on a regular basis. Similar reconciliations could include the treasurer reconciling the daily credit receipts log with the deposits for the same period and reconciling the accounts receivable control account with subsidiary accounts.

In this chapter we introduced you to some key points concerning cash and accounts receivable, including the methods available to account for uncollectible accounts. In addition, we provided some pointers for bank reconciliation preparation and setting up proper internal controls. Chapter 2 will examine the account usually listed as the third current asset—inventories.

QUIZ

1. Accounts receivable has a normal _____ balance, and you can decrease the account by _____ it.
   A. credit; crediting
   B. credit; debiting
   C. debit; crediting
   D. debit; debiting

2. All the following are considered cash *except*
   A. bank drafts.
   B. traveler's checks.
   C. coins.
   D. postdated checks.

3. Mulligan, Inc., established a petty cash account on February 10, 2010, in the amount of $150. During the remainder of the month, the following small expenditures were made by the company: office supplies, $25; break-room refreshments $15; and postage, $45. At the end of the month, $63 remained in the petty cash drawer. Based on this information, the cash short and over account will have which of the following balances?
   A. $2 credit balance
   B. $2 debit balance
   C. $20 debit balance
   D. A cash short and over account is not needed.

4. When performing a bank reconciliation, which of the following should be added to the bank's balance to reconcile it to the balance per the books?
   A. Interest earned on the account
   B. A service charge on the account
   C. Deposits in transit
   D. A debt the bank collected on behalf of the company

5. Pearson Company prepared its bank reconciliation at the end of the period. Given the following information and provided that the account is the only source of cash for the company, what amount should be recorded as cash on the balance sheet as of the period end? Cash balance per the bank statement, $83,500; deposits in transit, $1,600; outstanding checks, $1,250; $100 bank service charge; and $350 interest earned during the period.
   A. $84,100
   B. $83,850
   C. $83,500
   D. $83,750

6. Under the direct write-off method of accounting for accounts receivable, which of the following represents the journal entry that would be made to write off an account that is not expected to be paid?

    A. Debit bad debt expense and credit allowance for bad debts.
    B. Debit accounts receivable and credit bad debt expense.
    C. Debit bad debt expense and credit accounts receivable.
    D. Debit allowance for bad debt expense and credit accounts receivable.

7. L&P, Inc., accounts for its bad debts using the allowance method. On December 31, the company had gross accounts receivable recorded on its books of $25,870. On that date, the allowance for bad debts account had a credit balance of $450. During the year, the company had $100,000 in sales. Bad debts are calculated as 5 percent of net credit sales. What entry needs to be made to the allowance for bad debts account to record this information?

    A. A credit entry for $5,000
    B. A credit entry for $4,550
    C. A credit entry for $5,450
    D. A debit entry for $5,450

8. Burrs Company accounts for its bad debts using the allowance method. On December 31, the company had gross accounts receivable recorded on its books of $200,000. On that date, the allowance for bad debts accounts had a credit balance of $22,000. During the year, the company had $500,000 in sales. Bad debts are calculated as 5 percent of outstanding accounts receivable. What entry needs to be made to the allowance for bad debts account to record this information?

    A. A credit entry for $10,000
    B. A debit entry for $32,000
    C. A credit entry for $25,000
    D. A credit entry for $32,000

9. An individual responsible for recording a check received in the mail should not also perform which of the following tasks?

    A. Record a payable owed for inventory purchased from a vendor
    B. Prepare payroll checks
    C. Decide what checking account the funds will be deposited into
    D. Open the mail in which the check was received

10. On the balance sheet, assets are listed _____.

    A. in order of increasing magnitude
    B. in order of liquidity
    C. in order of decreasing magnitude
    D. alphabetically

chapter *2*

Inventory

CHAPTER OBJECTIVES

After completing this chapter, the student should

- Understand the financial statement presentation for inventories
- Account for inventories using the periodic system
- Account for inventories using the perpetual system
- Understand and account for four different cost flow assumptions for inventories
- Compute ending inventory using the dollar value LIFO method
- Understand the lower of cost or market method
- Compute ending inventory and cost of goods sold using two estimation methods
- Account for errors
- Understand internal controls over inventories

Overview

Have you ever really thought about all those items sitting on the shelves as you walk down each aisle of your local grocery store? How about the cars sitting on the lot of the dealership that you pass by each day on your way to work? What do those two seemingly very different situations have in common? In both cases, you are viewing inventory. That's right, you are exposed to hundreds, thousands, and sometimes even millions of dollars worth of inventory every day. That inventory represents an opportunity for its owner to benefit in the future, but only if and when the goods are actually sold. Just like you, businesses do not want to get stuck holding onto something that is of no value to them, so they will rely on eye-pleasing displays and incentives to persuade you to buy their products. We bet that you had no clue that accounting was the culprit of the lack of money in your pocketbook, did you?

Financial Statement Presentation

So those cans of soup on the shelf and Mercedes on the lot are each a part of their companies' inventories and, as inventories, are presented on the balance sheet under the classification of *current assets*. Considered to be less liquid than cash and accounts receivable, they are listed after both those other types of assets. While we have already described one type of business that uses inventories, a merchandising firm, there is another that holds a different kind of inventory, a manufacturing firm. Inventories of manufacturing firms, however, are more properly associated with cost accounting, so we will reserve our discussion only to inventories of merchandising firms in this book.

Like almost everything in accounting, inventories have a domino effect. They affect not one, but two financial statements—the balance sheet and the income statement. As a result, accurate valuation is imperative, and the resulting inventory value is almost always material. So how exactly are both financial statements affected? Well, before the time of sale, the cost of an item (inventory) is presented as an asset on the balance sheet. Then, when that good is sold, its cost is transferred to and expensed on the income statement as cost of goods sold (COGS). Think back to our example of the cars on the dealership's lot and even all the groceries that you pass by in the store. This should help you to understand the materiality of the dollar amounts involved.

So how do we account for this inventory? Several accounts, some of which are new, are involved. As always, you must understand those accounts' normal balances as well as where each is presented in the financial statements. The accounts that you should be concerned with for this chapter are presented below as well as in Appendix A.

Account	Normal Balance	Financial Statement Classification
Inventory	Debit	Current asset on balance sheet
Cost of goods sold (COGS)	Debit	Expense on income statement
Purchases	Debit	Part of computation of COGS on income statement
Purchase discounts	Credit	Part of computation of net purchases in COGS on income statement

Purchase returns	Credit	Part of computation of net purchases in COGS on income statement
Freight–in	Debit	Part of computation of net purchases in COGS on income statement
Freight–out	Debit	Operating expense on income statement—*not* COGS
Sales	Credit	Revenue on income statement
Sales discounts	Debit	Part of computation of net sales on income statement
Sales returns	Debit	Part of computation of net sales on income statement

In the next few pages we will bring you up to speed on two types of inventory systems, four different cost flow assumptions, one exception to the historical cost principle, two inventory estimation methods, inventory errors, and a few basic internal controls for inventories. And with that, your journey continues.

Inventory Systems

There are currently two different inventory systems in use. *Currently* really is not the correct term, though, because both systems, periodic and perpetual, have been around for many years. While technology has made the perpetual system more widely available and the system of choice for many businesses today, the periodic system is still used by some companies and industries. Because you never know who you might someday work for, the company you might audit, or even the company you might sell products to, you must understand the characteristics of each system and the differences and similarities in journal entries for each system.

Periodic System

The periodic system generally is used by smaller companies with less sophisticated inventory management systems. When using this system, you must remember a few points:

- The inventory account on the balance sheet reflects the *beginning balance.*
- An actual physical count of the inventory must take place at the end of the period to determine the amount of both ending inventory and cost of goods sold (COGS) until an actual count of inventory takes place at the end of the period.
- A journal entry is made to remove the beginning balance and to add the ending balance to the inventory account.
- COGS is computed and a journal entry is made to record it at the end of the period.

- A purchases account is used to record all purchases of inventory.
- The inventory account is not adjusted with each purchase and sale.
- Only one journal entry is made when a sale is recorded.

EXAMPLE 2-1

BLP, Inc., began the current year with an inventory of $10,000. Various purchase and sale transactions took place during the year and were reflected in the following journal entries:

1. During the year, BLP recorded purchases on account of $50,000. The payment terms were 2/10, n/30.

Purchases	50,000	
Accounts payable		50,000

2. During the year, BLP returned $5,000 of purchases originally made on account.

Accounts payable	5,000	
Purchase returns		5,000

3. During the year, BLP took advantage of cash discounts of $900 for early payment.

Accounts payable (in at gross, out at gross)	45,000	
Purchase discount (45,000 × 2%)		900
Cash (45,000 × 98%)		44,100

4. During the year, BLP paid freight charges of $2,000 to get the inventory to the company and ready to sell to customers.

Freight-in	2,000	
Cash		2,000

5. During the year, BLP sold $100,000 of inventory on credit with terms 2/10, n/30.

Accounts receivable	100,000	
Sales		100,000

6. During the year, BLP allowed $8,000 in returns of items sold.

Sales returns	8,000	
Accounts receivable (in at gross, out at gross)		8,000

7. During the year, BLP allowed customers to take advantage of early payment cash discounts of $1,840.

Cash (92,000 × 98%)	90,160	
Sales discounts (92,000 × 2%)	1,840	
Accounts receivable (in at gross, out at gross)		92,000

8. BLP paid $3,000 in freight charges to ship inventory items out to customers.

Freight-out	3,000	
Cash		3,000

9. BLP took a physical count of inventory on the last day of the current year and determined that it had $8,000 of inventory remaining.

10. COGS is determined as illustrated in Table 2-1.

TABLE 2-1 Income Statement with Computation under Periodic Inventory System

	Sales	100,000		
	– Sales returns	(8,000)		
	– Sales discounts	(1,840)		
	= Net sales			90,160
BI	Beginning inventory		10,000	
+ Net Pur	Purchases	50,000		
	– Purchase returns	(5,000)		
	– Purchase discounts	(900)		
	+ Freight–in	2,000	46,100	
= GA	Goods available		56,100	
– EI	Ending inventory		(8,000)	
= COGS	Cost of goods sold			(48,100)
	Gross profit			42,060
	Less: Operating expenses			
	Freight–out			(3,000)
	Net income			39,060

Perpetual System

The perpetual system generally is used by larger companies with more sophisticated inventory management systems. Think back again to your visit to the grocery store. What happens when you get ready to check out? Well, besides the fact that you leave with your wallet a little emptier than when you entered the store? That's right, your purchases are scanned into a computer system. Not only does the reading of the bar code on the product by the scanner allow the cashier to easily determine how much you owe, but that scanner also is connected to the store's computer inventory system. With each scan, an item is removed from the inventory quantity and a sale is recorded. The process occurs instantaneously and is thus a perpetual system. When using this system, you must remember a few points:

- The inventory account on the balance sheet reflects the *current balance* of inventory.

- A journal entry is made to record each purchase and each sale directly to the inventory account, so the adjustment is made immediately.

- COGS is an actual account with a balance and is recorded each time a sale is made.

- An actual physical count of the inventory still must take place at the end of the period to confirm the amount of both ending inventory and COGS.

- Two journal entries are made when a sale is recorded.

EXAMPLE 2-2

BLP began the current year with an inventory of $10,000. Various purchase and sale transactions took place during the year and were reflected in the following journal entries:

1. During the year, BLP recorded purchases on account of $50,000. The payment terms were 2/10, n/30.

Inventory	50,000	
Accounts payable		50,000

2. During the year, BLP returned $5,000 of purchases originally made on account.

Accounts payable	5,000	
Inventory		5,000

3. During the year, BLP took advantage of cash discounts of $900 for early payment.

Accounts payable (in at gross, out at gross)	45,000	
Inventory (45,000 × 2%)		900
Cash (45,000 × 98%)		44,100

4. During the year, BLP paid freight charges of $2,000 to get the inventory to the company and ready to sell to customers.

Inventory	2,000	
Cash		2,000

5. During the year, BLP sold $100,000 of inventory on credit with terms 2/10, n/30; the cost of the inventory sold was $49,000.

Accounts receivable	100,000	
Sales		100,000
COGS	49,000	
Inventory		49,000

6. During the year, BLP allowed $8,000 in returns of items sold; the cost of these items was $4,000.

Sales returns	8,000	
Accounts receivable (in at gross, out at gross		8,000
Inventory	4,000	
COGS		4,000

7. During the year, BLP allowed customers to take advantage of early payment cash discounts of $1,840.

Cash (92,000 × 98%)	90,160	
Sales discounts (92,000 × 2%)	1,840	
Accounts receivable (in at gross, out at gross)		92,000

8. BLP paid $3,000 in freight charges to ship inventory items out to customers.

Freight-out	3,000	
Cash		3,000

9. BLP took a physical count of inventory on the last day of the current year and determined that it had $8,000 of inventory remaining. Because the T account for inventory shows a balance of $11,100 at this point, an adjusting entry must be made to reflect the difference in the balance per the books and the actual amount of inventory on hand at the end of the year.

COGS	3,100	
Inventory		3,100

10. COGS is determined as illustrated in Table 2-2. (*Hint:* Prepare T accounts to determine the balances of the inventory and COGS accounts.)

TABLE 2-2 Income Statement with COGS under Perpetual Inventory System		
Sales	100,000	
– Sales returns	(8,000)	
– Sales discounts	(1,840)	
= Net sales		90,160
Cost of goods sold		(48,100)
Gross profit		42,060
Less: Operating expenses		
Freight–out		(3,000)
Net income		39,060

Cost Flow Assumptions

So do grocery stores sell the goods they have had on the shelves the longest first? We would hope so, but we also realize that such an order of sales does not always occur. We bet many of you look at the dates on food products as you shop, and like any sensible consumer, grab the package that has the latest date from the current date because you know that that particular product should stay fresh or last longer than one with a date that is sooner. However, the product with the latest date also is likely one of the most recently purchased by the store. Thus your practice of looking at the dates completely changes the normal flow of inventory items. Thankfully, the actual flow of inventory items out of the store *does not* have to match the flow of dollars on the financial statements. Can you imagine how much work it would be if it did, especially for a business with as many different types and large supplies of inventory as a grocery store?

Now, we know that this is a unique concept, but as we said, intermediate accounting is filled with a lot of little surprises! To help you better understand, we will proceed in discussing four cost flow assumptions: specific identification, FIFO, LIFO, and average costing.

Specific Identification

Specific identification is the cost flow assumption that a non-accountant intuitively would assume would be used. Under it, the actual flow of inventory items *exactly* matches the monetary flow on the financial statements. That jewelry store where you bought your wife's (or your own) diamond ring, that fur shop where you purchased your genuine mink coat, and even that favorite car dealership of yours are the primary users of this system. What do they all have in common? Each sells "big ticket" items that may differ significantly from one another. Thus it makes sense that each product is tracked individually via a specific identification number and its cost matched with its resulting sales proceeds. This process is fairly self-explanatory, so we will now turn our attention to the three assumptions that are a bit less intuitive, FIFO, LIFO, and average cost, and their variations. The data we will use for examples for each of these methods can be found in Table 2-3.

TABLE 2-3 Data for Cost-Flow-Assumption Examples			
	Units	**Cost**	**Total**
BI	100	10	1000
Pur 1–3	50	11	550
Pur 1–10	75	12	900
Pur 1–22	100	13	1300
GA: Goods available	325		3750
Sold 1–2	–100		
Sold 1–5	–25		
Sold 1–12	–75		
Sold 1–30	–50		
EI	75		

FIFO

FIFO, isn't that the name of your neighbor's dog? Well, it might be, but in accounting, this acronym stands for *first-in, first-out* inventory cost flow, as opposed to a slobbery kiss from the German shepherd next door. Using FIFO, the dollar flow can be determined by assuming that the first items of inventory into the store also will be the first items out of the store. Most textbooks show you how to compute either ending inventory (EI) or cost of goods sold (COGS) and then ask you to "plug," or solve for, the other. Being the accountants that we are, we personally feel that it is better if you actually compute both EI and COGS so that you can prove you are correct. Plus, the technique will help you to better understand the total concept and the interrelatedness of the numbers on the financial statements. The following are the steps that we use when working these problems:

Step 1: You *must* complete a basic information table consisting of beginning inventory and purchases with a total for goods available (GA) that looks similar to Table 2-3. It is very helpful if you list each purchase individually because you will need the individual numbers later in the problems. Also, it will be helpful later if you list each sale individually.

Step 2: Set up the basic format of your answer, showing *only* the units of EI and *only* the units of COGS that you know you will have at the end of the problem. Sometimes it is easier to start at the end and work backward.

Step 3: Compute the COGS numbers, and fill in the EI table with the inventory values that are remaining. Remember that you are using the FIFO method, so start with the first items purchased until you arrive at the proper number for COGS. The remaining inventory then is a part of EI. Make sure to complete the unit, unit cost, and total cost columns. Indicating which purchase each unit of COGS is coming from helps in better understanding and keeping track of the process.

Step 4: Always prove that EI units plus COGS units equal goods available units. Likewise, EI dollars plus COGS dollars also must always equal goods available dollars. Prove that the equality holds true in that case as well. This is the most important step, and it should be completed for *every* problem!

One last thing before we move on to LIFO. When you compute EI and COGS under the FIFO periodic system, you will arrive at the same numbers as when you compute EI and COGS under the FIFO perpetual system, so don't think that something is wrong or that you have come across some new phenomenon. When computing the COGS numbers for any perpetual system, though, you always must remember to look at both the dates for purchases and the dates for sales because it is impossible to sell what you do not have available in the store. Under any periodic system, though, the dates for both purchases and sales can be ignored. A periodic system does not take individual purchases and sales into consideration. Instead, all purchases are lumped together and assumed to be available for sale at any point during the time frame. Thus the periodic system transcends time. A purchase not made until January 10 still could be sold on January 5 despite what common sense would lead us to assume. See Table 2-4 for FIFO computations for both the periodic and perpetual systems.

TABLE 2-4 FIFO Periodic and Perpetual

FIFO Periodic	Ending Inventory				Cost of Goods Sold			
	Units	Cost/Unit	Total			Units	Cost/Unit	Total
					BI	100	$10	$1000
					Pur 1–3	50	11	550
					Pur 1–10	75	12	900
Pur 1–22	75	$13	$975		Pur 1–22	25	13	325
EI	75		$975		COGS	250		$2775

Proof:	Units	Total
EI	75	$975
COGS	250	2775
Goods available	325	$3750

FIFO Perpetual	Ending Inventory					Cost of Goods Sold			
	Units	Cost/Unit	Total				Units	Cost/Unit	Total
				Sale 1–2	BI		100	$10	$1000
				Sale 1–5	Pur 1–3		25	11	275
				Sale 1–12	Pur 1–3		25	11	275
					Pur 1–10		50	12	600
				Sale 1–30	Pur 1–10		25	12	300
Pur 1–22	75	$13	$975		Pur 1–22		25	13	325
EI	75		$975				250		$2775

Proof:	Units	Total
EI	75	$975
COGS	250	2775
Goods available	325	$3750

LIFO

Is it just us or does LIFO stir up thoughts of a big life preserver in the minds of anyone else? Actually, the acronym LIFO stands for *last-in, first-out* inventory method. LIFO assumes that the last items of inventory into the store will be the first items of inventory out of the store. Remember our grocery store example. Why would anyone buy a carton of milk with an August 8 date when they can get an equivalent with an August 15 date? Obviously, the August 8 carton was put on the shelf first, but consumers will purchase the August 15 carton because it has a better chance of lasting longer, having sat on the shelf for less time. There you have it, LIFO in real-world action. Again, most textbooks show you how to compute either EI or COGS and then ask you to "plug" the other. We suggest that you compute both EI and COGS so that you can prove you are correct. The technique will assist you in better understanding the total concept and the interrelatedness of the numbers on the financial statements. Use the same set of steps that we outlined for working FIFO problems in your attempt to calculate LIFO inventory. There is one important difference that you must remember, however. LIFO periodic and LIFO perpetual usually will *not* give you the same dollar amounts for EI and COGS. You can see this in Table 2-5. As with FIFO perpetual, when working LIFO perpetual problems, you *must* keep in mind the dates of both purchases and sales. As mentioned earlier, you cannot sell what you do not have available. Therefore, it is helpful to compute COGS by sale date(s) and to keep track of the purchase date(s) that each sale came from. You can see that we have included those columns in Table 2-5.

A third component of LIFO is known as *dollar-value LIFO*. Dollar-value LIFO takes into consideration the purchasing power, or inflation component, of dollars from different years. As you saw in LIFO periodic and perpetual, the dollars remaining in EI represented the oldest dollars from the earliest time periods. When LIFO has been applied for many years, the dollars in EI on the balance sheet represent dollars from the year LIFO was initially adopted. The inflationary effects of inventory value increases and decreases must be separated from actual quantity changes. In order to accomplish this task, you must first take the year-end cost and convert it to a base-year cost so that actual quantity changes can be determined. Then the base-year cost is reconverted back to dollars for each year using the previously created layer(s) starting with the oldest that is still available. The value calculated becomes the EI dollar amount that is reflected on the balance sheet. The steps we recommend for computing dollar-value LIFO are as follows:

Step 1: Prepare your spreadsheet or table with the following headings: Year, Year-End Cost, Index, Base-Year Cost, Layers × Index, and $LIFO = EI.

Step 2: Enter the year, year-end cost, and appropriate index for each year. Take the index and move the decimal point two places to the left. For example, an index of 120 will become 1.20 (120/100).

Step 3: Compute the base-year cost by dividing the year-end cost by the index.

Step 4: Compare the current year's base-year cost with the prior year's base-year cost to determine if inventory quantities increased or decreased. An increase indicates that there has been a real quantity increase in ending inventory. In other words, some of the inventory purchased in the current

TABLE 2-5 LIFO Periodic and Perpetual

LIFO Periodic	Ending Inventory				Cost of Goods Sold			
	Units	Cost/Unit	Total			Units	Cost/Unit	Total
					Pur 1–22	100	$13	$1300
					Pur 1–10	75	12	900
					Pur 1–3	50	11	550
BI	75	$10	$750		BI	25	10	250
EI	75		$750		COGS	250		$3000

Proof:	Units	Total
EI	75	$750
COGS	250	3000
Goods available	325	$3750

LIFO Perpetual	Ending Inventory					Cost of Goods Sold			
	Units	Cost/Unit	Total				Units	Cost/Unit	Total
				Sale 1–2	BI		100	$10	$1000
				Sale 1–5	Pur 1–3		25	11	275
Pur 1–3	25	$11	275						
				Sale 1–12	Pur 1–10		75	12	900
				Sale 1–30	Pur 1–22		50	13	650
Pur 1–22	50	$13	$650						
EI	75		$925				250		$2825

Proof:	Units	Total
EI	75	$925
COGS	250	2825
Goods available	325	$3750

period has not yet been sold. However, a decrease in inventory signals that the entire inventory layer for the current period has been consumed. Thus EI consists only of previously purchased goods that are still on hand. The current layer has been eliminated and cannot be used in future years.

Step 5: When completing the Layers × Index column, you must remember that the sum of the layers must equal the base-year cost.

Step 6: When completing the Layers × Index column, you must remember to use the index for the year the layer was created.

Step 7: The final column equals the sum of the Layers × Index for each year (see Table 2-6).

TABLE 2-6 Dollar-Value LIFO					
Year	**Year-End Cost**	**Index**	**Base-Year Cost**	**Layers × Index**	**$LIFO = EI**
1–1–X0	12,000	1.00	12,000	12,000 × 1.00	12,000
12–31–X0	14,100	1.05	13,429	12,000 × 1.00	
				1,429 × 1.05	13,500
12–31–X1	13,000	1.15	11,304	12,000 × 1.00	
			13,304	1,304 × 1.05	13,369
12–31–X2	16,000	1.20	13,333	12,000 × 1.00	*12 000*
				1,304 × 1.05	*1,369.*
				29 × 1.20	13,404

Average Cost

Okay, one more cost flow assumption and we will be on our way. Average cost, like FIFO and LIFO, can be computed two different ways. When using a periodic system, the average cost is called a *weighted average.* Alternatively, under a perpetual system, the average cost is known as a *moving average.* An example for both methods is given in Table 2-7.

Weighted average is simple. It is essentially exactly what its name implies. The total cost of goods is determined and divided by the total quantity of those goods to determine an average cost per unit. That average cost per unit then determines the EI and COGS values. Think of it this way: Typically, a store will purchase goods from its wholesaler or a wholesaler will purchase goods from a manufacturer, and such purchases will occur at different points in time. For instance, one purchase may have been made three weeks ago, one might be made today, and yet another might occur in eight days. The costs of goods in those purchases might be very volatile, so the unit cost may range from $1.00 to $2.25. Is each of those products earmarked so that the retailer and wholesaler can exactly match costs to associated revenues at the point of sale? No, probably not. One way to bypass this issue is to use the average cost of a unit instead so that the average of, say, $1.67 is associated with each unit whether it was purchased today or three weeks ago. Here are the steps to complete this process:

Step 1: Divide goods available dollars by goods available units to obtain an average cost per unit. It is best if you leave all the numbers in your calculator and round at the very end of your computations. This differs from most textbooks, which recommend rounding at the cost per unit point.

TABLE 2-7 Weighted Average and Moving Average

Weighted Average for Periodic System

GA $	$3750	=	$11.5384615–4
GA units	325		

EI	75	$11.53846154	$865.3846154
COGS	250	$11.53846154	2884.615385
	325		$3750

Moving Average for Perpetual System

Transaction	Units	Cost per Unit	Total = EI	COGS
BI	100	$10.00	$1000.00	
Less: Sale 1–2	–100	(10.00)	(1000.00)	$1000.00
Balance	0	$0.00	$0.00	
Add: Pur 1–3	50	11.00	550.00	
Balance	50	*$11.00*	$550.00	
Less: Sale 1–5	–25	(11.00)	(275.00)	275.00
Balance	25	$11.00	$275.00	
Add: Pur 1–10	75	12.00	900.00	
Balance	100	*$11.75*	$1175.00	
Less: Sale 1–12	–75	11.75	(881.25)	881.25
Balance	25	$11.75	$293.75	
Add: Pur 1–22	100	13.00	1300.00	
Balance	125	*$12.75*	$1593.75	
Less: Sale 1–30	–50	12.75	(637.50)	637.50
Balance	75	$12.75	$956.25	$2793.75

Proof:	Units	Total		
EI	75	$956.25		
COGS	250	2793.75		
Goods available	325	$3750.00		

Step 2: Multiply the cost per unit by EI units to determine the cost of EI.

Step 3: Multiply the cost per unit by COGS to determine the COGS dollar value.

Step 4: Remember to prove that EI units plus COGS units equals goods available (GA) units and that EI dollars plus COGS dollars equals GA dollars.

The downside to the periodic average cost is that the COGS and likewise the EI cannot be computed until the end of the period, when all purchases have been made. Still, the method is quite simple and intuitive.

Moving average, however, is a bit more complicated, but nothing you can't handle! The main difference is that a new average cost per unit must be calculated after every purchase. Here are the recommended steps for working moving average inventory problems:

Step 1: Create your spreadsheet or table with column headings for transactions, units, cost per unit, total (which will equal EI at any point in time), and COGS.

Step 2: Enter beginning inventory (BI) into the units, cost per unit, and total columns.

Step 3: Enter the first transaction into the units, cost per unit, and total columns.

Step 4: If the transaction is a sale, use the previous cost per unit as the sale price. Also, remember to put the total sold in the COGS column.

Step 5: If the transaction is a purchase, then you must compute a new average cost per unit by dividing the balance of total dollars by the balance of total units. This step must be completed after *every* purchase!

Step 6: Compute a balance for the unit, cost per unit, and total columns.

Step 7: Continue with each transaction until the end.

Step 8: The last number in the total column will represent the EI number to be reported on the balance sheet.

Comparison of FIFO, LIFO, and Weighted Average Periodic and Perpetual

As you may have figured out, there are some strategies and benefits to using one of the three inventory costing methods over the others, as well as to selecting the periodic or perpetual version. It all depends on what your company is trying to achieve. Please use Table 2-8 along with the following paragraphs for comparing the different methods.

TABLE 2-8 Comparison of FIFO, LIFO, and Average-Cost Assumptions			
	FIFO Periodic	**LIFO Periodic**	**Weighted Average**
EI	$975	$750	$865
COGS	2775	3000	2885
	FIFO Perpetual	**LIFO Perpetual**	**Moving Average**
EI	$975	$925	$956
COGS	2775	2825	2794

First, in a period of rising prices, FIFO always will result in higher EI than LIFO, and alternatively, use of FIFO always will result in a lower COGS than LIFO. Thus FIFO will allow a firm to achieve a higher net income in the current period because COGS, an expense, is based on the lower costs of the earlier inventory sold. Essentially, FIFO matches current revenues with historical costs, whereas LIFO matches current costs with current revenues.

Second, again, in a time of increasing prices, LIFO periodic will result in higher COGS and lower EI than LIFO perpetual because of the lack of focus on purchase and sale dates. For instance, the higher-cost inventory purchased last week may be matched with a sale that occurred two months ago under the periodic system, whereas under the perpetual system, calculations are not based on such an impossibility.

Third, in a period of rising prices, the moving-average method will produce results between those of FIFO and LIFO, and like LIFO, the perpetual (moving average) version will have a lower COGS and higher EI than the periodic (weighted average) version.

Finally, there is one caveat to using the LIFO method. When LIFO is used for tax purposes, it also must be used for financial statement presentation. Therefore, the benefit of having a lower net income on which to pay taxes is counterbalanced by the negative perceptions by investors of lower profits on the company's books.

Exception to the Historical Cost Principal

Inventories usually are shown at historical cost on the balance sheet. Suppose, however, that a once popular good has experienced bad news in the press recently or technology is making it obsolete. Music systems are a great example of this. For those of you who are older, you may remember when a night of musical entertainment included spinning a stack of your favorite bands' records on a turntable and dancing the night away. Those were the good old days, and you thought they would never end, right? Well, despite how much you wanted them to last forever, they ceased with the advent of the cassette player, and those days, too, were quickly replaced with the introduction of CD players. Now the latest and greatest MP3 player or portable device of the month has stolen the scene. Needless to say, that CD player you bought a few years ago is not worth nearly as much today as it was then. Stores have the same issue, so why would they keep such inventories on the books at the older, higher cost when they know they will never receive such a large future benefit. You're right—they wouldn't. When the replacement cost of the inventory falls below the historical cost, the historical cost principle is abandoned, and the inventory is shown at the lower of cost or market (LCM) on the balance sheet. The objective of the switch is to exercise conservatism. You do not want to falsely represent your financial position because so many internal and external parties rely on those financial statement numbers. The end result is that you indirectly show your loss so that such users will not be misled. An example is given in Table 2-9, but first is a list of the steps recommended for completing LCM problems:

Step 1: Obtain or compute the replacement cost, ceiling, and floor by using the formula in Table 2-9.

Step 2: Choose the middle value from the replacement cost, ceiling, and floor. Throw out the highest and lowest numbers.

Step 3: Call the middle value *market*.

Step 4: Compare *market* with *cost*.

Step 5: Choose the lower value.

Step 6: Apply the lower value to the inventory. You can apply it by individual item, by inventory category, or for the inventory as a whole. The most conservative result always occurs as a result of applying LCM on an individual item basis, though.

TABLE 2-9 Formula for LCM			
	Case A	**Case B**	**Case C**
Selling price	100	100	100
Less: Cost of completion	−2	−5	−10
Less: Cost of disposal	−1	−2	−8
= NRV (ceiling)	97	93	82
Less: Normal profit margin	−10	−10	−10
= Floor	87	83	72
Replacement cost	95	80	90
Market	95	83	82
Cost	85	85	85
LCM	85	83	82

Two Estimation Methods

Have you ever wondered what would happen if inventory were destroyed in a fire, flood, or other natural disaster or if the person in charge of keeping records up to date purposely removed a portion of those records to hide his or her illegal acts? How would the company ever determine the value of its EI? There are times like these when taking a physical inventory count is either impossible or impractical. Under such conditions, companies will estimate their EI by using the gross profit or the retail inventory method. Both those approaches provide an estimate of EI. In addition to the instances previously identified, such estimates also can be used when preparing interim period financial statements, when an auditor is checking the reasonableness of EI, or during the budgeting process when EI and COGS predictions are made.

Gross Profit Method

The gross profit method uses the format illustrated in Table 2-1 for the periodic system. When working gross profit problems, *always* set up the basic format, fill in the numbers you know, and then solve for the unknown. The objective is usually to determine the dollar amount of EI. An important item to understand is that gross profit can be presented either as a percentage of sales or as a percentage of COGS. If gross profit is a percentage of sales, then sales is designated as 100 percent. Alternatively, if gross profit is a percentage of COGS, then COGS is designated as 100 percent. Remember to use your knowledge of algebra (yes, algebra—and you thought your days of math beyond adding and subtracting were over) to determine COGS when gross profit is stated as a percentage of COGS. If, as in the following example, gross profit is 30 percent of cost, then the algebraic equation would be cost × 1.30 = sales. This equation can be reduced to cost = sales/1.30.

EXAMPLE 2-3

BLP, Inc., had net sales for the current year of $100,000. The company began the year with $10,000 in inventory and had net purchases of $80,000. Determine the EI under the following assumptions: Case A, gross profit is 30 percent of sales; Case B, gross profit is 30 percent of cost. The solution can be found in Table 2-10.

TABLE 2-10 Gross Profit Method

Case A: Gross profit is 30% of sales

100%	Sales		100,000
	BI	10,000	
	+ Net Pur	80,000	
	= GA	90,000	
	– EI (plug)	*(20,000)*	
70%	= COGS (compute as 100,000 x 70%)	70,000	(70,000)
30%	GP		30,000

Case B: Gross profit is 30% of cost

130%	Sales		100,000
	BI	10,000	
	+ Net Pur	80,000	
	= GA	90,000	
	– EI (plug)	*(13,077)*	
100%	= COGS (compute as 100,000/1.30)	76,923	(76,923)
30%	GP		23,077

Retail Inventory Method

Companies will use the retail method for all the same estimation reasons as noted previously for the gross profit method. Some key points regarding the retail inventory method include

- The objective is to determine EI *at cost* because that is the number that ultimately will appear on the balance sheet.
- The basic format for determining COGS under the periodic method as illustrated in Table 2-1 is used.
- The cost to retail percentage is the key number in all these computations.
- *EI at retail* is computed, and then the cost percentage is used to convert *EI at retail* to *EI at cost*.

There are four different applications of the retail inventory method. The key differences between each method revolve around what is included in the cost percentage and what the cost percentage is applied to. Following is a summary of these points:

Cost Flow Assumption	BI	Net Purchases	Net Markups	Net Markdowns	Application of Cost Percentage
FIFO	No	Yes	Yes	Yes	Multiplied by EI at retail
Average cost	Yes	Yes	Yes	Yes	Multiplied by EI at retail
LCM	Yes	Yes	Yes	No	Multiplied by EI at retail
LIFO	Yes, separate percentage	Yes	Yes	Yes	Separate cost percentage computed for both BI and other three components (see the following explanation)

LIFO's cost percentage must be computed for both the BI layer and the net purchases layer. If the LIFO EI at retail is *less than* the BI at retail, then multiply the BI cost percentage by EI at retail to determine EI at cost. If the LIFO EI at retail is *more than* the BI at retail, then add together the products of BI at retail times the BI cost percentage and the purchases layer added this year times the purchases cost percentage to determine EI at cost.

EXAMPLE 2-4

To illustrate the four different retail methods, use the following data for BLP, Inc., for the current year, and refer to Table 2-11.

BI at cost is $40 and at retail is $70.

Net purchases at cost are $80 and at retail are $150.

Net markups at retail only are $10.

Net markdowns at retail only are $15.

Sales at retail only are $135.

TABLE 2-11 Retail Methods

FIFO

	Cost	Retail	
Net purchases	$80	$150	
Add: Net markups	0	10	
Less: Net markdowns	0	(15)	
Compute cost to retail ratio	80	145	0.5517
Add: BI	40	70	
Less: Net sales		(135)	
EI at retail		$80	
Times the cost percentage			0.5517
EI at cost		$44	

LIFO

	Cost	Retail	
Net purchases	$80	$150	
Add: Net markups	0	10	
Less: Net markdowns	0	(15)	
Compute cost to retail ratio	80	145	0.5517
Add: BI	40	70	0.5714
Less: Net sales		(135)	
EI at retail		$80	

	Retail		Cost
BI layer	70	0.5714	$40
Purchases layer	10	0.5517	6
EI at cost	$80		$46

Average Cost

	Cost	Retail	
BI	$40	$70	
Add: Net purchases	80	150	
Add: Net markups	0	10	
Less: Net markdowns	0	(15)	
Compute cost to retail ratio	120	215	0.558
Less: Net sales		(135)	
EI at retail		$80	
Times the cost percentage			0.5581
EI at cost		$45	

LCM

	Cost	Retail	
BI	$40	$70	
Add: Net purchases	80	150	
Add: Net markups	0	10	
Compute cost to retail ratio	120	230	0.5217
Less: Net markdowns	0	(15)	
Less: Net sales		(135)	
EI at retail		$80	
Times the cost percentage			0.5217
EI at cost		$42	

Errors

Wouldn't it be nice if we were all perfect and errors never occurred? Life would be so much easier. Unfortunately, though, even accountants and businesspeople frequently err when it comes to accounting for inventories. In order to save yourself from many headaches, it is imperative to correct an error as soon as it is discovered. To do this, you must understand the effect an error has on every aspect of the financial statements. The method that will be presented here will work for many types of accounting mistakes, but it is especially effective for use with inventory errors. First, determine the formula you need for the particular error. For inventory errors, always assume use of the periodic computation for COGS, as illustrated in Table 2-1. Next, randomly select a set of base numbers and enter them into the formula. Finally, determine what the error is, and make another column of numbers with the error substituted into the formula while holding all the other numbers constant. You then can easily determine the effect of the error on several key financial statement components. Table 2-12 offers an example of this method.

TABLE 2-12 Errors	Base	Comparison
BI	100	100
Add: Net purchases	300	250
GA	400	350
Less: EI	–150	–150
COGS	250	200
Result:		
BI is OK		
Purchases are understated		
COGS is understated		
Net Income (NI) is overstated		

Internal Controls

Establishment of Responsibility and Segregation of Duties

Before a purchase of inventory can be made, a requisition must be submitted to an authorized individual such as a manager by the department desiring the materials. Depending on the type of business, the requisition may be generated by an actual person, or in the case of highly automated systems and especially just-in-time setups, a requisition may be sent automatically to the individual with authorization responsibilities when the inventory drops to a certain set level or a certain point in the month is reached. Once the requisition is approved, a purchase order can be prepared by the purchasing department. When the goods ordered arrive, the receiving department handles them and thus has custody duties. Finally, the company must note its responsibility for future payment as well as actually pay the vendor when required to do so. These responsibilities are considered to be a part of recordkeeping and are delegated to the accounts payable and accounting departments.

Documentation Procedures and Physical, Mechanical, and Electronic Controls

A considerable amount of documentation is prepared in regard to inventory, and rightly so. Remember, inventory usually constitutes a very material amount of a company's assets. First, the manager or other individual who approves the requisitions must provide some permanent indication of his or her authorization of the purchase, such as a signature on the requisition document. Second, the requisitions should be prenumbered in order to better ensure that all order requests are accounted for and to provide a later check that something has not been ordered without proper approval. Third, purchase orders are created to both send to the desired vendor and keep within the company as proof that the company entered into a particular transaction. Like requisitions, purchase orders should be prenumbered. Fourth, at the time of arrival, goods are noted by quantity, description, and so on on a receiving report. Fifth, an invoice is received from the vendor and is kept on hand for later internal verification and payment authorization. Sixth, the accounts payable department prepares and approves a voucher for payment, and a copy of that voucher is forwarded to the treasurer for future payment, and another copy is filed for future reference. Finally, once the payment is remitted, the voucher package is canceled so that the payment will not be processed a second time.

In terms of physical controls, inventory is one area that is given significant focus. Have you ever heard the expression, "Inventory is walking out the back door"? For many businesses, inventory "walking out" either the back or even the front door is a significant concern. Both employees and customers, especially in retail situations, are capable of stealing from the business. Inventory items that are small and easily hidden are particularly susceptible to pilferage (a fancy word for stealing). However, it is not unheard of for employees to take items as large as large-screen television sets when no one is watching or to create false purchases and have such purchases sent to addresses where they themselves will receive the goods but will never pay the business for them. Sometimes employees reconcile their guilt by telling themselves that they are undercompensated for their work or that they are being treated poorly, so the business deserves to be punished. In any case, such losses must be controlled through physical controls.

A perfect example of physical controls in the retail sector is the use of ink tags on certain items of clothing. I think you will agree with us when we say that those ink tags are very annoying! How many times have you walked out of a store having paid for your goods only later to find out at home that the cashier forgot to remove the ink tag? If you're like us, probably quite a few times! So what happens? Well, in an effort to prevent your new pair of dress pants from becoming soaked in permanent ink, you return to the store and explain your situation to the cashier, who then proceeds to use a special tool to remove the tag, and once again, you are on your way. There are two things that should be noted here. First, the ink tag was placed on the garment in an effort to deter a shopper from walking out of the store without paying for the piece of clothing. It acts as a physical control. Second, no alarm buzzed when you walked out of the store. The system, like many, is not effective 100 percent of the time. Still, the mere presence of the ink tag and the chance that the alarm may go off when the item is taken from the store may be enough to reduce or even eliminate the pilferage. Other physical and electronic controls that may be in use to prevent loss of inventory include locks and alarms on storefronts, locks on stockrooms, and passwords known only by authorized individuals to change inventory quantities in the business's computer system.

Independent Internal Verification

Independent internal verification uses the paperwork established during documentation procedures to further safeguard a company's assets and ensure that illegal acts are discovered as soon as possible. First, the receiving department receives a copy of the purchase order. The actual goods that arrive thus can be compared with those indicated on the purchase order. Second, the accounts payable department also receives the purchase order and requisition from purchasing, as well as the receiving report from receiving and the invoice from the vendor. That department ensures that all those documents match before payment is authorized and a voucher is prepared. Finally, accounts payable must reconcile the daily purchases summary with the journal entries posted to the purchases journal, whereas the accounting department is in charge of ensuring that the monthly statements received from the vendor match the entries posted to the accounts payable master file.

This discussion concludes our investigation of current assets. This chapter provided some greater insights into the various inventory accounting methods available under the periodic and perpetual methods, including FIFO, LIFO, and average cost. It also introduced some procedures to estimate inventory and presented the lower of cost or market concept, as well as briefly mentioned errors and internal controls. In Chapter 3 we will move on to the first type of long-term assets—long-term receivables.

QUIZ

1. Which of the following statements is *not correct* concerning the periodic and perpetual inventory systems?

   A. Under the perpetual system, COGS is a real account with a balance that is updated as each sale is made.

   B. Two entries are made to record a sale under the periodic inventory system.

   C. The inventory amount found on the balance sheet under the periodic system is the beginning balance, which is replaced with the physically counted amount at the end of the period.

   D. A physical count of inventory must be taken under the perpetual inventory system.

2. On July 6, Mac, Inc., a science supply wholesaler, sold $35,000 of inventory on account for $60,000. What entry (entries) would be made to record the sale using the perpetual inventory system?

A. Accounts receivable	60,000	
Sales		60,000
Cost of goods sold	35,000	
Inventory		35,000
B. Accounts receivable	35,000	
Sales		35,000
Cost of goods sold	35,000	
Inventory		35,000
C. Cost of goods sold	35,000	
Sales		35,000
D. Accounts receivable	60,000	
Sales		60,000

3. On October 2, 2010, Corr's Autobody purchased some radiators at a total purchase price of $300,000 from the company's supplier on account with terms of 2/15, n/30. The company uses a periodic inventory system and has a policy of not recording discounts until taken. Corr's paid off the payable on October 13, 2010. Based on this information, what amount should be credited to cash to record the transaction?

   A. $300,000

   B. $6,000

   C. $294,000

   D. $255,000

4. **Which of the following products is most likely to use the specific identification cost flow assumption?**

   A. Cans of peas
   B. Mass-produced anniversary clocks
   C. A newly released DVD
   D. A jeep

5. **Which of the following cost flow assumptions will produce the highest net income assuming a period of rising prices?**

   A. LIFO periodic
   B. Average cost perpetual
   C. FIFO perpetual
   D. LIFO perpetual

6. **Using the information in the following table, what would the COGS be under the LIFO perpetual system?**

	Units	Cost
BI	75	$5
Purchase 2/3/10	100	$7
Purchase 2/16/10	25·	$6
Sold 2/1/10	50	
Sold 2/20/10	75	

   A. $825
   B. $850
   C. $725
   D. $750

7. **Using the data from question 6, what would the EI be under the FIFO periodic system?**

   A. $500
   B. $375
   C. $350
   D. $725

8. **Using the data from question 6, what would be the COGS under the periodic average-cost system?**

   A. $766
   B. $459
   C. $750
   D. $825

9. Given the following data and the fact that the year-end cost on January 1, 2010, was $10,000, what would be the EI under the dollar-value LIFO inventory method on December 31, 2012?

Year	Year–End Cost	Index
2010	$12,000	1.05
2011	$11,500	1.10
2012	$13,000	1.15

A. $14,950
B. $11,477
C. $11,454
D. $11,500

10. A certain product has a selling price of $30, disposal costs of $5, a normal profit margin equal to 10 percent of the selling price, a replacement cost of $29, and a historical cost of $28. Under the lower of cost or market, what should be the product cost?

A. $22
B. $25
C. $28
D. $29

11. A fire destroyed part of the inventory of the McGuire Company. For the current year, the company had net sales of $120,000 and began the year with $40,000 in inventory with $60,000 in additional purchases during the year. If gross profit is 25 percent of sales, what would be the company's EI?

A. $90,000
B. $100,000
C. $30,000
D. $10,000

chapter 3

Long-Term Receivables

CHAPTER OBJECTIVES

After completing this chapter, the student should

- Understand the financial statement presentation for long-term receivables
- Understand and account for long-term receivables
- Amortize premiums and discounts on long-term receivables
- Understand internal controls over long-term receivables

Overview

While we have already discussed a short-term type of receivable, a company also may allow customers to extend their time of payment beyond a month. Have you ever purchased a "big ticket" item such as a large screen television and had the opportunity to opt in for a payment plan? If so, you know that rather than paying the full amount up front, you were allowed to pay off the balance in installments. It is likely that along with the principle, though, you also were required to pay interest. For doing you (a less than rich customer) a favor by allowing you to spread out your payments, the company expects some compensation—interest—in return. As a result, both you and the company receive a type of benefit.

Financial Statement Presentation

The focus in this chapter will be on those long-term receivables, specifically long-term notes receivable. To help you to better understand the process of accounting for such receivables, let's begin with an example. Assume that BLP, Inc., has one particular customer to which it has loaned a substantial amount of money to finance the purchase of startup inventory. This *long term note receivable* (LTNR) will be listed on BLP's balance sheet as a long-term asset and will have a normal debit balance.

Another new account that should be noted for its association with LTNR is *discount on LTNR*. The account has a normal credit balance and is presented as a contra account to LTNR, so the net of the two accounts represents the present value of the LTNR.

Journal Entries

The LTNR should be recorded at whichever of the following is most reliable:

- The full fair market value (FMV) of the property, goods, or services
- The FMV of the note itself
- The present value of the note using the borrower's incremental interest rate

 **EXAMPLE 3-1**

To continue with our example on January 1, BLP, Inc., sold $500,000 of clothing to DotCom, Inc., in exchange for a $500,000 LTNR with an interest rate of 6 percent. Payments of $10,000 plus any accrued interest will be made semiannually on June 30 and December 31. In this case, we have valued the note at the FMV of the property exchanged, which is known and thus is the most reliable measurement.

The initial journal entry would be

Jan 1:

Long-term notes receivable	500,000	
Inventory		500,000

The journal entries for BLP for year 1 would be

June 30:

Cash	25,000	
Interest revenue (500,000 × 6% × ½)		15,000
Long-term notes receivable		10,000

Dec 31:

Cash	24,700	
Interest revenue (490,000 × 6% × ½)		14,700
Long-term notes receivable		10,700

EXAMPLE 3-2

Now let's change the conditions a bit and look at how the note would be accounted for *if* the FMV of the property and the FMV of the note were *not* reliable. On January 1, BLP, Inc., sold $500,000 of clothing to DotCom, Inc., in exchange for a five-year non-interest-bearing LTNR. DotCom's incremental borrowing rate is 8 percent. The accrued interest will be recorded annually on December 31. In this case, the note must be valued at the present value of the note using the borrower's incremental interest rate.

The first step is to determine the present value of the LTNR. The present value of the note would be $340,291, which was determined by multiplying the face value of $500,000 by the present value factor for five years at 8 percent (0.680583). We have included present-value tables in Appendix B. If time value of money tables are not handy, however, formulas also may be used. The present value (of a single-sum) interest factor (PVIF) of 0.680583 also can be obtained from the following calculation: $1/(1 + 0.08)^5$.

Now that we have thoroughly confused you, you are likely asking, "Why do I need to know the present value of the note when I already know the face value?" The answer is twofold. First, generally accepted accounting principles (GAAP) require that the accrual basis be used, meaning that revenues must be reported in the period earned. Second, in reality, a non-interest-bearing note does not actually exist. If it did, we would all want one of those! No matter what is stated, there always will be interest implied in every note. Thus, if there really is interest included in the $500,000 note, it must be removed initially and included as revenue when earned. The effective interest method may be used to calculate the amount of interest earned each year. To perform the calculation, multiply the *implied interest* rate of 8 percent times the present value of the LTNR at the beginning of the year.

TABLE 3-1 Amortization Schedule Using Effective Interest Method for LTNR

Date	Debit Discount on LTNR	Credit Interest Revenue	Present Value of LTNR
		8%	
01.01.×1			340,291
12.31.×1	27,223	27,223	367,514
12.31.×2	29,401	29,401	396,915
12.31.×3	31,753	31,753	428,669
12.31.×4	34,293	34,293	462,962
13.31.×5	37,038	37,038	500,000

Now, you are ready to complete an amortization schedule for the life of the note receivable. Please refer to Table 3-1 for this schedule and note the following:

- At the date the note is exchanged, the present value is $340,291.
- The credit to interest revenue each year is calculated as 8 percent times the previous present value.
- The debit to discount on the LTNR is the same amount as the credit to interest revenue.
- In year 5, $1 is added to the interest revenue as a rounding figure to make the present value of the note equal to the face value of $500,000.

The journal entries for the first year for this example would be

Jan. 1:

LTNR	500,000	
Inventory		340,291
Discount on LTNR		159,709

Dec. 31:

Discount on LTNR	27,223	
Interest revenue		27,223

On December 31 of year 1 the long-term assets section of the balance sheet would include the following for the notes receivable:

Long-term notes receivable	500,000
Less: Discount on long-term notes receivable	(132,486)
Net long-term notes receivable	367,514

Internal Controls

Internal controls for LTNRs are very similar in nature to controls used for accounts receivable. The most important item to remember is that you should maintain segregation of duties. Thus there should be an employee who authorizes the extension of credit and approves the related terms, an employee who records all the related transactions in the books, and an employee who actually receives the principle and interest payments when they arrive. It is imperative that, if practical, none of these functions be performed by the same individual.

This was quick and painless, wasn't it? Now that you know more about the accounting for long-term receivables, their financial statement presentation, and the amortization of related premiums and discounts, all while resting up a bit, we can move on to a bit more involved topic—investments.

QUIZ

1. A long-term note receivable is a _____ asset and has a normal _____ balance.
    A. fixed, debit
    B. long-term, debit
    C. long-term, credit
    D. fixed, credit

2. Cuso, Inc., sold books valued at $45,000 to Nusch, Inc., in exchange for an LTNR with a 5 percent interest rate. It was indeterminable what the value of the note would be in the marketplace, but another seller is willing to accept the note in exchange for $60,000 worth of goods. Payments of $5,000 along with accrued interest will be made semiannually. Given this information, at what value should the LTNR be recorded?
    A. $45,000
    B. $60,000
    C. $47,250
    D. $52,500

3. GBW, Inc., has a five-year $250,000 outstanding note receivable at an interest rate of 5 percent. Interest is paid semiannually on June 30 and December 31. What amount would be recorded as interest revenue on June 30 of the current year?
    A. $12,500
    B. $6,250
    C. $0
    D. $1,250

4. On January 1, 2010, LJ, Inc., sold $250,000 of clothing to GBW, Inc., in exchange for a five-year non-interest-bearing LTNR. GBW's incremental borrowing rate is 7 percent. What will be the present value of the note receivable?
    A. $250,000
    B. $233,645
    C. $178,247
    D. $232,500

5. Using the same information as in question 4, the credit to discount on notes receivable on January 1 would be which of the following?
    A. $71,753
    B. $250,000
    C. $16,355
    D. $17,500

6. Using the same information as in question 4, the debit to discount on long-term notes receivable on December 31, 2011, would be which of the following? (*Hint:* Use the effective interest method.)

   A. $12,477
   B. $13,351
   C. $14,000
   D. $16,355

7. Using the same information as in question 4, the net long-term notes receivable recorded on LJ's balance sheet on December 31, 2013, would be closest to which of the following? (*Hint:* Use the effective interest method.)

   A. $250,000
   B. $190,724
   C. $233,646
   D. $178,247

8. At the end of the term of an LTNR but before receiving payment, the present value or net value of the note is equal to

   A. the amount of the original discount on long-term notes receivable.
   B. the face value of the note.
   C. $0.
   D. the same net amount as at the establishment of the note.

9. Discount on long-term notes receivable is a(n) _____ account to long-term notes receivable.

   A. expense
   B. complementary
   C. contra
   D. control

10. A three-year non-interest-bearing LTNR is received in exchange for some goods held by LR, Inc. The company has an incremental borrowing rate of 6 percent. Interest revenue from the note will accrue annually. In order to value the LTNR properly on the company's books at the date of inception, which of the following time value of money factors would need to be used?

    A. The present value of an ordinary annuity at three periods and a 6 percent rate
    B. The present value of a single sum at six periods and a 3 percent rate
    C. The present value of a single sum at three periods and a 6 percent rate
    D. The present value of an annuity due at three periods and a 6 percent rate

chapter 4

Investments

After completing this chapter, the student should

- Understand the financial statement presentation for investments
- Understand what securities are included in each category of investments
- Account for trading securities
- Account for available-for-sale securities
- Account for debt securities held to maturity
- Understand internal controls over investments

Overview

We would be willing to bet that most of you currently hold or have held at least one type of investment. You might have invested in the stock market, purchased corporate or government bonds, placed money in an interest-bearing savings account at your local bank, provided money to an entrepreneur and his or her startup company claiming to be the next "gold mine," and so on. Why would you make such investments? Because you are just a nice person and want to be a Good Samaritan to those people who need to use your funds, right? Well, maybe you are a kindhearted person; we do not in any way intend to question your compassion in this area. However, even if you do see your investment as a good deed, you likely still have some ulterior motives for giving up use of your cash for awhile.

So what exactly are those motives? When cash is left sitting idle, an opportunity to earn additional money is lost. In all types of investments, those who provide the investment funds expect some type of return in exchange for allowing the other party to use their money. The magnitude of the return expected depends on the safety of the investment. While we have just applied the process to individuals, the same is true for businesses. One business may buy stock in another company, purchase bonds, and/or use a number of other investment strategies to try to obtain the greatest return for owners (in the case of corporations, stockholders). How much idle cash a business has on hand and how soon it expects to need to use those funds determine the duration period of its investment. For instance, an outdoor amusement park in Colorado might be open only five months of the year (May through September). It is therefore considered a seasonal establishment. From May through September, money is paid out for employee wages, food, prizes for midway games, additional electricity to operate the rides and other contraptions, fees for performers, and fees for other types of entertainment along with other expenses. During those five months, idle money may be sparse. However, throughout the remaining months of the year, there are fewer expenses, so extra money may be available for investments. The park could just leave the money sitting around to collect dust until the next season, but based on the reasons already noted, it probably wouldn't. Rather, the park would choose an investment vehicle and try to multiply its earnings. Depending on the success and magnitude of such investments, park goers just might be able to experience the thrill of a new roller coaster next season.

So what types of investments will be covered in this chapter? As we alluded to earlier, there are two main types of investments—debt and equity—and it is those two types that will be the focus of the next few pages. An example of a debt security is a purchased bond, whereas an example of an equity security is stock ownership in another company. In regard to stock ownership, there are three different levels based on the percentage of ownership in the other firm: less than 20 percent, 20 to 50 percent, and greater than 50 percent. In this chapter we will focus solely on stock ownership of less than 20 percent.

Terminology

Before continuing, we will offer some definitions for and explanations of the differences between the three types of securities—trading, available for sale, and debt held to maturity. The first type, *trading securities,* can be either debt or equity, but management must intend to sell the securities in the near future for proper placement in this category. The second type, *available-for-sale securities,* are comprised of two items: debt securities that are *not* classified as held to maturity and both debt and equity securities that are *not* classified as trading securities. The final type, *debt securities held to maturity,* consists of debt securities that management intends to hold until their maturity dates.

Financial Statement Presentation

Not only do the definitions of the three types of securities differ, but they also have different classifications on the balance sheet. Trading securities are considered to be current assets. Securities available-for-sale and debt held to maturity securities, on the other hand, are categorized as long-term assets. Regardless of classification, however, a normal debit balance is common to all.

For the remainder of this chapter we will separate our discussion in terms of each of the three securities. For each type of security we will list the rules based on generally accepted accounting principles (GAAP) and then provide a comprehensive example of each.

Trading Securities

Recall that trading securities can consist of both debt and equity. Thus, with trading securities, both interest and dividends may be available to investors. GAAP rules include the following:

- The initial purchase of trading securities is recorded at cost.
- Any dividend revenue received is reported on the income statement.
- Any interest revenue received is also reported on the income statement.
- Realized gains and losses from the sale of trading securities are reported on the income statement.
- Trading securities are reported on the balance sheet at *fair market value* (FMV), not cost.
- Any unrealized gains and losses are reported in net income.

 **EXAMPLE 4-1**

On February 2, BLP, Inc., had an extra $10,000 available for five months. (*Note:* The period of time is less than one year, which would indicate near term.) The company invested in 200 shares of ABC at a cost of $20 per share. BLP also bought 400 debt securities in DEF for $15 per security. The journal entry to record this transaction would be

Feb. 2:

Trading securities, ABC (200 shares × $20)	4,000	
Trading securities, DEF (400 shares × $15)	6,000	
Cash		10,000

On March 31, BLP received two checks in the mail, one from ABC for $40 (dividends) and the other one from DEF for $30 (interest). The journal entry to record these transactions would be

March 31:

Cash	70	
Dividend revenue		40
Interest revenue		30

Because March 31 also signals the end of a quarter, BLP, Inc., a corporation, must publish its first-quarter financial statements for the year (January through March). According to the rule, trading securities must be reported at FMV on each balance sheet date. As a result, the FMV of each security must be determined. The controller for BLP has determined that the FMV of each share of ABC was $19 and the FMV of each security of DEF was $16. The journal entry to record the change in FMV would be

March 31:

Trading securities, DEF (400 shares × $1)	400	
Trading Securities, ABC (200 shares × $1)		200
Unrealized gain on trading securities		200

During May, an unexpected problem arose for BLP, and the company needed the $10,000 it had invested on February 2. BLP decided to sell all of its trading securities effective May 15. The ABC stock sold for $22 a share, and the DEF securities sold for $17 a share. The journal entry to record such sales would be

May 15:

Cash (200 shares × $22) + (400 shares × $17)	11,200	
Trading securities, ABC (200 shares × $19)		3,800
Trading securities, DEF (400 shares × $16)		6,400
Realized gain on sale of trading securities		1,000

To see how the dividend revenue, interest revenue, and realized gain would be reported on the income statement, please refer to Table 4-1. The manner in which the unrealized gain would be reported on the balance sheet may be seen in Table 4-2.

TABLE 4-1 BLP, Inc., Income Statement, Fiscal Year Ending December 31	
Sales	
Cost of goods sold	
Gross profit	
Operating expenses	
Operating income	
Other items	
Interest revenue	30
Dividend revenue	40
Realized gain on sale of trading securities	1000
Unrealized gain on trading securities	200
Pretax income from continuing operations	
Tax expense	
Income from continuing operations	
Results from discontinued operations	
Income before extraordinary items	
Extraordinary items	
Net income	

TABLE 4-2 BLP, Inc., Balance Sheet, December 31	
Assets:	
Current assets:	
Long-term assets:	
Liabilities:	
Current liabilities:	
Long-term liabilities:	
Stockholders' equity:	
Contributed capital:	
Retained earnings:	
Other comprehensive income:	

Available-for-Sale Securities

Recall that available-for-sale securities can be both debt and equity securities. Therefore, both interest and dividends can be received. GAAP rules include the following:

- The initial purchase of available-for-sale securities is recorded at cost.

- Any dividend revenue received is reported on the income statement.

- Any interest revenue received is also reported on the income statement.

- Realized gains and losses are reported on the income statement.

- The realized gain or loss is equal to the selling price less the original cost.

- Available-for-sale securities are reported on the balance sheet at FMV, not cost.

Unrealized holding gains and losses are reported on the balance sheet. During the first year, they are reported in other comprehensive income (OCI), and in subsequent years, they are shown in accumulated other comprehensive income (AOCI), a stockholders' equity account, located on the balance sheet.

Helpful Hints

It is easier to follow the examples if you keep separate accounts for each security for both of the following accounts: allowance to value available-for-sale securities and unrealized increase/decrease in value of available-for-sale securities.

- Start at the beginning of each example and create an allowance to value and unrealized increase/decrease T-account for each security. Such T accounts will help immensely when computing the proper numbers for the balance sheet and income statement and will help in determining the entry that needs to be made when selling part or all of a particular security. The T-accounts for Example 4-2 can be found in Table 4-3.

- Abbreviations will be used for some accounts: allowance to value of available-for-sale securities (allowance), unrealized increase/decrease in value of available-for-sale securities (unrealized I/D), available-for-sale equity securities (AS, EQ), and available-for-sale debt securities (AS, DT).

- Prepare a table reflecting the cost and FMV of each investment at year-end (or each Balance Sheet date if more frequent). The table will assist in the determination of the required year-end journal entries that must be made to properly record the FMV of each security. The table for Example 4-2 is given in Table 4-4.

EXAMPLE **4-2**

Note: Follow the example using the T-accounts found in Table 4-4. The cost and FMV of the securities at year end are located in Table 4-3.

On January 15, xxx2, BLP, Inc., had an extra $25,000 available for three years. (*Note:* The holding period is more than one year, so the securities will not necessarily be sold in the near future, and debt will not be held until maturity.) The company invested in 300 equity shares of GHI and paid $30 per share. The company also invested in 400 debt securities of JKL and paid $40 for each security. The journal entry to record the initial purchase at cost would be

January 15, xxx2:

AS, EQ—GHI (300 shares × $30)	9,000	
AS, DT—JKL (400 shares × $40)	16,000	
Cash		25,000

During the month of December xxx2, dividends of $90 were received from GHI along with interest of $100 from JKL. The journal entry to record the receipt of interest and dividends would be

December xxx2:

Cash	190	
Interest revenue		100
Dividend revenue		90

On December 31, xxx2, the FMV of the GHI equity securities was $8,400 and the FMV of the JKL debt securities was $16,400. Remember that the financial statements should reflect the FMV on the balance sheet date. Currently, the cost is reflected in the T-accounts; therefore, a journal entry must be made so that the accounts reflect the FMV of each security.

December 31, xxx2:

Unrealized I/D—GHI	600	
Unrealized I/D—JKL	400	
Allowance—GHI		600
Allowance—JKL		400

The value of the GHI equity securities continued to decline, so BLP decided on March 17, xxx3 to sell all the GHI securities. The proceeds received were $25 per share. Because there were three permanent accounts associated with GHI, all those accounts must be eliminated to record the sale.

Refer to the T-accounts in Table 4-3 to see the balances in each account. Please note that the plug in this case is a realized loss of $1,500.

March 17, xxx3:

Cash	7,500	
Realized loss	1,500	
Allowance—GHI	600	
AS, EQ—GHI		9,000
Unrealized I/D—GHI		600

BLP identified MNO as another equity security worthy of investment on April 3, xxx3, and purchased 200 shares at $37 per share. The journal entry to record this initial purchase at cost would be

April 3, xxx3:

AS, EQ—MNO	7,400	
Cash		7,400

During the month of December xxx3, dividends of $90 were received from MNO along with interest of $100 from JKL. The journal entry to record the receipt of interest and dividends would be

December xxx3:

Cash	190	
Interest revenue		100
Dividend revenue		90

On December 31, xxx3, the FMV of the MNO equity securities was $8,400 and the FMV of the JKL debt securities was $17,200. Again, remember that the financial statements should reflect the FMV on the balance sheet date. Currently, the FMV on December 31, xxx3, is reflected in the T-accounts; therefore, a journal entry must be made so that the accounts reflect the FMV of each security as of December 31, xxx3.

December 31, xxx3:

Allowance—MNO (7400 – 8400)	1,000	
Unrealized I/D—MNO		1,000
Allowance—JKL (16,400 – 17,200)	800	
Unrealized I/D—JKL		800

An unexpected need for cash arose in March xxx4, so BLP decided to sell half the investment in JKL for $45 per share on March 10, xxx4. Remember that there are three permanent accounts associated with JKL, and half of each account will need to be removed when half the investment is sold. *Note:* The plug in this journal entry is the realized gain.

March 10, xxx4:

Cash (200 shares × $45)	9,000	
Unrealized I/D—JKL (0.5 × 1200)	600	
AS,DT—JKL (200 shares × $40)		8,000
Realized gain		1,000
Allowance—JKL (0.5 × 1200)		600

During the month of December xxx4, dividends of $90 were received from GHI along with interest of $50 from JKL. The journal entry to record the receipt of interest and dividends would be

December xxx4:

Cash	140	
Interest revenue		50
Dividend revenue		90

On December 31, xxx4, the FMV of the MNO equity securities was $8,800 and the FMV of the JKL debt securities was $9,400. Remember that the financial statements should reflect the FMV on the balance sheet date. Currently, the FMV on December 31, xxx3, is reflected in the T-accounts along with the sale of half the JKL shares; therefore, to make the accounts reflect the FMV for each security as of December 31, xxx4, a journal entry is needed.

December 31, xxx4:

Allowance—MNO (8400 – 8800)	400	
Unrealized I/D—MNO		400
Allowance—JKL (9400 – 8600)	800	
Unrealized I/D—JKL		800

As noted previously, the T-accounts for Example 4-2 are reflected in Table 4-4, whereas the related balance sheet and income statement appear in Tables 4-5 and 4-6, respectively. *We urge you to reread and study this example until you fully understand it before moving on to the next topic.*

TABLE 4-3   T-Accounts for Example 4-2

	Cost	FMV		
		December 31, xxx2	December 31, xxx3	December 31, xxx4
AS, EQ—GHI	9,000	8,400		
AS, DT—JKL	16,000	16,400	17,200	9,400
AS, EQ—MNO	7,400		8,400	8,800

TABLE 4-4   FMV as of December 31 of the Three Years of Example 4-2

AS, EQ—GHI		Allowance—GHI		Unrealized I/D—GHI	
1/15/xxx2 9,000		12/31/xxx2	600	12/31/xxx2 600	
12/31/xxx3	9,000	3/17/xxx3 600		3/17/xxx3	600

AS, DT—JKL		Allowance—JKL		Unrealized I/D—JKL	
1/15/xxx2 16,000		12/31/xxx2 400		12/31/xxx2	400
3/10/xxx4	8,000	12/31/xxx3 800		12/31/xxx3	800
		3/10/xxx4	600	3/10/xxx4 600	
		12/31/xxx4 800		12/31/xxx4	800

AS, EQ—MNO		Allowance—MNO		Unrealized I/D—MNO	
4/03/xxx3 7,400		12/31/xxx3 1,000		12/31/xxx3	1,000
		12/31/xxx4 400		12/31/xxx4	400

TABLE 4-5 BLP, Inc., Balance Sheet as of December 31 of the Three Years of Example 4-2

	December 31, xxx2	December 31, xxx3	December 31, xxx4
Current assets:			
Long-term assets:			
AS, EQ—GHI, at cost	9,000		
Less: Allowance—GHI	(600)		
AS, EQ—GHI, at FMV	8,400		
AS, DT—JKL, at cost	16,000	16,000	8,000
Add: Allowance—JKL	400	1,200	1,400
AS, DT—JKL, at FMV	16,400	17,200	9,400
AS, EQ—MNO, at cost		7,400	7,400
Add: Allowance—MNO		1,000	1,400
AS, EQ—MNO, at FMV		8,400	8,800
Total long-term assets	24,800	25,600	18,200

TABLE 4-6 BLP, Inc., Income Statement for the Three Years of Example 4-2

	December 31, xxx2	December 31, xxx3	December 31, xxx4
Other items:			
Interest revenue	100	100	50
Dividend revenue	90	90	90
Realized gain on sale of available-for-sale securities			1,000
Realized loss on sale of available-for-sale securities		(1,500)	

Debt Securities Held to Maturity

Recall that debt securities held to maturity can be only debt securities such as bonds. Additionally, it must be management's intent to hold the securities until they mature. GAAP rules include the following:

- The initial purchase is recorded at *cost,* which is not necessarily the face value (FV) of the bond.

- All subsequent reporting at each balance sheet date is at *amortized cost*, not FMV and not cost.

- All discounts and premiums are amortized directly to the investment in debt held to maturity account.

- All discounts and premiums are amortized over the remaining life of the bond.

- Unrealized holding gains and losses are not recorded.

- Interest revenue is reported on the income statement.

We will offer you five different examples for accounting for debt held to maturity (debt—HM) securities. The number of possible scenarios and treatments necessitate the number of examples. First, debt securities may be purchased at either a premium or a discount, so examples for both will be provided. Second, there are two ways to amortize any premiums and discounts, the straight-line method and the effective interest method, so both methods will be demonstrated. Finally, a debt security may be sold before it actually matures, so we will provide the journal entries to simulate that occurrence as well.

Straight-Line Amortization of a Premium

 EXAMPLE 4-3

On January 1, 2010, BLP, Inc., invested in bonds that the company's management intends to hold until their maturity date of January 1, 2013. BLP paid $102,531.25 for the $100,000 face-value bonds. The bonds carry a stated interest rate of 10 percent and have an effective rate of 9 percent.

Notice that the price paid for the bonds is greater than the face value, signifying a premium. In this example we will amortize the premium of $2,531.25 using the straight-line method. So let's get the purchase recorded.

January 1, 2010:

Investment in debt—HM	102,531.25	
Cash		102,531.25

Because the interest is paid only once per year on January 1, the interest revenue must be accrued on each balance sheet date. We will assume that financial statements are issued only once per year on December 31. When we accrue the interest revenue, we also will make the journal entry to amortize the premium. The premium is currently a part of the investment in debt—HM account, and our goal is to reduce that account to the face value of the bonds of $100,000 by the date of their maturity. Additionally, we want the interest revenue account to reflect the effective rate of interest rather than the stated rate of interest in order to achieve a proper matching of revenues and expenses each year.

Please note that the stated rate of interest reflects the amount of actual cash that will always be received by the company. However, the amount of interest actually recognized is based on the *effective rate of interest*, which takes into consideration the extra amount of money beyond the face value of the bonds that was paid at the time of purchase. That purchase price reflects the interest rates that were found in the market at the purchase date. Bonds will be sold at a premium when their stated rates are larger than the going interest rates for bonds carrying a similar risk in the marketplace. When investors are offered a higher return than they otherwise would obtain for similar bonds, they will be willing to pay more than face value for those securities, which results in a premium. That premium is reduced gradually over the life of the bond, and the interest revenue recognized is the difference between the amount of cash received and the premium reduction.

Because in this example the effective rate of interest (9 percent) is less than the stated rate of interest (10 percent), the interest revenue recognized in our journal entry will be less than the cash actually received for the interest. Since we are using the straight-line method of amortization, the total amount of the premium, $2,531.25, will be reduced in equal amounts each year until the 2013 maturity date. Therefore, the total premium is divided by the three-year remaining life of the bond to arrive at the premium amortization of $843.75. In the straight-line method, this amount will never change, which is different from the treatment under the effective method, as we will see shortly. The journal entry for both the accrual of interest revenue at year-end and the amortization of the premium using the straight-line method would be

December 31, 2010:

Interest receivable	10,000	
Interest revenue (plug)		9,156.25
Investment in debt—HM		843.75

When we accounted for investments in debt and equity available-for-sale securities, we needed the FMV at year end so that we could adjust the account to reflect the FMV at year end. However, when we account for investments in debt—HM, we want the securities to appear at amortized cost on each financial statement. Because we amortized the premium to the investment account, the balance in the investment account will reflect the new amortized cost of $101,687.50 (102,531.25 – 843.75).

On January 1, 2011, when we receive the interest, we will make the following journal entry:

January 1, 2011:

Cash	10,000	
Interest receivable		10,000

We will make the same journal entry on December 31 of each year for the life of the bonds to amortize the premium and record the accrual of interest revenue. Then, on January 1 of each year, we will make the same journal entry as shown above to record the receipt of the interest revenue. These journal entries are illustrated below:

December 31, 2011:

Interest receivable	10,000	
Interest revenue		9,156.25
Investment in debt—HM		843.75

Now the amortized cost of the investment in debt—HM is $100,843.75 ($101,687.50 – 843.75), and it will be reflected on the December 31, 2011, balance sheet.

January 1, 2012:

Cash	10,000	
Interest receivable		10,000

December 31, 2012:

Interest receivable	10,000	
Interest revenue		9,156.25
Investment in debt—HM		843.75

Now the amortized cost of the investment in debt—HM is $100,000 ($100,843.75 – 843.75), and it will be reflected on the December 31, 2012, balance sheet.

January 1, 2013:

Cash	10,000	
Interest receivable		10,000

Recall from the beginning of this example that the bonds have a three-year life. We have amortized the premium over three years, and if all has gone according to plan, the amortized cost of the bonds should equal their face value. A quick look shows that they do—both are $100,000.

On January 1, 2013, the bonds will be redeemed for their maturity value, and the event will be recorded on the books using the following journal entry:

January 1, 2013:

Cash	100,000	
Investment in debt—HM		100,000

For some people, it is easier to prepare the amortization schedule first and then make the journal entries directly from the information in the amortization schedule. As a result, we have included the schedule along with the numbers from this example in Table 4-7. Try it and see what works best for you.

TABLE 4-7 Investment in Debt—HM Premium Amortization Table: Straight-Line Method (Example 4-3)

	10%[a] Dr Cash or Interest Receivable	Difference[c] Cr Interest Revenue	Premium/Life[b] Cr Investment in Debt—HM	Amortized Cost of Investment in Debt—HM[d]
1/1/12				102,531.25
12/31/10	10,000.00	9,156.25	843.75	101,687.50
12/31/11	10,000.00	9,156.25	843.75	100,843.75
12/31/12	10,000.00	9,156.25	843.75	100,000.00

Note: Cr refers to credit and Dr refers to debit in all amortization schedules used in this book.
[a]Stated rate (10%) times FV of bonds ($100,000).
[b]$2,531.25/three–year life of bonds.
[c]Difference between amount from footnote a and footnote b.
[d]Previous investment balance minus the amount from footnote b.

Effective Interest Amortization of a Premium

EXAMPLE 4-4

Two methods are used to amortize the premiums and discounts for investments in debt—HM. This example will illustrate the journal entries and amortization schedule using the effective interest method. Hopefully, we can keep the example easy for you by using the same dollar amounts as we did in Example 4-3. The only amount that will change will be the amortization of the premium, which, in turn, as we mentioned earlier, will change the amount of interest revenue reported each year. The amortization schedule may be found in Table 4-8.

TABLE 4-8   Investment in Debt—HM Premium Amortization Table: Effective Interest Method (Example 4-4)

	10%[a] Dr Cash or Interest Receivable	9%[b] Cr Interest Revenue	Premium/Life[c] Cr Investment in Debt—HM	Amortized Cost of Investment in Debt—HM[d]
1/1/10				102,531.25
12/31/10	10,000.00	9,227.81	772.19	101,759.06
12/31/11	10,000.00	9,158.32	841.68	100,917.38
12/31/12	10,000.00	9,082.62	917.38	100,000.00

[a]Stated rate (10%) times FV of bonds ($100,000).
[b]Effective rate (9%) times the previous amortized cost.
[c]Difference between amount for footnote a and footnote b.
[d]Previous investment balance minus the amount from footnote c.
Note: The interest revenue for 12/13/2013 was rounded by 0.06 to make the ending amortized cost equal the FV of the bonds.

Please note that the amount of interest revenue recognized each year is calculated as the amortized cost times the effective interest rate. As under the straight-line method, the company always will receive the same amount of actual cash, which is calculated as the face value of the bonds times the stated interest rate and in this case is $10,000. The difference between the actual amount of cash received and the interest revenue is the amount of premium that is amortized for the year. Because the amortized cost changes each year, the amount of interest revenue recognized and thus the amortization amount for each year differ. However, the total premium on the bonds still must be completely eliminated by the time of their maturity.

To record the purchase of the investment in debt—HM:

January 1, 2010:

| Investment in debt—HM | 102,531.25 | |
| Cash | | 102,531.25 |

To accrue the interest revenue and amortize the premium at the end of year 1 (2010):

December 31, 2010:

Interest receivable	10,000	
Interest revenue		9,227.81
Investment in debt—HM		772.19

To receive the first of three interest payments:

January 1, 2011:

| Cash | 10,000 | |
| Interest receivable | | 10,000 |

To accrue the interest revenue and amortize the premium at the end of year 2 (2011):

December 31, 2011:

Interest receivable	10,000	
Interest revenue		9,158.32
Investment in debt—HM		841.68

To receive the second of three interest payments:

January 1, 2012:

| Cash | 10,000 | |
| Interest receivable | | 10,000 |

To accrue the interest revenue and amortize the premium at the end of year 3 (2012):

December 31, 2012:

Interest receivable	10,000	
Interest revenue		9,082.62
Investment in debt—HM		917.38

To receive the third of three interest payments:

January 1, 2013:

| Cash | 10,000 | |
| Interest receivable | | 10,000 |

All that is left is to make the journal entry to redeem the bonds for their maturity value:

January 1, 2013:

| Cash | 100,000 | |
| Investment in debt—HM | | 100,000 |

Straight-Line Amortization of a Discount

Investments in debt—HM also can be purchased at a discount. A discount will result when the face value of the bonds is greater than the purchase price of the bonds. Bonds will be sold at a discount when their stated rates are smaller than the going interest rates for bonds carrying a similar risk in the marketplace. When investors are offered a lower return than they otherwise would obtain for similar bonds, they will not be willing to pay the full face value for those securities, which results in a discount. The discount is eliminated gradually over the life of the bond by increasing the investment in the debt—HM account through amortization of the discount. The reduced price of the securities effectively compensates for the lower interest that actually will be received, and the discount amortization essentially recognizes the extra interest that is effectively earned beyond the amount of cash actually received.

The next two examples illustrate the journal entries for these situations.

 EXAMPLE 4-5

We will use most of the same assumptions from Example 4-4 here. However, the three-year bonds now will be purchased for $95,196.31, which reflects a discount of $4,803.69. The stated rate of interest will be 10 percent, as before, but the effective rate of interest now will be 11 percent. The face value of the bonds will still be $100,000. The amortization schedule may be found in Table 4-9.

TABLE 4-9 Investment in Debt—HM Discount Amortization Table: Straight-Line Method (Example 4-5)

	10%[a] Dr Cash or Interest Receivable	Sum[c] Cr Interest Revenue	Premium/Life[b] Cr Investment in Debt—HM	Amortized Cost of Investment in Debt—HM[d]
1/1/10				95,196.31
12/31/10	10,000.00	11,601.23	1,601.23	96,797.54
12/31/11	10,000.00	11,601.23	1,601.23	98,398.77
12/31/12	10,000.00	11,601.23	1,601.23	100,000.00

[a]Stated rate (10%) times FV of bonds ($100,000).
[b]$4,803.69/three-year life of bonds.
[c]Sum of amount for footnote a and footnote b.
[d]Previous investment balance plus the amount from footnote b.

Please note that the stated interest rate, 10 percent, is lower than the effective or market interest rate, 11 percent. Thus investors will be willing to purchase the securities only at a discount. Additionally, under the straight-line method, the amount of the discount, $4,803.69, must be evenly distributed over the three years until maturity, so the amount of the amortization each year is $1,601.23. This amount plus the cash actually received, $10,000, results in the amount of interest revenue that is recognized each year, $11,601.23.

To record the purchase of the securities:

January 1, 2010:

Investment in debt—HM	95,196.31	
Cash		95,196.31

To accrue the interest earned and amortize the discount at the end of year 1 (2010):

December 31, 2010:

Interest receivable	10,000.00	
Investment in debt—HM	1,601.23	
Interest revenue		11,601.23

To record the first of three interest payments:

January 1, 2011:

Cash	10,000	
Interest receivable		10,000

To accrue the interest earned and amortize the discount at the end of year 2 (2011):

December 31, 2011:

Interest receivable	10,000.00	
Investment in debt—HM	1,601.23	
Interest revenue		11,601.23

To record the second of three interest payments:

January 1, 2012:

Cash	10,000	
Interest receivable		10,000

To accrue the interest earned and amortize the discount at the end of year 3 (2012):

December 31, 2012:

Interest receivable	10,000.00	
Investment in debt—HM	1,601.23	
Interest revenue		11,601.23

To record the third of three interest payments:

January 1, 2013:

Cash	10,000	
Interest receivable		10,000

All that is left is to make the journal entry to redeem the bonds for their maturity value.

January 1, 2013:

Cash	100,000	
Investment in debt—HM		100,000

Effective Interest Method of Discount Amortization

EXAMPLE 4-6

Again, we will show the effective interest method for the amortization of a discount using the same assumptions. The amortization schedule may be found in Table 4-10. Refer to the amortization schedule for the numbers for each of the following journal entries.

TABLE 4-10 Investment in Debt—HM Discount Amortization Table: Effective Interest Method (Example 4-6)

	10%[a] Dr Cash or Interest Receivable	12%[b] Cr Interest Revenue	Premium/Life[c] Cr Investment in Debt—HM	Amortized Cost of Investment in Debt—HM[d]
1/1/10				95,196.31
12/31/10	10,000.00	11,423.56	1,423.56	96,619.87
12/31/11	10,000.00	11,594.38	1,594.38	98,214.25
12/31/12	10,000.00	11,785.75	1,785.75	100,000.00

[a]Stated rate (10%) times FV of bonds ($100,000).
[b]Effective rate (12%) times the previous amortized cost.
[c]Difference between amount for footnote a and footnote b.
[d]Previous investment balance plus the amount from footnote c.
Note: The interest revenue for 12/13/2012 was rounded by 0.04 to make the ending amortized cost equal the FV of the bonds.

Please note that the amount of interest revenue recognized each year is calculated as the amortized cost times the effective interest rate. As under the straight-line method, the company always will receive the same amount of actual cash, which is calculated as the face value of the bonds times the stated interest rate and in this case is $10,000. The difference between the interest revenue and the actual amount of cash received is the amount of discount that is amortized for the year. Because the amortized cost changes each year, the amount of interest revenue recognized and thus the amortization amount for each year differ. However, the discount still must be eliminated completely and the bonds carried at face value by the date of their maturity.

To record the purchase of the securities:

January 1, 2010:

Investment in debt—HM	95,196.31	
Cash		95,196.31

To accrue the interest earned and amortize the discount at the end of year 1 (2010):

December 31, 2010:

Interest receivable	10,000.00	
Investment in debt—HM	1,423.56	
Interest revenue		11,423.56

To record the first of three interest payments:

January 1, 2011:

Cash	10,000	
Interest receivable		10,000

To accrue the interest earned and amortize the discount at the end of year 2 (2011):

December 31, 2011:

Interest receivable	10,000.00	
Investment in debt—HM	1,594.38	
Interest revenue		11,594.38

To record the second of three interest payments:

January 1, 2012:

Cash	10,000	
Interest receivable		10,000

To accrue the interest earned and amortize the discount at the end of year 3 (2012):

December 31, 2012:

Interest receivable	10,000.00	
Investment in debt—HM	1,785.75	
Interest revenue		11,785.75

To record the third of three interest payments:

January 1, 2013:

Cash	10,000	
Interest receivable		10,000

All that is left is to make the journal entry to redeem the bonds for their maturity value:

January 1, 2013:

Cash	100,000	
Investment in debt—HM		100,000

Before beginning our final example, there is one more point that needs to be emphasized. Although we have presented both the straight-line and effective interest methods for amortization, GAAP prescribes that the effective interest method, because it properly matches expenses with revenues, be used unless the straight-line method results in interest revenue amounts that are not materially different.

Sale of Debt Held to Maturity Security Prior to Maturity

 EXAMPLE **4-7**

Let's refer to Table 4-10, the amortization schedule for Example 4-6, to see the amortized cost as of December 31, 2011 ($98,214.25). On June 30, 2012, six months prior to the bonds maturing, BLP, Inc., decided to sell the bonds for $99,500.00 plus accrued interest.

Just as depreciating an asset up to the date of sale is required, we also must amortize the premium/discount up to the date of sale and accrue the interest revenue. Please note that the amount of cash to be received, the interest receivable, is only half of what would have been received had the bonds been held for the entire year ($100,000 × 0.1 × 0.5 = $5,000). Additionally, the interest revenue is calculated in a similar manner. The amortized cost still is multiplied by the effective interest rate, but now that amount also must be multiplied by 0.5 because the interest is accruing for only 6 months ($98,214.25 × 0.12 × 0.5 = $5,892.86). As always, the amortization amount is the difference between the interest revenue recognized and the interest to be received, which in this case is $892.86. The journal entry to record the discount amortization and accrue the interest revenue would be

June 30, 2012:

Interest receivable	5,000.00	
Investment in debt—HM	892.86	
Interest revenue		5,892.86

This brings the amortized cost of the investment in debt—HM account to $99,107.11 ($98,214.25 + 892.86). The realized gain or loss on the sale is the difference between the amortized cost and the selling price ($99,500 − $99,107.11 = $392.89). The journal entry to reflect the sale of the securities is

June 30, 2012:

Cash ($99,500 + $5,000)	104,500.00	
Investment in debt—HM		99,107.11
Interest receivable		5,000.00
Gain on sale of investment in debt—HM		392.89

Internal Controls

Establishment of Responsibility and Segregation of Duties

As with most other areas of business operations, investments require a clear establishment of responsibility and segregation of duties. First, the board of directors or a similar designated party should be in charge of authorizing investment purchases and sales. Second, another party, preferably an unrelated one, should be responsible for the actual physical care of the assets. Finally, yet a different individual should be selected to record the investments in the books. As a result of such segregation, hiding investments for personal gain or stealing assets of the company can be better precluded.

Documentation Procedures and Physical, Mechanical, and Electronic Controls

If the board of directors is responsible for approving the purchase and sale of securities, the protocol for such approvals should be noted in the organization's bylaws. Additionally, when approvals actually are voted on, the minutes of the board should document such authorizations. In order to better physically safeguard the securities, a safe-deposit box at a bank may be used for their storage.

Independent Internal Verification

Internal parties may verify that the investments noted on the company's records actually are held by the company and, likewise, that investments that are held in the company's name have been recorded on the books. Such reconciliations help to ensure accuracy and to prevent fraud. Also, internal personnel, in addition to independent parties, should perform recalculations of any investment gains and losses, dividends and interest received, and discount and premium amortization determinations.

In this chapter we have identified and thoroughly described the accounting treatment for the various types of investments: trading, available-for-sale, and debt held to maturity. In Chapter 5 we will continue with another long-term asset. This one, though, might take up a bit more physical space—property, plant, and equipment.

QUIZ

1. **Which of the following types of investments cannot include equity securities?**

   A. Trading securities
   B. Available-for-sale securities
   C. Securities with the intent to sell in the near future
   D. Held-to-maturity securities

2. **The two types of securities that are recorded on the balance sheet at fair market value are**

   A. Trading securities and debt held to maturity.
   B. Available-for-sale securities and debt held to maturity.
   C. Trading and available-for-sale securities.
   D. None of the above.

3. **On May 14, 2010, the Jeffres Company invested in 100 shares of A company stock at $30 per share. The company also bought 200 debt securities in B company at $20 per security. The company intended to sell the securities in the near future. At the end of the year, the value per share of A was $35, and the value per security of B was $14. On December 31, 2010, the balance sheet date, the investments would be recorded on the balance sheet at _____ and _____, respectively.**

   A. $3,500; $2,800
   B. $3,000; $4,000
   C. $2,800; $3,500
   D. $500; $1,200

4. **Based on the information in question 3, the journal entry to record the change to fair market value would include**

   A. A debit to trading securities A for $3,500 and a credit to trading securities B for $2,800.
   B. A debit to trading securities A for $500 and a credit to trading securities B for $2,800.
   C. A credit to trading securities B for $1,200 and a debit to unrealized loss on trading securities for $700.
   D. A credit to trading securities B for $1,200 and a credit to unrealized gain on trading securities for $700.

5. **Using the same information as in question 3, the Jeffres Company sold all the A securities on May 9, 2011, for $37 per share. The value of the securities did not change from December 31, 2010. What would be the realized gain or loss on the sale, and where would it be reported?**

   A. A realized loss of $200 reported on the income statement
   B. A realized gain of $200 reported in other comprehensive income
   C. A realized loss of $200 reported in other comprehensive income
   D. A realized gain of $200 reported on the income statement

6. On April 5, 2010, LJ, Inc., purchased 500 equity securities in GBW, Inc., at $5 per share that it classified as available for sale. On December, 31, 2010, as it was preparing its financial statements, LJ, Inc., determined that the fair market value of the securities had increased to $15 per share. What would be the journal entry to adjust the value of the securities?

   A. A debit to available-for-sale securities—GBW for $5,000 and a credit to unrealized gain for $5,000

   B. A debit to unrealized increase/decrease—GBW for $7,500 and a credit to allowance to value AFS securities for $7,500

   C. A debit to unrealized increase/decrease—GBW for $5,000 and a credit to allowance to value AFS securities—GBW for $5,000

   D. A debit to allowance to value AFS securities—GBW for $5,000 and a credit to unrealized increase/decrease—GBW for $5,000

7. On January 15, 2015, LJ, Inc., sold half the GBW securities described in question 6. Immediately before the sale, the securities had been revalued on the company's books at $25 per share. LJ, Inc., sold the shares for $23 each. The entries to the unrealized increase/decrease and the realized gain/loss accounts would be

   A. a debit to unrealized increase/decrease—GBW for $5,000 and a credit to realized gain of $4,500.

   B. a debit to unrealized increase/decrease—GBW for $10,000 and a credit to realized gain of $9,000.

   C. a debit to realized loss of $9,000 and a credit to unrealized increase/decrease—GBW for $10,000.

   D. a debit to realized loss of $4,500 and a credit to unrealized increase/decrease—GBW for $4,500.

8. On January 3, 2010, GBW, Inc., purchased bonds from LJ, Inc., that it intends to hold to their maturity date of January 1, 2015. GBW paid $91,889.09 for the $100,000 face-value bonds. The bonds carry a stated interest rate of 6 percent and have an effective rate of 8 percent. The interest on the bonds is to be paid semiannually. What is the amount of interest revenue that should be recorded on December 31, 2010, using the straight-line method?

   A. $811.09

   B. $2,188.91

   C. $3,000.00

   D. $3,811.09

9. Using the same information as in question 8, what is the amount of interest revenue that should be recorded on December 31, 2010, using the effective interest method?

    A. $2,188.91
    B. $702.59
    C. $3,000.00
    D. $3,702.59

10. Using the same information as in question 8, what is the amortized cost of the bonds on December 31, 2012, if the effective interest method is used?

    A. $96,370.09
    B. $96,755.64
    C. $3,821.93
    D. $93,267.24

chapter 5

Property, Plant, and Equipment

CHAPTER OBJECTIVES

After completing this chapter, the student should

- Understand the financial statement presentation for property, plant, and equipment
- Account for six different ways to acquire property, plant, and equipment
- Calculate depreciation expense using four different methods
- Understand capitalizing versus expensing expenditures
- Account for the elimination of assets
- Understand internal controls over property, plant, and equipment

Overview

What would a business do without a building, machines, furniture, vehicles, and so on? Now don't get us wrong, there are some businesses that do not need many of the physical assets that historically have been essential to business operations. Especially in this electronic and virtual age, where employees and even owners of companies work from their homes and transport information and products all across the world with just a single click, businesses gradually have been downscaling their physical presence along with the associated big-dollar-value assets and costs. However, what we in the accounting world refer to as *property, plant, and equipment* (PPE) is still quite plentiful and still constitutes a large portion of companies' assets (especially manufacturing companies) on their balance sheets. Therefore, it is less than surprising that the proper accounting for these items is essential both for external use by creditors and investors and for the company's well-being. In fact, it is in this very area and with the decision whether to capitalize as PPE or expense the costs of certain items that companies have wound up in trouble and involved in scandals in recent years. Because of such monetary magnitude, such choices open an easy avenue for earnings manipulation on the income statement.

Financial Statement Presentation

BLP, Inc., has several buildings that are completely furnished with desks, filing cabinets, computers, and equipment. The company also has a fleet of cars and trucks for its salespeople to use. All these items are considered property, plant, and equipment (PPE). Because they are owned by the company and represent a future benefit to the organization, they will appear as assets on the balance sheet. Additionally, because such assets all have expected useful lives of more than one year, their proper classification more specifically falls under long-term assets. Like all other assets, the PPE accounts have normal debit balances. It is important to note, however, that besides having useful lives of more than one year, there are two other characteristics that must be met in order for an item to be deemed PPE. First, it must be tangible, or, in layperson's terms, must have the ability to be seen and touched, which all the items mentioned at BLP appear to be, and second, it must be used in the company's operations. Again, the building, desks, filing cabinets, computers, and other equipment of the company are indeed used in this capacity.

There are two additional types of assets that we need to discuss here. You might inadvertently classify them as PPE, but such classification would be incorrect. This may sound very strange to you, but it really is logical. Here is the explanation: These assets are held only for future use (investment purposes) or are allowed to sit idle without use. Remember, to be classified as PPE, the asset *must be used* in operations. Since these two assets are not being used in operations, they may not be classified as PPE. Instead, they are classified as long-term investments and other assets, respectively.

Let's go back to PPE. As a result of their longer-than-one-year useful lives, all the PPE assets, except for land (more about land in a bit), can be depreciated. Essentially, depreciation allows for the allocating of the cost of an item over a certain time period or in terms of its varied use. Thus, even though the entire cost of the purchase may be paid out immediately at the time of purchase or acquisition, that cost is recognized in the books over a longer time frame in an effort to match expenses with related revenues. Remember that we said that, as an asset, the item held future benefit for the company, which, depending on the item, may be increased production capability for a larger number of sales or increased communication abilities and connections with customers across the world, and so on. Those benefits are not all obtained at the time of purchase, so the cost of obtaining those benefits similarly should be spread out. The journal entry to account for the depreciation is considered an adjusting journal entry and, like most other adjusting entries, involves both a balance sheet account (accumulated depreciation) and an income statement account (depreciation expense). The accumulated depreciation account has a normal credit balance and is presented as a contra account to each asset or category of assets on the balance sheet. Table 5-1 provides a visual example of the balance sheet presentation for PPE along with the corresponding accumulated depreciation accounts.

TABLE 5-1   Balance Sheet: Property, Plant, and Equipment

Assets:		
Current assets:		
Long-term assets:		
Land		50,000
Buildings	300,000	
Less: Accumulated depreciation: Buildings	(100,000)	200,000
Furniture and fixtures	200,000	
Less: Accumulated depreciation: Furniture and fixtures	(75,000)	125,000
Equipment	400,000	
Less: Accumulated depreciation: Equipment	(125,000)	275,000
Vehicles	250,000	
Less: Accumulated depreciation: Vehicles	(225,000)	25,000
Total property, plant, and equipment		675,000
Liabilities:		
Current liabilities:		
Long-term liabilities:		
Stockholder's equity:		
Contributed capital:		
Retained earnings:		
Other comprehensive income:		

Now, as promised, let's investigate land in a bit more detail. The main reason for depreciation is to recognize that assets do have limited lives and thus have only a certain time frame in which they can be used and benefit the company. Land, with an unlimited useful life, does not meet such criteria. Now, we know what you are thinking: A company doesn't always hold onto a piece of land forever. Yes, we agree. Companies relocate all the time. However, even though a company may use the land for a limited time frame, land in and of itself has an unlimited life and therefore is not depreciable.

In the next few pages we will do more with PPE than you ever thought imaginable. We will acquire it, depreciate it using various methods, put additional money into PPE that is already owned, and eliminate it, and, of course, discuss some basic internal controls.

Acquisition of Property, Plant, and Equipment

So what is the difference between capitalizing and expensing? When you spend money, you will have a credit to one of three accounts—cash, accounts payable, or notes payable—that is a given. The debit, however, requires a bit more thought and is a choice between an asset or an expense. *If you debit an asset*, you are *capitalizing* the expenditure because the total cost is first recorded on the balance sheet and, over time, is transferred to the income statement via depreciation expense. *If you debit an expense*, though, you are *expensing* the expenditure because the total cost is recognized immediately on the income statement and never appears on the balance sheet.

Now that you have an understanding of this basic concept, let's spend some time acquiring assets. We will discuss six different ways that long-term assets can be acquired: purchase as a single asset, purchase as a group of assets, acquire by making deferred payments, acquire by issuing securities, acquire by donation, and acquire by exchanging assets with another company.

Purchase as a Single Asset

If you are purchasing a building that already has been constructed, the contract price constitutes the cost of the building. The costs of any remodeling or reconditioning work that must be completed before the building is ready for use also must be capitalized to the building account. However, if construction of the building has not yet commenced, the capitalized cost will include the cost of excavation work, including digging through the ground to prepare the land for the foundation of the building. The capitalized cost also will include any architectural costs incurred and building permits obtained in connection with the initiative. Often companies will have to borrow money to help finance the construction of a building. The interest charges incurred during the construction period (while expenditures for construction are being made, activities are being undertaken to get the building ready for its use, and related interest is being incurred, but before the building is substantially complete and ready for its prespecified use) also will have to be capitalized. Finally, any unanticipated costs that result from the condition of the land, such as removing rocks, will be capitalized to the building account.

If you are purchasing land intended to be the site of construction for a building, the cost of the land will include the purchase price and any closing costs associated with obtaining title to the land. Closing costs usually include the commission paid to the real estate agent, lawyer's fees, title search fees, and any delinquent (past due) taxes that must be paid before title legally can change hands. Costs incurred in connection with surveying the land also will be capitalized to the land account. Finally, the costs associated with preparing the land for its intended use, such as the removal of an existing building to make room for the new structure, will appear as part of the cost of the land on the balance sheet.

EXAMPLE 5-1

BLP, Inc., decided to relocate to a new area of the city to keep pace with the city's expanding growth. The company incurred several costs associated with the purchase of the land and construction of a building. As we discussed earlier, it is important to distinguish which costs are capitalized to the land account and which are capitalized to the building account. Table 5-2 shows the costs BLP incurred. Please pay particular attention to the account (land or building) to which each cost is capitalized.

TABLE 5-2 Costs for Acquisition of Land and Construction of a Building (Example 5-1)

	Land	Building
Purchase price of land	40,000	
Real estate agent commission	2,400	
Legal fees associated with changing title to the land	5,000	
Other closing costs	600	
Cost to remove an old building	2,000	
Cost of building plans		20,000
Contract price paid to the construction contractor		200,000
Interest costs during the construction period		30,000
Unanticipated costs resulting from the condition of the land:		
There was a large layer of rock that had to be removed		50,000
	50,000	300,000

The journal entry to record the purchase of the land and the construction of the building would be

March 30, 2010:

Land	50,000	
Building	300,000	
Cash		350,000

Purchase as a Group of Assets

Recall that land is not depreciable, but buildings are. Because of this, it is extremely important that the costs associated with the purchase of a group or bundle of assets be allocated appropriately to each of the assets included in the group. You do not want a depreciable expenditure capitalized to the land account and, as a result, understate depreciation. Likewise, you do not want to depreciate, as part of the building, a nondepreciable expenditure.

When assets are acquired as part of a group purchase, the total cost must be allocated to each asset based on the total fair market value (FMV) of the entire group. If any appraisals are required to determine the FMV of the assets, then the costs associated with such appraisals are also part of the total allocable cost.

EXAMPLE 5-2

BLP, Inc., located a piece of property in a high-growth area of its city that, for the most part, conformed to its desires. The property included land, a building, and equipment that could be used in BLP's business. The current owner was offering to sell all the items as a group to the same buyer for a total cost of $500,000. In the process of deciding whether or not to purchase the items, BLP obtained appraisals for all three items and discovered that the total FMV was $700,000. Additionally, the cost of the appraisals amounted to $50,000. Identifying the purchase as a good deal, BLP decided to follow through with the purchase of the land, building, and equipment. Table 5-3 lists the allocation of the purchase price to each asset based on the total FMV. Please note that the cost allocated to each new asset is the FMV of each individual asset divided by the total FMV of the asset group times the total cost to be allocated.

The journal entry to record the purchase of the land, building, and equipment would be

March 30, 2010:

Land	78,571	
Building	314,286	
Equipment	157,143	
Cash		550,000

TABLE 5-3 Lump-Sum Purchase (Example 5-2)

| | | | FMV/Total FMV × Cost to Be Allocated | |
	FMV	FMV of Each Asset	Total FMV (Group FMV)	Cost to be Allocated ($500,000 Purchase Price + $50,000 Appraisal Fees)	Cost
Land	$100,000	$100,000	$700,000	$550,000	$78,571
Building	400,000	400,000	700,000	550,000	314,286
Equipment	200,000	200,000	700,000	550,000	157,143
Total	$700,000				$550,000

In the preceding example, the FMV of all the assets in the group were obtained. This is a best-case scenario that sometimes does not occur in the real world. If the FMV of only one or two of the assets is available, the appraised values of those assets are assigned to their accounts, and the remainder of the cost is apportioned to the other assets.

Acquire by Making Deferred Payments

Sometimes companies need to purchase assets by making deferred payments. If the note that is signed is a non-interest-bearing note and the FMV of the asset being purchased is not known, then the asset must be recorded at the present value of the future note payments.

EXAMPLE 5-3

BLP, Inc., contracted with another company on January 2, 2010, to purchase some equipment. The agreement was that BLP would pay the other company $5,000 at the end of each year for the next five years. The market rate of interest was 10 percent. The present value of $5,000 for five years at 10 percent is $18,954 ($5,000 × 3.790787 – present value of an ordinary annuity interest factor, as found in Appendix B), and this will be debited to the equipment account. The total amount to be paid was $25,000 ($5,000 × 5 payments), and this will be credited to notes payable. Everything is great, and we are done accounting for this, right? Wrong! Now the debits do not equal the credits, and that invalidates the journal entry.

So what should we do? We will have to use a new account to make the journal entry balance. It is called *discount on notes payable* and has a normal debit balance. Each year, as a payment is made, the discount on notes payable account will be reduced with a credit, and the corresponding debit will be to interest expense. The note that was signed was effectively a non-interest-bearing note, and as we all know, such notes do not truly exist. If they did, everyone would want to borrow money. We're not sure that there would be that many willing lenders, however. So the difference between the total amount to be paid ($25,000) and the present value of the payments ($18,954), $6,046, in reality reflects the interest on the note. If the straight-line method of amortization is used, each year when a payment is made, $1,209.20 ($6,046/5) will be taken from the discount on notes payable account and put into interest expense.

The journal entry to record the purchase of the equipment would be

January 2, 2010:

Equipment	18,954	
Discount on notes payable	6,046	
Notes payable		25,000

The journal entries that will be made at the end of each year would be

December 31, 2010, 2011, 2012, 2013, 2014:

Notes payable	5,000.00	
Cash		5,000.00
Interest expense	1,209.20	
Discount on notes payable		1,209.20

Acquire by Issuing Securities

Sometimes a company will give up some of its ownership rights to obtain a much-needed asset. The main issue associated with such situations is determination of the proper amount to be debited to the asset account. Generally accepted accounting principles (GAAP) state that the asset should be debited for the FMV of the asset or the FMV of the securities, whichever is more clearly determinable. Therefore, whichever valuation is most "outside the company" or "at arm's length" is likely the best estimate. For instance, the FMV of securities traded on the New York Stock Exchange is more reliable than the FMV determined by one of the company's board of directors and thus should be used. Additionally, an appraisal of the asset by an "independent" appraiser is more reliable than an appraisal by an employee or owner of one of the companies.

 **EXAMPLE 5-4**

On April 15, 2010, BLP, Inc., wanted to exchange 1,000 shares of its common stock for a piece of much-needed equipment from Jones Company.

The stock had a par value of $5 per share but was not publicly traded on a stock exchange. The last time it was sold was five months ago at a price of $40 per share. The Jones Company firmly believed that its equipment had a FMV of $50,000. BLP hired an independent appraiser, and the appraiser valued the equipment at $45,000. So what value is most appropriate for the equipment? The sale price of $40 for the common stock five months prior is not a reliable estimate of the current value. The $50,000 the Jones Company "believed" the equipment was worth was not an "outside the company," "arm's length" value. The "independent" appraiser provided the best FMV of the three choices given. The equipment should be debited for the $45,000. The common stock should be credited for $5,000 (1,000 shares × $5 par value), leaving another credit of $40,000 needed. Additional paid-in capital: Common stock should be credited for the balance, $40,000.

April 15, 2010:

Equipment	45,000	
Common stock		5,000
Additional paid-in capital: Common stock		40,000

Acquire by Donation

Often cities and counties will donate a piece of land or a building to entice a company to relocate to their area. In return for the land and/or building, the municipality will require the company to employ a certain number of people for a certain amount of time. The company obtaining the asset will debit the asset for its FMV, and a balancing credit will be made to *donated capital*. The donated capital account will be reported in the stockholders' equity section of the balance sheet.

Acquire by Exchanging Assets with Another Company

A final method used to acquire assets is to exchange one of your company's assets for an asset from another company. It is important to note that the rules for asset exchanges for financial statement purposes are different from the rules for asset exchanges for federal income tax return purposes. The following will cover only the rules for asset exchanges for financial statements.

It is helpful to use a step-by-step system to account for asset exchanges. As long as you follow each step precisely, the numbers will always be correct. Before beginning the step-by-step system, develop a chart that lists the two parties to the transaction and indicates what each is giving up and receiving in return. Table 5-4 presents such a chart.

TABLE 5-4 Asset Exchanges

	Given Up	Received
Cost		
Less: Accumulated depreciation		
Equals: Book value		
FMV		
Cash		

Now, for the step by step system:

Step 1: Determine the *realized* gain or loss. Start with the FMV of the asset surrendered, and subtract the book value (BV) of the asset surrendered. The difference is the realized gain or loss.

Step 2: Determine the *recognized* gain or loss. The recognition rules have changed many times over the years. Currently, life is quite easy: Everything gets recognized for financial statement purposes.

Step 3: Determine the cost of the asset acquired. Start with the FMV of the asset surrendered, and then either subtract any cash you received or add any cash you paid. The result is the cost of the new asset.

Step 4: Prepare the journal entry to eliminate the old asset, add the new asset, record any cash transfer, and record any recognized gain or loss. After you have determined each number and recorded each part of the journal entry, the entry should balance.

Table 5-5 offers a template for this technique.

EXAMPLE 5-5

BLP, Inc., agreed to exchange buildings with Jones Company. The building that BLP is surrendering cost the company $175,000 and has a current book value of $110,000. The FMV of this building is $250,000, whereas the FMV of the building Jones Company is giving up is $300,000. Because the FMVs of the two buildings are not equal, BLP has agreed to also pay Jones Company $50,000 in addition to giving the company the building. Table 5-6 provides a chart with numbers, and Table 5-7 shows the step-by-step format with numbers.

TABLE 5-5 Asset Exchanges

Step 1: Determine realized gain or loss

FMV of asset surrendered

Less: BV of asset surrendered

Equals: Realized gain or loss

Step 2: Determine recognized gain or loss

Recognize everything

Step 3: Determine cost of asset acquired

FMV of asset surrendered

Less: Cash received

Add: Cash paid

Equals: Cost of new asset

Step 4: Prepare journal entry

Dr Cost of new asset

Dr Accumulated depreciation of old asset

Dr Cash received

Dr Recognized loss

Cr Recognized gain

Cr Cost of old asset

Cr Cash paid

TABLE 5-6 Asset Exchanges (Example 5-5)

	BLP, Inc.	
	Given Up	Received
Cost	175,000	
Less: Accumulated depreciation	(65,000)	
Equals: Book value	110,000	
FMV	250,000	300,000
Cash	50,000	

TABLE 5-7 Asset Exchanges (Example 5-5)		
Step 1: Determine realized gain or loss		
FMV of asset surrendered	250,000	
Less: BV of asset surrendered	(110,000)	
Equals: Realized gain or loss	140,000	
Step 2: Determine recognized gain or loss		
Recognize everything	140,000	
Step 3: Determine cost of asset acquired		
FMV of asset surrendered	250,000	
Less: Cash received		
Add: Cash paid	50,000	
Equals: Cost of new asset	300,000	
Step 4: Prepare journal entry		
Dr Cost of new asset	300,000	
Dr Accumulated depreciation of old asset	65,000	
Dr Cash received		
Dr Recognized loss		
Cr Recognized gain		140,000
Cr Cost of old asset		175,000
Cr Cash paid		50,000

Depreciation

We now have successfully acquired several assets, and the related costs have been capitalized to long-term asset accounts. Now it is time to learn how to depreciate those items. As we mentioned previously, the purpose of depreciation is to allocate the cost of a long-term asset over its useful life. In this chapter we will explain four different methods to calculate depreciation: straight-line, units-of-output, sum of the years' digits, and declining-balance methods. For each method, there is one firm rule that you *must* remember: *Do not depreciate below the salvage value.* You also can use this rule to deduce a couple of check figures for yourself. First, the total accumulated depreciation at the end of the asset's useful life always will equal the cost of the asset minus the salvage value. Second, the book value (BV) at the end of the asset's useful life always will be the salvage value of the asset. If either of these two check figures does not match up, you have done something wrong. Check for these two items in each of the examples in this section.

Another point to consider is the time of year the asset is purchased. Companies must be consistent in their application of depreciation methods. Company A may choose to depreciate for a full year any asset purchased in the first half of the year and depreciate for only a half a year any asset purchased in the last half of the year. Company B may choose to depreciate based on how many actual months the asset was owned during the year. Company C may choose to depreciate based on how many actual days the asset was owned during the year. It doesn't matter what system is used as long as it is used consistently.

To record the journal entry for depreciation, debit *depreciation expense* and credit *accumulated depreciation*. Recall that depreciation expense is a temporary account reported on the income statement and has a normal debit balance. Also recall that accumulated depreciation is a permanent account on the balance sheet with a normal credit balance. The accumulated depreciation account will "accumulate" all the depreciation expense for the asset for each year of the asset's useful life.

For each example, we will use the same basic set of information so that you can compare each of the methods with one another. The information may be found in Table 5-8.

Another useful tool when learning the different methods of depreciation is to set up a chart that shows the date, depreciation expense, accumulated depreciation, and BV for each year of the asset's life. Such a chart may be found in Table 5-9.

TABLE 5-8 Depreciation Basic Information

Cost, January 2, 2010	110,000
Salvage value	10,000
Useful life	4 years
Total units of output each year:	
Year 1	33,000
Year 2	30,000
Year 3	25,000
Year 4	12,000
Total units of output	100,000

TABLE 5-9 Depreciation Column Headings

Date	Formula	Depreciation Expense	Accumulated Depreciation	Book Value

TABLE 5-10 Straight-Line Depreciation				
Date	Formula	Depreciation Expense	Accumulated Depreciation	Book Value
1/2/10				110,000
12/31/10	(110,000 – 10,000)/4	25,000	25,000	85,000
12/31/11	(110,000 – 10,000)/4	25,000	50,000	60,000
12/31/12	(110,000 – 10,000)/4	25,000	75,000	35,000
12/31/13	(110,000 – 10,000)/4	25,000	100,000	10,000
		100,000		

Straight-Line Depreciation

The straight-line depreciation method achieves a uniform expensing of the cost of the asset on the income statement for each year of the asset's life. The formula is cost minus salvage value divided by the life of the asset [(cost – salvage value)/useful life] to arrive at depreciation expense for the year. Table 5-10 shows the related depreciation calculation.

Units-of-Output Depreciation

The units-of-output depreciation method models the assumption that a piece of equipment has a definite capacity (measured in number of units that can be produced) that represents its useful life. The cost of the asset should be allocated (matched) to depreciation expense based on how many units are produced by the asset each year (or period). The formula is cost minus salvage value times units produced this year divided by total units produced over the life of the asset [(cost – salvage value) × (units produced this year/total units produced over life of asset)]to arrive at depreciation expense for each year. Table 5-11 shows the related depreciation calculation.

Sum of the Years' Digits Depreciation

The sum of the years' digits depreciation method models the assumption that a company will get more use and benefit out of an asset in the early years of its life than it will in the later years. Using this method, a greater proportion of the asset's cost is expensed through depreciation in the early years than in later years. The formula is cost minus salvage value times a fraction. The numerator of the fraction is the remaining life at the beginning of the year. The denominator of the fraction is the sum of years of the asset's life. There are two ways to determine the denominator. First, you can simply add the number of years of life together. For our basic example with a useful life of four years it would be

TABLE 5-11 Units-of-Output Depreciation

Date	Formula	Depreciation Expense	Accumulated Depreciation	Book Value
1/2/10				110,000
12/31/10	(110,000 – 10,000) × (33,000/100,000)	33,000	33,000	77,000
12/31/11	(110,000 – 10,000) × (30,000/100,000)	30,000	63,000	47,000
12/31/12	(110,000 – 10,000) × (25,000/100,000)	25,000	88,000	22,000
12/31/13	(110,000 – 10,000) × (12,000/100,000)	12,000	100,000	10,000
		100,000		

$1 + 2 + 3 + 4 = 10$. Second, and sometimes easier and quicker, especially when the useful life is long, you can use the formula $[n \times (n + 1)]/2$, where n is the life of the asset. In our basic example it would be $[4 \times (4 + 1)]/2 = 10$. Table 5-12 shows the related depreciation calculation.

Recall that we talked about purchasing assets during the year and not always at the beginning of a year. When this occurs, the only method that requires substantial adjustment is the sum of the years' digits method. You *must* ensure that you have a full 12 months at each fraction.

TABLE 5-12 Sum of the Years' Digits Depreciation

Date	Formula	Depreciation Expense	Accumulated Depreciation	Book Value
1/2/10				110,000
12/31/10	(110,000 – 10,000) × (4/10)	40,000	40,000	70,000
12/31/11	(110,000 – 10,000) × (3/10)	30,000	70,000	40,000
12/31/12	(110,000 – 10,000) × (2/10)	20,000	90,000	20,000
12/31/13	(110,000 – 10,000) × (1/10)	10,000	100,000	10,000
		100,000		

TABLE 5-13	Sum of Years' Digits Depreciation with Purchase on July 1, 2010				
Date	Formula	Depreciation Expense	Accumulated Depreciation	Book Value
7/1/10					110,000
12/31/10	(110,000 – 10,000) × (4/10) × 1/2 year	20,000	20,000	20,000	90,000
12/31/11	(110,000 – 10,000) × (4/10) × 1/2 year	20,000			
	(110,000 – 10,000) × (3/10) × 1/2 year	15,000	35,000	55,000	55,000
12/31/12	(110,000 – 10,000) × (3/10) × 1/2 year	15,000			
	(110,000 – 10,000) × (2/10) × 1/2 year	10,000	25,000	80,000	30,000
12/31/13	(110,000 – 10,000) × (2/10) × 1/2 year	10,000			
	(110,000 – 10,000) × (1/10) × 1/2 year	5,000	15,000	95,000	15,000
12/31/14	(110,000 – 10,000) × (1/10) × 1/2 year	5,000	5,000	100,000	10,000
			100,000		

EXAMPLE 5-6

If in our basic example the asset was purchased July 1, 2010, instead of January 2, 2010, the 2010 depreciation expense would be six months at 4/10. The 2011 depreciation would be the sum of six months at 4/10 and six months at 3/10. For a better understanding, Table 5-13 shows the related depreciation calculation. Notice that six months depreciation expense remains to be taken in 2014 as well.

Declining-Balance Depreciation

The purpose of the declining-balance depreciation method is very similar to the purpose of the sum of the years' digits method. The method assumes that a company will get more use out of an asset in the early years than it will in the later years. Thus a larger proportion of the cost is allocated to the early years than to the later years. The formula is (Be careful here because this one is different from the rest!) *book value* (not cost minus salvage value) times the declining-balance percentage. The table that you have been using throughout this

TABLE 5-14 Declining-Balance Depreciation

Date	Formula	Depreciation Expense	Accumulated Depreciation	Book Value
1/2/10				110,000
12/31/10	110,000 × 0.5	55,000	55,000	55,000
12/31/11	55,000 × 0.5	27,500	82,500	27,500
12/31/12	27,500 × 0.5	13,750	96,250	13,750
12/31/13	Plug	3,750	100,000	10,000
		100,000		

depreciation section will especially be helpful with this method. First, to determine the declining-balance percentage, you have to know which declining-balance percentage you are using. There are three declining-balance percentages commonly used: 125 percent, 150 percent, and 200 percent. The 200 percent version is called the double-declining-balance (DDB) method because it is exactly double the straight-line rate. The DDB method is the most commonly used of the declining-balance methods and is the one that we will illustrate in Table 5-14. To determine the DDB percentage, use the following formula: 1/ life of the asset times two. For our basic example, the DDB percentage would be 50 percent [1/4 = 25 percent (the straight-line rate) × 2.00 = 50 percent]. Table 5-14 shows the related depreciation calculation.

Notice that the formula was used in the first three years but *not* in the last year. Recall that the total depreciation expense must equal cost minus salvage value. As can be seen from Table 5-14, because of the nature of its formula, the declining-balance method allows for the indefinite depreciation of the asset. However, because the asset has a definite life, expensing the cost through depreciation must cease at the end of the asset's useful life. Therefore, the last year's depreciation expense must be plugged so that the total depreciation expense for the asset equals cost minus salvage value.

Putting More Money into Existing Assets

Now that we have acquired our assets and depreciated them for a few years, it is time to perform some repair and maintenance on them or maybe even splurge and do some upgrades. So the question of the day becomes, How do we account for these additional expenditures on already capitalized assets? Remember our conversation earlier in this chapter regarding capitalizing versus expensing expenditures? The same basic principles apply here as well.

The first situation we will discuss relates to the materiality of the amount of the expenditure. Many companies have a set dollar amount that they consider to be material. Let's say that BLP, Inc., has set its materiality limit at $2,000. Any expenditure on an existing asset that is below the $2,000 limit will be automatically expensed to the repair and maintenance account. Any amount over the $2,000 limit will be evaluated to determine if it should be expensed or capitalized.

Let's now consider the second situation, where BLP, Inc., has spent over its $2,000 limit and must decide if the expenditure should be capitalized. If the expenditure represents a totally new asset, it should be capitalized. An example would be a new wing on an existing building. If, however, the expenditure represents an improvement to an existing asset or a replacement of an existing asset, there are three possible treatments: substitution, the reduction of accumulated depreciation, or an increase to the asset account.

Substitution Method

When the expenditure is above the set materiality limit and the BV of the old asset is known, then the BV of the old asset is removed, and the new asset is recorded.

 EXAMPLE 5-7

During the summer of 2010, BLP, Inc., noticed that the air-conditioning system in its building was not working well. BLP called the repair company and, after a technician looked at the system, was told that the compressor was beyond repair and that the company needed a completely new system. The cost of the old system was $10,000, and its value remaining on the books was $4,000. The cost of the new system was $15,000. The journal entry to reflect the transaction would be

Summer 2010:

New air-conditioning (AC) system	15,000	
Accumulated depreciation: Old AC system	6,000	
Loss on old AC system	4,000	
Old AC System		10,000
Cash		15,000

Reduce Accumulated Depreciation

When the expenditure is above the set materiality limit and the BV of the old asset is *not* known and some of the service potential that was previously written off has been restored, then the best reporting alternative is to reduce the accumulated depreciation account that is associated with the asset account.

This process will effectively place back on the books some of the service potential that was previously expensed and that has now been restored.

 EXAMPLE 5-8

During the summer of 2010, BLP, Inc., noticed that the air-conditioning system in its building was not working well. BLP called the repair company and, after a technician looked at the system, was told that the compressor needed a new part. The technician assured BLP that after the part was replaced, the system would function as well as it did when it was new. The cost of the old system was $10,000. The cost of the new part was $2,100. The journal entry to reflect the transaction would be

Summer 2010:

Accumulated depreciation: Old AC system	2,100	
Cash		2,100

Increase the Asset Account

When the expenditure is above the set materiality limit and the BV of the old asset is *not* known and an addition to the service potential of the asset has been made, the best choice is to increase the asset account. The asset account is increased because the benefits of the asset have been increased above those originally expected.

 EXAMPLE 5-9

During the summer of 2010, BLP, Inc., noticed that the air-conditioning system in its building was not working well. BLP called the repair company and was told the compressor needed two new parts. The two parts would allow the system to work for another five years beyond the system's original useful life. The cost of the old system was $10,000. The cost of new parts was $5,100. The journal entry to reflect this transaction would be

Summer 2010:

Old AC System	5,100	
Cash		5,100

Eliminate Assets

So far we have acquired assets, depreciated them, and repaired or replaced parts in them. So what's left? Yep, that's right. Now that we have taken on, used, and nurtured these assets and they have become like our very own children, frustrating us some days but making us proud most others (just like children who go off to college and then begin new journeys in their lives), it is time to say farewell to those assets. Although there are other ways to dispose of assets, in this book we will focus solely on the sale of assets.

The chief item to remember is to depreciate the asset up to the date of sale. Then, when the asset is sold, simply eliminate the asset account and its related accumulated depreciation account, record the cash received, and book the difference as a gain or loss on the sale of the asset.

EXAMPLE 5-10

BLP, Inc., sold some equipment on December 30, 2012. Let's assume that it was the same equipment that was being depreciated in Table 5-10. If you look back at the table, you will notice that the cost of the equipment was $110,000, and the accumulated depreciation on December 31, 2011, was $50,000. Before BLP sells the equipment, the company must record the depreciation for 2012. The journal entry would be

December 30, 2012:

Depreciation expense	25,000	
Accumulated depreciation		5,000

The journal entry to record the sale of the equipment for $30,000 would be

December 30, 2012:

Accumulated depreciation	75,000	
Cash	30,000	
Loss on sale of equipment	5,000	
Equipment		110,000

Internal Controls

Establishment of Responsibility and Segregation of Duties

The board of directors, which is responsible for approving the capital budget, in effect is the body that approves the acquisition of PPE. While, depending on company policy, certain expenditures may be authorized by other personnel without specific approval from the board, normally a certain dollar threshold is established by the company, and any single capital expenditure that exceeds that amount must be endorsed individually by the board. In order to prevent employees from concealing the removal of PPE items from the property or other fraudulent acts, those individuals who work directly with the equipment on a daily basis should not play any part in the recording of related transactions or other events that pertain to the assets. For instance, accounting personnel, rather than individuals on the production line in a manufacturing facility, should be responsible for counting PPE inventory, properly valuing and recording all purchases, classifying equipment based on expected useful lives, and periodically reassessing the appropriateness of the depreciation calculations. Identifying obsolete or scrapped equipment as well as impaired assets and then writing those assets down on the books while relying on some input from those who use the equipment to make such judgments also should be carried out by the accounting department. Additionally, when assets are disposed of, those who authorize the disposals should not be the same individuals who physically remove the assets nor the same individuals who update the accounting records.

Documentation Procedures and Physical, Mechanical, and Electronic Controls

Because of the large dollar value of PPE on a company's balance sheet, it is imperative that such assets be physically safeguarded. To ensure that all equipment in a plant is properly accounted for and to be able to easily identify if one or more items are missing, each piece of equipment should be issued an identification number, and that number should be permanently affixed to the item. The identification number then should be listed in the accounting records along with a description of the item. Periodic physical inspections are necessary to ensure that all items listed in the records can be located on the plant floor or be otherwise accounted for.

Certain events and transactions related to PPE also should be documented properly. Capitalization policies and materiality thresholds, as mentioned throughout this chapter, as well as chosen depreciation methods, should be documented in written form so that personnel understand the policies they are required to follow, and independent parties are able to assess the company's procedures and ensure that they are applied properly as well. At the time of acquisition, a special requisition form should be filed with top management. Information provided in the requisition should include a description of the item, the purpose of the acquisition, and the cost. At the time of retirement, certain documents should be filed as well. A work order for disposal should be issued and should contain the reasoning for the disposal as well as proper authorization. The work order then is used as a basis to adjust the books and record proceeds, if any, received.

Independent Internal Verification

As mentioned previously, the PPE on hand should be traced back to the accounting records, and likewise, the PPE listed in the accounting records should be located in the company's facilities or otherwise be accounted for (vouched). Sometimes a subsidiary ledger is maintained listing the specific details for a particular asset, including description, location, date of acquisition, cost, depreciation method, and so on. That ledger can be used to verify the PPE listed on the year-end balance sheet.

Wow! What a chapter, huh? We included everything you would ever want to know about property, plant, and equipment, right? Various acquisition methods, the calculation of depreciation expense under various models, the differences between capitalization and expensing, and the accounting treatment for the sale of assets were just some of the many items covered in the last few pages. In Chapter 6 we will introduce you to a type of asset that is a bit more difficult to grasp, physically that is—intangible assets.

QUIZ

1. Property, plant, and equipment accounts should be presented in the financial statements
   A. net of accumulated amortization.
   B. net of accumulated depletion.
   C. net of accumulated depreciation.
   D. as expenses.

2. Capitalizing an expenditure means
   A. the expenditure is debited to an asset account.
   B. the expenditure is debited to an expense account.
   C. the expenditure is credited to an expense account.
   D. the expenditure is credited to property, plant, and equipment.

3. BLP, Inc., purchased land and a building for $100,000. The fair market value of the land was $25,000, and the fair market value of the building was $90,000. The book value on the seller's books of the land was $15,000, and the building was $82,000. The journal entry BLP will make to record the purchase will include
   A. a debit to cash of $100,000.
   B. a debit to land of $15,000.
   C. a debit to building of $82,000.
   D. a debit to land of $21,739.

4. BLP, Inc., wants to exchange 500 shares of its common stock for a piece of machinery. The stock has a par value of $1 per share but is not traded on a public stock exchange. The last time it was sold was six months ago for $50 per share. BLP hired an independent appraiser, and the appraiser valued the equipment at $30,000. The selling company believed that the equipment was worth $35,000. BLP should record the equipment at which value?
   A. $500
   B. $25,000
   C. $30,000
   D. $35,000

5. BLP, Inc., exchanged buildings with Jones Company. BLP's building cost $120,000 and has a current book value of $90,000 and a fair market value of $100,000. The Jones building has a fair market value of $120,000. BLP gave Jones its building along with cash of $20,000. The journal entry BLP will record includes
   A. a debit to cash of $20,000.
   B. a credit to cash of $20,000.
   C. a credit to accumulated depreciation of $30,000.
   D. a debit to the gain on sale of asset account of $10,000.

Questions 6, 7, and 8 are based on the following data:

BLP, Inc., purchased a piece of equipment on January 2, 2010, for $120,000. The company determined that it will have a useful life of five years and will be worth $20,000 at the end of that time. BLP decided to depreciate this asset using the sum of the years' digits method. (*Hint:* Prepare a complete depreciation schedule for this asset for each year of its life prior to answering the following questions. Make certain that your schedule shows the date, depreciation expense, accumulated depreciation, and book value for each year of the asset's life.)

6. **The depreciation expense for 2012 will be**
   A. $33,333
   B. $26,667
   C. $20,000
   D. $13,333

7. **The accumulated depreciation as of December 31, 2011, will be**
   A. $33,333
   B. $60,000
   C. $80,000
   D. $93,333

8. **The book value as of December 31, 2014, will be**
   A. $60,000
   B. $40,000
   C. $26,667
   D. $20,000

9. **The formula to compute double-declining-balance depreciation is**
   A. cost minus salvage value divided by life.
   B. cost minus salvage value times remaining life at the beginning of the year divided by the sum of the years' digits.
   C. cost minus salvage value times double the straight-line rate.
   D. book value times double the straight-line rate.

10. **Which of the following statements is *false* regarding internal controls over property, plant, and equipment?**
    A. The accounting department should authorize the purchase of PPE.
    B. Certain expenditures below a threshold dollar amount may be approved by management.
    C. When assets are disposed of, those who authorize the disposals should not be the same individuals who physically remove the assets.
    D. When assets are disposed of, those who authorize the disposals should not be the same individuals who update the accounting records.

chapter 6

Intangibles

CHAPTER OBJECTIVES

After completing this chapter, the student should

- Understand the financial statement presentation for intangibles
- Understand and account for four different ways to acquire intangibles
- Understand and apply amortization rules for intangibles
- Account for seven different types of intangibles
- Understand internal controls over intangibles

Overview

Have you ever thought of a new useful or innovative item? How about that made-at-home toy that you just loved as a child? You should have patented that trinket and made millions, right? Have you ever seen something on TV or in a catalog and exclaimed, Why didn't I think of that? Haven't we all had those or similar thoughts at some point in our lives? What would cashing in on those ideas have been worth to us? The answer is part of the accounting for intangibles.

Financial Statement Presentation

Intangibles, by their very nature, are unique assets. Like all assets, however, they are reported on the balance sheet, usually after property, plant, and equipment (PPE). Recall that we reported the accumulated depreciation related to PPE on the face of the balance sheet. Intangibles are a bit different. Even though intangibles are amortized, there is no separate accumulated amortization account for each intangible on the face of the statement.

In this chapter we will discuss the characteristics of intangibles, four different acquisition methods, amortization rules, specific accounting requirements for certain types of intangibles, and finally, some basic internal controls related to these items.

Characteristics of Intangibles

Intangibles, as a general rule, cannot be seen or touched. For the most part, their value is related to a particular company. The value may fluctuate from year to year. The length of benefit to a company is often uncertain, resulting in the opportunity for intangibles to have definite and indeterminate, although not necessarily indefinite, lives.

Because of the magnitude of uncertainties, the accounting for intangibles is different for each and every intangible. Thus these differences will be highlighted in this chapter. Before we get there, though, you need to understand some basic concepts regarding the acquisition and amortization of intangibles.

Acquisition Methods

There are four different situations related to the acquisition of intangibles. Has the intangible been purchased or internally developed? Is it identifiable or unidentifiable? The answers to these questions will direct you to the proper accounting for the intangible in terms of capitalization and expensing.

Purchased Identifiable Intangibles

Despite its success with a product, a company, for one reason or another, may wish to sell an intangible that it currently holds. A purchase acquisition is as simple as another company agreeing to pay for the intangible from the one wishing to sell it. When this occurs, the recorded and capitalized cost consists of the purchase price. Examples of possible identifiable intangibles are patents and copyrights.

Purchased Unidentifiable Intangibles

Take the same scenario as last time, but this time let's imagine that the company is purchasing an unidentifiable intangible. Again, the purchase price becomes the capitalized cost. A good example of an unidentifiable intangible is goodwill. We will discuss goodwill in greater detail in the individual intangible section of this chapter.

Internally Developed Identifiable Intangibles

Now let's propose that rather than another company being creative, you have hired some talented individuals of your own and have obtained some intangibles from internal development. Usually such intangibles are developed by performing research and development (R&D) activities related to a new product or process. The R&D costs associated with internal development are expensed as incurred. After the product or process development is complete, lawyers are brought in to file the required paperwork, and if everything goes as planned, a patent or copyright is obtained. Legal fees for these activities will be considered part of the cost of the intangible and are capitalized.

Internally Developed Unidentifiable Intangibles

Remember the goodwill that we mentioned earlier. Instead of purchasing goodwill from another company, goodwill also can be developed internally. Internally developed goodwill may consist of excellent customer service, a great location, or even superior sales personnel. As you might imagine from the preceding description, it is extremely hard to identify any particular cost associated with internally developed goodwill; therefore, there are no costs to capitalize. Any costs associated with the internal development are expensed in other appropriate areas of the income statement such as salaries and wages expense. The benefits of internally developed goodwill include increased revenues, an increased selling price when and if the company is sold, and possibly higher stock prices if the company is publicly held.

Amortization Rules

Accounting is never simple, right? With intangible amortization, this statement may be incorrect. There are only three amortization rules. First, only amortize intangibles that have a definite life. Second, use the straight-line method to amortize the intangibles unless another method provides a better matching of revenues and expenses. Finally, amortize over the lesser of 40 years, the useful life of the intangible, or the legal life of the intangible. This is all there is to it!

Now what about the journal entry? All that is required is a debit to *amortization expense* and a credit to the particular intangible account. As we mentioned previously, GAAP does not require accumulated amortization to be reported on the face of the balance sheet. Therefore, most companies leave it out.

Individual Intangibles

In this section we will discuss seven individual intangibles: patents, copyrights, franchises, computer software costs, internal-use software costs, trademarks and trade names, and finally, goodwill.

Patents

After the R&D work has been completed on a new product or process, an attorney will file paperwork with the federal government asking for a patent to be granted. If the patent is granted, the company will have control over the manufacture, sale, or any other use for a period of 20 years from the date the request is filed. For amortization purposes, the legal life of a patent is 20 years. If a company decides to sell the patent after owning it for 5 years, then the legal life of the intangible acquired by the new company will be 15 years (20-year original life – 5 years) for amortization purposes.

Copyrights

Copyrights are different from patents because they deal only with literary or artistic products instead of manufacturing products or processes. Your favorite musical stars have copyrights on their songs and albums, just as authors have copyrights protecting their words. Legally, the life of a copyright is the life of the author plus 70 years. Because the legal life is much greater than 40 years, any copyrights will be amortized over the lesser of 40 years or the useful life of the copyright.

Franchises

You are probably familiar with many franchises. They are all around us. Maybe you had lunch today at McDonald's or Burger King, or maybe you stayed at a chain hotel on your recent vacation. These are all examples of franchises. These corporations give individuals and companies the right to sell their products for a certain amount of time. The right is called a *franchise*.

The contract between the two parties determines the terms of the franchise. If the franchise is granted in perpetuity, then the life of the franchise is indefinite, precluding amortization. Instead, each year the franchise agreement must be evaluated to determine if there is any impairment (loss of value) that should be recognized in the financial statements. On the other hand, if the contract states a certain life for the franchise, then it can be amortized over the lesser of the legal life, useful life, or 40 years.

Computer Software Costs

Have you ever thought of what goes into the development and marketing of the software you use every day? Have you pondered the hours and hours spent grueling over the source code, graphics, and user-interaction tools that are commonplace in the electronic age these days? Consider all the different software packages you have used since your first days behind a computer desk. It is not hard to see that software production is big business today. If you don't believe us, simply consider the Microsoft Corporation and all the software it has developed over the years.

So what does accounting have to do with all this? Accounting practices must keep up with all these technological revolutions. This represents just one example of how accounting is ever changing, dynamic, and an interesting field of study to pursue. Just think, as an accountant, you could be on the cutting edge of making the financial rules for all the latest and greatest innovations. You could be right there on the scene and even be a star. Identifying the proper accounting methods for this technology just may be your claim to fame. Now who said accounting wasn't exciting?

Enough of this stardom talk. Let's get back to the actual accounting for computer software costs. There are three associated categories of costs: software production costs, the unit cost of reproducing the software, and finally, the maintenance and customer-support costs. We will discuss what is involved with each of these costs in the next few paragraphs.

Software Production Costs

Software production costs can be thought of as the development stage of the software. These costs relate to designing the software, coding the software, testing the software, and preparing the documentation and training materials. It is crucial to identify the date of technological feasibility. What is *technological feasibility*? When a company has a program design that is detailed or the company has completed a working model of the software program, what is known as *technological feasibility* has been achieved. Any costs incurred *prior* to that date are expensed to R&D expense as incurred. Any costs incurred *after* that date are capitalized and amortized over the expected life of the product, which is usually five years or less.

Unit Cost of Reproducing the Software

The unit cost of reproducing the software would include any costs associated with duplicating the software, packaging the software for sale, and reproducing any training or documentation materials packaged and sold with the computer disks.

Because a company is selling the software, the software is considered inventory to the company. As inventory, the costs are capitalized and reported on the balance sheet as assets. At the time the inventory is sold, the asset (inventory) is removed, and the cost is transferred to the income statement as cost of goods sold.

Maintenance and Customer-Support Costs

Maintenance and customer-support costs include any costs incurred after the software is released to the general public. How many times have you purchased new software and run into a problem and had to call the company's customer-service department? These are the exact costs we are talking about! Because these are ordinary and necessary business expenses, they are expensed as incurred.

Internal-Use Software Costs

Instead of developing the software for sale to customers, what happens to the costs if the company is developing the software to be used by the company internally? First, all preliminary development costs are expensed as incurred, just like a normal R&D cost. Next, after the preliminary work is completed *and* management has agreed to fund the software development project *and* it is probable the project will be completed *and* the software will be used as intended, then the costs are capitalized. The costs to be capitalized include any external direct costs of both materials and services used when developing the software, along with the payroll costs of the employees directly associated with the project and any interest costs incurred during the development of the software.

Trademarks and Trade Names

You probably are quite familiar with trademarks and trade names. When you think of Nike, do you visualize the Swoosh symbol that is associated with Nike products? When you think of a soda, does Coca-Cola come to mind? These are examples of trademarks and trade names, respectively. Why is it important for companies to obtain trademarks and trade names? The trademark or trade name gives a company the exclusive right to use a particular name or symbol to represent its product. No other company can infringe on the protected name or symbol and use it as part of its product. The legal life of both trademarks and trade names is 20 years, and both are renewable indefinitely. So, as long as you renew it, once you have established your trademark or trade name, no other company can ever use it. Because they are both renewable indefinitely, they are considered to have indefinite lives and are not amortized. However, at least once per year, they must be reviewed for impairment.

Goodwill

Have you ever thought about why you like to shop at your favorite store? Is it because of its great location? How about its fabulous customer service? Maybe it's the quality of its products that keeps you coming back? Possibly the store's name brands bring out your shopping weakness? All these items can be considered goodwill.

There are two ways to acquire goodwill. First, goodwill can be developed internally over a company's years of operation. Any costs associated with such internally developed goodwill are expensed as incurred. The second way to acquire goodwill is as part of the purchase of another company. To calculate purchased goodwill, start with the purchase price of the company, and then subtract the fair market value (FMV) of the net assets acquired. The difference can be booked as goodwill.

Let's review what is meant by net assets. *Net assets* are assets minus liabilities. By definition, and from the basic accounting equation, it is equivalent to stockholders' equity. Remember, with net assets, you subtract the FMV and not the book value of the net assets. The *book value* (BV) is what the company has recorded on its books for the assets, liabilities, and equity. It is important to note that the BV does not necessarily equal the FMV for each of these items.

 EXAMPLE 6-1

Let's assume that BLP, Inc., is considering purchasing ABC, Inc., on February 1, 2010, for $250,000. BLP requested a copy of ABC's balance sheet. This balance sheet is shown in Table 6-1.

TABLE 6-1 Purchased Goodwill (Example 6-1)

	BV	FMV
Cash	5,000	5,000
Accounts receivable	6,000	6,000
Inventory	7,000	12,000
Equipment, net	15,000	20,000
Building, net	100,000	150,000
Total assets	133,000	193,000
Accounts payable	15,000	15,000
Notes payable	75,000	75,000
Stockholders' equity	43,000	103,000
Total liabilites and stockholders' equity	133,000	193,000
Purchase price of ABC, Inc.		250,000
Less: FMV of net assets		(103,000)
Goodwill		147,000

Notice that there are two columns, one for BV and one for FMV. When computing the amount of goodwill, you must subtract the FMV of the net assets ($103,000) from the purchase price ($250,000).

The journal entry BLP would record for the purchase of ABC would be

February 1, 2010:

Cash	5,000	
Accounts receivable	6,000	
Inventory	12,000	
Equipment, net	20,000	
Building, net	150,000	
Goodwill	147,000	
Accounts payable		15,000
Notes payable		75,000
Cash		250,000

Having the purchase price of a company available and recording the purchase are, as we have seen, not too difficult. Unfortunately, you may not always know the purchase price of the company. Instead, you may know the FMV of the net assets and may be negotiating the price. Being able to compute goodwill under different scenarios, therefore, is not just about accounting; it also will help you to be a better negotiator. Before we get into the specifics, think about why you want to purchase a particular company and why you are willing to pay more for the company than the current value of the net assets. Is it because of the company's location, customer service, quality, or brand name? If you find value in any of these items, you likely will be more willing to pay bigger bucks for the company than the net assets are actually worth. Why, exactly, is this the case? Simply speaking, you will pay more because you believe that the company has the ability to earn a higher than normal rate of return on the FMV of its net assets. We will illustrate this with two different examples. First, we will ask you to assume that the goodwill will last forever. Second, we will put a time limit on the goodwill's benefit. Both examples will use a discount rate. The *discount rate* is the interest rate that BLP can obtain for long-term debt.

EXAMPLE 6-2

We will continue the preceding example by assuming that BLP, Inc., is negotiating to purchase ABC, Inc. The FMV of ABC's net assets is $103,000, and the discount rate to be used is 5 percent. ABC's future earnings are $15,000. BLP is attempting to determine a purchase price for ABC, Inc. In this example, BLP will assume that any goodwill will last forever. The computation of ABC's normal earnings is the product of the discount rate (5 percent) times the FMV of the company's net assets ($103,000). Thus the normal earnings are $5,150. The excess earnings are the future earnings

TABLE 6-2 Goodwill Will Last Forever (Example 6-2)		
Future earnings		15,000
Less: Normal earnings	103,000 × 0.05	(5,150)
Excess earnings		9,850
Divided by the discount rate		5.00%
Equals: Goodwill		197,000
Add: FMV of net assets		103,000
Equals: Purchase price of the company		300,000

($15,000) minus the normal earnings ($5,150). Thus the excess earnings are $9,850. Because the assumption is that the goodwill will last forever, the computation of goodwill is excess earnings ($9,850) divided by the discount rate (5 percent)—formula for present value of a perpetuity. Thus goodwill is $197,000. To determine a possible purchase price for ABC, Inc., add the goodwill of $197,000 to the FMV of the net assets of $103,000. Thus a possible purchase price for ABC, Inc., is $300,000. Table 6-2 shows these computations.

EXAMPLE 6-3

We will continue the preceding two examples by assuming that BLP, Inc., is negotiating to purchase ABC, Inc. The FMV of ABC's net assets is $103,000, and the discount rate to be used is 5 percent. ABC's future earnings are $15,000. BLP is attempting to determine a purchase price for ABC, Inc. In this example, BLP will assume that any goodwill will last for five years only. The computation of ABC's normal earnings is the product of the discount rate (5 percent) times the FMV of the company's net assets ($103,000). Thus the normal earnings are $5,150. The excess earnings are the future earnings ($15,000) minus the normal earnings ($5,150). Thus the excess earnings are $9,850. Because the assumption is that the goodwill will last for five years only, the computation of goodwill is excess earnings ($9,850) multiplied by the present value of an ordinary annuity for five years at 5 percent (4.329477) as found in Appendix B. Thus goodwill is $23,163. To determine a possible purchase price for ABC, Inc., add the goodwill of $23,163 to the FMV of the net assets of $103,000. Thus a possible purchase price for ABC, Inc., is $145,645. Table 6-3 shows these computations.

Whenever negotiating the purchase price of a company, completing a sensitivity analysis for the goodwill computations is essential. A *sensitivity analysis* consists of several goodwill computations that use different discount rates and different numbers of years. For instance, in Example 6-2, you might complete the computations using discount rates of 5, 6, and 7 percent. In Example 6-3,

TABLE 6-3 Goodwill Will Last Five Years (Example 6-3)		
Future earnings		15,000
Less: Normal earnings	103,000 × 0.05	(5,150)
Excess earnings		9,850
Multiply by PV of annuity for 5 years at 5%		4.329477
Equals: Goodwill		42,645
Add: FMV of net assets		103,000
Equals: Purchase price of the company		145,645

you might use 5 percent for five years, 5 percent for ten years, or 6 percent for eight years. The bottom line is better negotiating skills equate to better purchase prices.

Internal Controls

Establishment of Responsibility and Segregation of Duties

Intangible assets are a bit more complicated than tangible assets to account for and control properly. Think about it. A company may hold a patent on its unique product, but that patent cannot be observed physically. There is likely some documentation that has a physical substance, but the patent itself is invisible. The efforts of R&D can be observed, but deciding which of the related costs should be capitalized or expensed is somewhat tricky. In terms of responsibility, management should be responsible for proper valuation of intangibles. While the actual positions of the individuals who decide when to capitalize or expense R&D costs, the useful lives of intangibles, the existence of impairments, and many other matters regarding these items may vary from company to company, the decision makers may consult with but should not be the same individuals who are directly involved with the recording of the intangibles on the books. Likewise, individuals actually working on or having custody of the items on a day-to-day basis should not be involved in any related authorizations or recordings.

Documentation Procedures and Physical, Mechanical, and Electronic Controls

Because of the nature of intangibles, the need for physical, mechanical, or electronic controls is very limited. Proper checks should be built into computer systems and programs on a general basis to ensure that no alterations of files occur. In the process, such controls should prevent any unauthorized changes to the intangible records as well. Additionally, some physical controls may be needed for supplies purchased in association with R&D to ensure that employees do not steal such items for personal use.

Documentation should be maintained on all intangible assets held by a company, including acquisition dates, related costs, and descriptions of the items. Additionally, amortization, capitalization, and impairment policies should be documented and made available so that those in charge of keeping the related records understand how to account for the items properly.

Independent Internal Verification

A third party within an organization should ensure that all intangibles recorded on the books actually are held by the organization, in addition to making sure that none have been inadvertently or fraudulently omitted. Additionally, impairment and amortization calculations should be verified by an otherwise uninvolved party to validate the proper carrying value of the items on the company's books.

This chapter has offered you information concerning the acquisition and amortization procedures involving intangibles, as well as a classification system composed of seven categories. This completes our coverage of assets. We will now move on to what you or your company owes—liabilities, current liabilities to be specific.

QUIZ

1. **Which of the following statements regarding intangibles is _false_?**
    A. Intangibles are presented on financial statements as an asset.
    B. Intangibles are presented on financial statements net of any amortization.
    C. Accumulated amortization for intangibles is presented on the face of the balance sheet.
    D. Intangibles are presented on the balance sheet.

2. **Which of the following statements regarding intangibles is _true_?**
    A. Only purchased goodwill can be recorded in the accounting records.
    B. Both purchased and internally developed goodwill can be recorded in the accounting records.
    C. Neither purchased nor internally developed goodwill can be recorded in the accounting records.
    D. Only internally developed goodwill can be recorded in the accounting records.

3. **The general rule for recording amortization on intangibles is**
    A. only intangibles with an indefinite life should be amortized.
    B. only the double-declining-balance method of amortization is allowed.
    C. never amortize over more than three years.
    D. amortize over the lesser of useful life, legal life, or 40 years.

4. **Which of the following statements is _true_?**
    A. A patent gives a company control over the manufacture, sale, or any other use of a product or process.
    B. A patent deals with literary or artistic products.
    C. The life of a patent is the life of the author plus 70 years.
    D. A patent gives individuals and companies the right to sell a particular product for a certain amount of time.

5. **Which of the following statements is _false_?**
    A. Trademarks and trade names give a company the exclusive right to use a particular name or symbol to represent its product.
    B. Trademarks and trade names should be amoritized over 20 years.
    C. Trademarks and trade names have an indefinite life.
    D. Trademarks and trade names are not amortized.

6. **Net assets are**
    A. assets plus liabilities.
    B. assets minus liabilities.
    C. assets plus stockholders' equity.
    D. assets minus revenues.

7. **Goodwill**
   A. can only be recorded if it is developed internally.
   B. can be amortized over five years.
   C. has a definite life.
   D. has an indefinite life.

8. **Why would you want to perform many different calculations of goodwill using various scenarios?**
   A. So that you can be a better negotiator
   B. To keep your accountant busy
   C. To determine the *only* price you will pay for a company
   D. So that you can determine the normal rate of return for your company

9. **BLP, Inc., has decided to purchase JKL Company for $500,000. The book value of JKL Company's net assets is $349,500, and the fair market value of those same assets is $426,000. BLP should record goodwill at**
   A. $150,500.
   B. $74,000.
   C. $426,000.
   D. $500,000.

10. **Regarding internal controls over intangibles, which of the following statements is *false*?**
   A. Management is responsible for proper valuation of intangibles.
   B. Computer systems and programs should not allow alterations of the value of intangibles.
   C. There is no need for any independent internal verification of intangibles.
   D. Documentation should be maintained on all intangible assets, including acquisition date, related costs, and descriptions of each intangible.

Part II

The Balance Sheet: Liabilities—What Do I Owe?

chapter **7**

Current Liabilities

CHAPTER OBJECTIVES

After completing this chapter, the student should

- Understand the financial statement presentation for current liabilities
- Understand the definition for and characteristics of current liabilities
- Account for six current liabilities that are based on set contract amounts
- Account for four current liabilities that are based on operations
- Account for two current liabilities that are based on estimates
- Understand and account for contingencies
- Understand internal controls over current liabilities

Overview

Up to this point, we have focused exclusively on what you own—assets. What resources did you use to acquire those assets, or what resources did you use to pay your bills as they came due? Maybe you had enough cash on hand or in your bank account to pay for your supplies out of pocket, or maybe you paid interest to your creditors immediately rather than allowing the liability to accrue. In such a situation, you may not have any current liabilities. In the case of a corporation, however, it is much more realistic to assume that when supplies are purchased in bulk from the office supply store, payment initially is on account. Now, by *account*, we do not mean that a credit card was used. Payment via a credit card is synonymous with cash. An *account* is established by your supplier acknowledging that you have been deemed creditworthy and will be allowed to take your goods now and pay for them later. Additionally, you may have a policy to pay interest only at year end. In this case, interest expense is incurred every quarter but is not paid at those intervals. Instead, an amount will appear in the interest payable account, and at the end of the year; the total will be cleared by using cash to pay the amount that has accrued. In both the preceding cases, current liabilities in the form of accounts payable and interest payable are involved.

Hopefully, from the preceding, you have determined what a liability is. You got it! A *liability* is something you owe that, when paid, will result in either a decrease in your assets or an incurrence of another liability. We will provide you with a more specific definition of a current liability in a bit.

Financial Statement Presentation

Current liabilities (CL) have a normal credit balance and are reported on the face of the balance sheet. A CL represents the amount of money owed to your short-term creditors. The most common current liabilities are accounts payable (AP), short-term notes payable (STNP), taxes payable, and salaries payable.

In this chapter we will discuss the characteristics of CL and identify and account for CL that are based on set contract amounts, those that are based on operations, and still others that are based on estimates. We also will discuss contingencies and conclude with some basic internal controls over CL.

Characteristics of CL

Current liabilities may be satisfied with either current assets or the creation of other current liabilities. For example, when you pay off an account payable you usually use cash, which is a current asset. However, in some instances, you may not have the available cash, or you may find that issuing a short-term note payable offers you a greater advantage. In such a case, another CL is created to satisfy the original.

The nature of current liabilities conforms to the definition of liabilities as a whole. First, you normally have no option to avoid CL; they must be paid. Second, a transaction already has occurred causing the incurrence of the debt. Interestingly, however, a legally enforceable claim does not need to exist for a liability to be recognized and placed on the balance sheet. Such a condition is known as a *probable-loss contingency*, and we will discuss it and other types of contingencies in more depth later in this chapter.

CL That Are Based on Set Contract Amounts

In this section we will discuss six different CL that are based on set contract amounts: trade accounts payable, notes payable, the currently maturing portion of long-term debt, dividends payable, accrued liabilities, and unearned revenues.

Trade Accounts Payable

A *trade account payable* is a nonwritten promise to pay a certain amount at a definite time. Trade accounts payable (AP) arise during the normal course of business (i.e., from selling products or services on a credit basis). They are usually repaid within 30 to 60 days from the date of purchase.

 EXAMPLE 7-1

BLP, Inc., purchased $7,000 of inventory on credit from DEF, Inc., on May 1, 2010. The journal entry made by BLP would be

May 1, 2010:

Inventory	7,000	
Accounts payable		7,000

Notes Payable

A *note payable* (NP) is a *written* promise to pay a certain amount at a definite time. The due date for a short-term note payable is usually 60 days to one year from the date of signing. As with trade accounts payable, short-term notes payable usually arise from the sale of products or services in the normal course of business.

One feature that distinguishes a note payable from an account payable, however, is interest. A note payable usually has interest, whereas an account payable does not—unless the account is overdue. Even though notes payable usually have an interest charge associated with them, there is a non-interest bearing note payable as well. In this section we will provide you with examples of both interest bearing and non-interest bearing types.

Interest Bearing Notes Payable

Let's start with the easier of the two, an interest bearing note payable. The interest is a percent of the face value of the NP. Remember, the interest rate is always stated as an annual rate. Therefore, if the interest is only for six months, you must adjust the formula to reflect only that percentage (in this case, six months) of interest. The formula to determine interest expense is principle × interest rate × time ($P \times R \times T$).

EXAMPLE 7-2

BLP, Inc., purchased $7,000 of inventory on credit from DEF, Inc., on May 1, 2010. The company signed a short-term note payable indicating an interest rate of 6 percent with payment due on October 31, 2010. The interest expense is $210 ($7,000 × 6% × ½ year). The journal entries made by BLP would be

May 1, 2010:

Inventory	7,000	
Short-term note payable		7,000
October 31, 2010:		
Short-term note payable	7,000	
Interest expense	210	
Cash		7,210

Non-Interest Bearing Notes Payable

A non-interest bearing note? Where can I get one of those? Okay, so we all know that a non-interest bearing note is nonexistent, a mere figment of accountants' imaginations, if you will. So if it is not non-interest bearing, what is it, then? All that happens with a note of this type is that the lender simply gives the borrower less money up front. Put another way, interest is included in the face value of the STNP. Because recording the interest expense before it has been incurred would be a violation of the matching principle (revenues should be recorded in the same period as the expenses incurred to achieve them), a new account must be created and used—*discount on STNP*. This account has a normal debit balance and is reported on the balance sheet as a contra account to the STNP figure. When the note is repaid, the discount on STNP is eliminated, and the interest expense is recorded. The process can be seen in the following example.

EXAMPLE 7-3

BLP, Inc., purchased inventory on credit from DEF, Inc., on May 1, 2010. The company signed a six-month non-interest-bearing short-term note payable of $7,000. The note is to be discounted at 6 percent with payment due on October 31, 2010. The interest expense is $210 ($7,000 × 6% × ½ year). The journal entries made by BLP are

May 1, 2010:

Inventory	6,790	
Discount on STNP	210	
STNP		7,000

October 31, 2010:

STNP	7,000	
Interest expense	210	
Cash		7,000
Discount on STNP		210

Currently Maturing Portion of Long-Term Debt

There are some forms of long-term debt that require payments each year. In this case, the portion of long-term debt that will come due and will be paid in the following year should be reclassified as a CL because the amount will be paid with the company's current assets.

Dividends Payable

There are five possible kinds of dividends. We will return to this topic again in Chapter 11. For now, though, we will list the types and briefly discuss their relationship to CL. The five kinds of dividends are cash, property, scrip, stock, and undeclared dividends in arrears. Only the cash and scrip dividends are considered CL at the date of declaration. The property dividends may or may not be CL depending on whether the property being used as a dividend is a current asset (CA) or a noncurrent asset. From the process of elimination, you probably have inferred that stock and undeclared dividends in arrears do not show up in the bottom portion (liability section) of the balance sheet, and you are absolutely correct!

Accrued Liabilities

An *accrued liability* is a liability that has been incurred but not yet paid. Additionally, it usually has not been recorded. In order to abide by the matching principle, all accrued liabilities must be recorded on the balance sheet date so that they will appear in the proper period in which they were incurred, just as all other revenues, expenses, assets, and liabilities for the period must be recorded on the financial statements at or by that time.

Examples of liabilities that are normally accrued are unpaid salaries at year end and interest or rent expense that has been incurred but not yet paid.

EXAMPLE 7-4

What if, in Example 7-2, the inventory was purchased on August 1, 2010, and the STNP was due January 31, 2011? A year-end *adjusting journal entry* (AJE) would need to be made on December 31, 2010, to record the interest that had accrued from August 1, 2010, to December 31, 2010 ($7,000 × 6% × 5/12 = $175). The journal entries to reflect this situation would be

August 1, 2010:		
Inventory	7,000	
STNP		7,000
December 31, 2010:		
Interest expense	175	
Interest payable		175
January 31, 2011:		
STNP	7,000	
Interest payable	175	
Interest expense	35	
Cash		7,210

Unearned Revenues

Unearned revenues are considered CL if they will be earned within one year or the operating cycle, whichever is longer. Unearned revenue is revenue that has been collected but not yet earned. Additionally, the unearned revenue usually has not been recorded. Examples include gift certificates and rent.

 EXAMPLE 7-5

Assume that BLP, Inc., sold gift certificates valued at $1,000 during December 2010. The gift certificates had an expiration date of January 31, 2011. No revenue would be earned in 2010, even though money was received. BLP still would owe the certificate holders merchandise equal to the certificates' value. Until redemption of the gift certificates for merchandise, BLP would have an obligation, a liability, to the holders. Assume that all the gift certificates were redeemed by January 31, 2011. The journal entries to reflect the transactions would be

December 2010:		
Cash	1,000	
Unearned gift certificate revenue		1,000
January 2011:		
Unearned gift certificate revenue	1,000	
Gift certificate revenue		1,000

CL That Are Based on Operations

In a business setting, there are various taxes that must be paid. Such taxes are normally based on operations in some manner. Sales taxes and income taxes are examples. When a company employs individuals, various liabilities related to the payroll, known as *payroll taxes*, must be accounted for and paid. Additionally, depending on the business and its operational success over the previous period, some employees may receive a bonus that is based on the magnitude of that success. Each of these items will be discussed below.

Sales Taxes

Sales tax is so common that many of us don't even think about it anymore when we shop. As we are browsing the store and see an item for $5 that we want to buy, we place it in our shopping cart, and when we proceed to the checkout, we take out a $10 bill, knowing that the price that will be charged cannot be covered by the $5 bill sitting next to the $10 bill in our wallet. Except in a few special circumstances, every time a purchase is made, sales tax is paid. Normally, both local and state sales taxes exist. The store, though, is just the intermediary. Although the store would like to be adding on the extra costs to make an even higher profit, what is really happening is that the store is collecting the sales tax for the city and the state. Once the store has collected the sales tax, it has an obligation (CL) to remit the sales tax to those governmental entities.

EXAMPLE 7-6

Assume that BLP, Inc., had sales of $1,000 and collected $50 of state sales tax in connection with those sales on November 1, 2010. BLP then remitted the $50 to the state on November 5, 2010. The journal entries to reflect these transactions would be

November 1, 2010:

Cash	1,050	
Sales		1,000
Sales tax payable		50

November 5, 2010:

Sales tax payable	50	
Cash		50

The preceding example reflects the most common method of handling sales taxes. However, in some instances, the sales tax is already included in the purchase price of the product.

EXAMPLE 7-7

Instead of what we noted in the preceding example, assume that BLP, Inc., does not compute the sales tax on the products it sells separately. Additionally, assume that the sales tax in the state in which the company operates is imposed at a rate of 5 percent. Using this information, if BLP sold $1,000 worth of merchandise, the amount recorded as sales would be

$952 ($1,000/1.05). Likewise, the amount recorded as sales tax would be $48 ($952 × 0.05). The journal entries to reflect these transactions would be

November 1, 2010:

Cash	1,000	
Sales		952
Sales tax payable		48

November 5, 2010:

Sales tax payable	48	
Cash		48

Income Taxes

Just like individuals, businesses owe a duty to Uncle Sam via the payment of income taxes. Such taxes may be imposed at the city, state, and federal levels and must be reported on the financial statements. We will discuss income taxes more thoroughly in Chapter 13. For now, though, it will be helpful for you to be familiar with the basic journal entry to record the income tax payable on the books. An example to better your understanding is presented below.

EXAMPLE 7-8

BLP, Inc., has determined its taxable income to be $100,000. Since it has a tax rate of 15 percent, its income tax payable at year end would be $15,000 ($100,000 × 0.15). This amount must be accrued, recorded, and reported on the financial statements on December 31, 2010. The adjusting journal entry needed to record this liability would be

December 31, 2010:

Income tax expense	15,000	
Income tax payable		15,000

Payroll Liabilities

Surely at some point in your life, as an employee, you have received a paycheck. Did you know that it costs money for a company to pay you? That is, in addition to the amount of your paycheck? Let us explain. There are some taxes that employees are responsible for paying and others that are the employer's responsibility.

The employee is responsible for paying one-half of the Federal Income Contribution Act (FICA) tax, which currently totals 7.65 percent of gross wages. Of that 7.65 percent, 6.2 percent is remitted for Social Security. There is a maximum wage (which typically changes each year) that is subject to the 6.2 percent. For 2010, the maximum wage subject to the 6.2 percent is $106,800. The other 1.45 percent represents charges for Medicare. There is no maximum wage that is subject to the 1.45 percent. The entire gross wages are taxable.

The employer is responsible for paying the other half of the FICA tax. The process works in exactly the same manner as the employee's share. Additionally, the employer is responsible for paying into the Federal Unemployment Tax Act (FUTA) and the State Unemployment Tax Act (SUTA) funds. Both those funds provide unemployment benefits to employees who have been laid off. FUTA is based on the first $7,000 of an employee's wages. The tax rate is 0.8 percent (0.008). Each state has its own rules for SUTA. For example, Colorado's SUTA for 2010 is based on the first $10,000 of wages per employee and has a tax rate of 2.52 percent. In most states, companies that have very few layoffs will pay a smaller percentage of SUTA in future years.

So how are all these taxes paid? First, the employee's portion of the FICA tax is withheld by the employer. Then the employer remits both the employee's and the employer's share, along with the employer's FUTA and SUTA funds to the proper agencies. There are severe penalties if an employer keeps the employee's share and does not remit it. This type of employer is *not* one who you want to work for!

EXAMPLE 7-9

Let's assume that BLP, Inc., is located in the state of Colorado and has two employees, Andrea and Bob. For the year 2010, Andrea made $110,000 and Bob made $80,000. From the journal entries below, you can see that in addition to salaries, it cost BLP $14,952.60 to have two employees. The journal entries to record the payment of wages, payroll tax expense, and payment to the agencies would be

Payment of wages:

Wage expense	190,000.00	
FICA pay A (106,800 × 0.062)		6,621.60
FICA pay B (80,000 × 0.062)		4,960.00
FICA pay A (110,000 × 0.0145)		1,595.00
FICA pay B (80,000 × 0.0145)		1,160.00
Cash		175,663.40

Record payroll expense:

Payroll tax expense (sum of all the credits)	14,952.60	
FICA pay A (106,800 × 0.062)		6,621.60
FICA pay B (80,000 × 0.062)		4,960.00
FICA pay A (110,000 × 0.0145)		1,595.00
FICA pay B (80,000 × 0.0145)		1,160.00
FUTA A&B (14,000 × 0.008)		112.00
SUTA A&B (20,000 × 0.0252)		504.00

Payment of payroll taxes:

FICA payable (total of A&B)	28,673.20	
FUTA payable	112.00	
SUTA payable	504.00	
Cash		29,289.20

Bonuses

Isn't it great to receive a bonus at the end of the year! Bonuses can be computed based on just about any number in the financial statements. One important point to remember is that bonuses are tax deductible. There are two common computations that are covered in traditional intermediate accounting textbooks, and we will discuss both those methods here.

With the first computation, the bonus (B) is paid on net income (NI) after deducting the income taxes (T) but before deducting the bonus. The algebraic computation is

$$B = \text{bonus percentage} \times (NI - T)$$

$$T = \text{tax rate} \times (NI - B)$$

Because you have two simultaneous equations, you must substitute the income tax formula (T) into the bonus formula. The equation now looks like this:

$$B = \text{bonus percentage} \times \{NI - [\text{tax rate} \times (NI - B)]\}$$

EXAMPLE 7-10

BLP, Inc., has NI of $100,000 that is taxed at a rate of 30 percent, and the company has agreed to pay Andrea a bonus of 15 percent of NI after deducting the income taxes. Her bonus is determined to be $10,995, and the calculation is shown below:

$$B = 15\% \times \{\$100,000 - [0.30 \times (\$100,000 - B)]\}$$
$$B = 15\% \times (100,000 - 30,000 + 0.3B)$$
$$B = 15,000 - 4,500 + 0.045B$$
$$0.955B = 10,500$$
$$B = \$10,995$$

Proof:

$$B = 0.15 \times \{100,000 - [0.3 \times (100,000 - 10,995)]\}$$
$$B = 0.15 \times (100,000 - 26,702)$$
$$B = 0.15 \times 73,298$$
$$B = 10,995$$

BLP's taxes are computed as follows:

$$T = 0.30 \times (100,000 - 10,995)$$
$$T = \$26,702$$

With the second common computation method, the bonus (B) is paid on net income (NI) after deducting both the income taxes (T) and the bonus. The algebraic computation is

$$B = \text{bonus percentage} \times (NI - B - T)$$

$$T = \text{tax rate} \times (NI - B)$$

Because you have two simultaneous equations, you must substitute the income tax formula (T) into the bonus formula. The equation now looks like this:

$$B = \text{bonus percentage} \times \{NI - B - [\text{tax rate} \times (NI - B)]\}$$

EXAMPLE 7-11

BLP, Inc., has NI of $100,000, which is taxed at a rate of 30 percent, and the company has agreed to pay Andrea a bonus of 15 percent of NI after deducting both the income taxes and the bonus. Her bonus is determined to be $9,502, and the calculation is shown below:

$$B = 15\% \times \{\$100,000 - B - [0.30 \times (\$100,000 - B)]\}$$
$$B = 15\% \times (100,000 - B - 30,000 + 0.3B)$$
$$B = 15\% \times (70,000 - 0.7B)$$
$$B = 10,500 - 0.105B$$
$$1.105B = 10,500$$
$$B = \$9,502$$

Proof:

$$B = 0.15 \times \{100,000 - 9,502 - [0.3 \times (100,000 - 9,502)]\}$$
$$B = 0.15 \times [90,498 - (0.3 \times 90,498)]$$
$$B = 0.15 \times (90,498 - 27,149)$$
$$B = 0.15 \times 63,349$$
$$B = 9,502$$

BLP's taxes are computed as follows:

$$T = 0.30 \times (100,000 - 9,502)$$
$$T = \$27,149$$

CL That Are Based on Estimates

Sometimes you need to record a CL before you know the actual amount. In such instances, you will need to record an estimated CL and then adjust what you have recorded when the actual amount becomes available. We will discuss two types of estimated CL—property taxes and warranty obligations.

Property Taxes

For purposes of discussion, we will assume that the lien date is May 1 and the billing date is October 1. These two dates are important because you need to record the liability as of the lien date, but you won't know the actual amount of the liability until the billing date. The accrual of property tax expense is usually performed monthly. So, from May through September, you will be accruing the property tax expense based on last year's amount of property taxes. Then, from October through December, you will be accruing the property taxes on an adjusted amount.

**EXAMPLE 7-12**

The 2009 property taxes for BLP, Inc., were $4,000. The lien date for the property taxes is May 1, 2010, and the billing date is October 1, 2010. From May through September, a monthly accrual of $500 ($4,000/8 months) should be made by debiting property tax expense and crediting property tax payable. The estimate of $500 per month is based on the time period May through December even though we will only be estimating the amount for the time period May through September. In October, when the bill arrives, it reflects a total of $4,400. At that time, five months (May through September) of $500 each will have been accrued, totaling $2,000. Since the actual bill is $4,400 and we have accrued $2,000, $2,400 remains to be recorded during October through December, or $800 each month. At the end of December, all $4,400 will have been recorded properly as property tax expense.

Warranty Obligations

The second type of CL that is based on estimates is warranty obligations. How many times have you purchased an appliance, a computer, or a car and been asked if you want to also purchase additional warranty coverage?

There are three different methods for handling warranties—the expense warranty accrual method, the sales warranty accrual method, and the modified cash basis method. We will discuss each method below.

Expense Warranty Accrual Method

The expense warranty accrual method is the theoretically correct method. The main point to remember is that in the period of sale, you must record both an expense and a liability.

EXAMPLE 7-13

BLP, Inc., sells a product in 2010 for $5,000. The product is sold with a one-year warranty. Past experience indicates the warranty cost for each product sold is about $200. During 2010, BLP sold 100 of these products. During 2010, BLP spent $9,900 on warranty repairs, and in 2011, the company spent $10,200. The journal entries required to reflect these transactions would be as follows:

Record the sale of 100 products at $5,000 each:

Cash or accounts receivable	500,000	
Sales		500,000

Recognize warranty expense at time of sale:

Warranty expense	20,000	
Estimated warranty liability		20,000

Recognize 2010 warranty expenditures:

Estimated warranty liability	9,900	
Cash		9,900

December 31, 2010 balance sheet:

Estimated warranty liability	<u>10,100</u>	

Recognize 2011 warranty expenditures:

Estimated warranty liability	<u>10,100</u>	
Warranty expense	100	
Cash		10,200

Sales Warranty Accrual Method

The main point to remember under the sales warranty accrual method is that the sale of the product is reflected separately from the sale of the warranty. The company is really selling two items—the product and the warranty. Until the warranty revenue is earned, the unearned warranty revenue is reflected as a liability on the balance sheet.

EXAMPLE 7-14

BLP, Inc., sells a product in 2010 for $5,000 with a one-year warranty valued at $200 that is included in the $5,000 purchase price. During 2010, BLP sold 100 of these products. During 2010, the company spent $9,900 on warranty repairs, and in 2011, it spent $10,200. The journal entries required to reflect these transactions would be as follows:

Record the sale of the product and the sale of the warranty:

Cash or accounts receivable	500,000	
Sales		480,000
Unearned warranty revenue		20,000

Record warranty expense for 2010:

Warranty expense	9,900	
Cash		9,900

Record warranty revenue earned in 2010:

Unearned warranty revenue	9,900	
Warranty revenue		9,900

December 31, 2010 balance sheet:

Unearned warranty revenue	10,100	

Record warranty expense for 2011:

Warranty expense	10,200	
Cash		10,200

Record warranty revenue earned in 2011:

Unearned warranty revenue	10,100	
Warranty revenue		10,100

Modified Cash Basis Method

The modified cash basis method is the *only* method accepted for federal income tax purposes. Therefore, it is the most widely used of the three methods. The main point to remember under the modified cash basis approach is that no liabilities are accrued. A company will record expenses only when they are actually incurred.

 EXAMPLE 7-15

BLP, Inc., sells a product in 2010 for $5,000 with a one-year warranty. During 2010, BLP sold 100 of these products. During 2010, BLP spent $9,900 on warranty repairs, and in 2011 the company spent $10,200. The journal entries required to reflect these transactions would be as follows:

Record sale of product:

Cash or accounts receivable	500,000	
Sales		500,000

Record warranty expense for 2010:

Warranty expense	9,900	
Cash		9,900

December 31, 2010 balance sheet:

No liabilities related to the warranty are recorded.

Record warranty expense for 2011:

Warranty expense	10,100	
Cash		10,100

Contingencies

A *contingency* is a situation that involves uncertainty as to whether it will result in a possible gain or loss based on the outcome of a future event. There are three possible types of contingencies—probable, reasonably possible, and remote. With all the contingencies, either a gain or a loss could result.

Probable

For a contingency to be probable, the event must be *likely* to occur. For example, assume that BLP, Inc., sued one of its suppliers for failure to follow the contract. BLP, in conjunction with its attorneys, determined that it was probable that the company would win the suit in court. The accounting result would be a *probable gain contingency.* The attorneys and BLP would not need to determine a dollar amount to be reported on the balance sheet at year end. According to generally accepted accounting principles (GAAP), conservatism rules: In an effort to avoid inflating income, probable gain contingencies are to be disclosed only in the footnotes to the financial statements rather than actually being recorded on the face of the statements.

The treatment is different for a *probable loss contingency.* For example, assume that one of BLP's customers purchased a defective product and was seriously hurt by the item. If the customer sued BLP to recover damages, provided that BLP actually sold the customer the defective product and the customer actually was injured by the item, the company would have a probable loss contingency. The attorneys and BLP would have to determine a dollar amount to be reported on the face of the balance sheet at year end to reflect the loss. Additionally, a footnote to the financial statements would be required describing the event.

Reasonably Possible

To be reasonably possible, an event must have been more than remote and less than likely. Don't you just love definitions like this! A *reasonably possible gain contingency* and a *reasonably possible loss contingency* must be disclosed only. Therefore, when such contingencies are present, a footnote is included in the financial statements explaining the situation.

Remote

To be remote, the chance of a future event occurring must be *slight.* If the contingency is a *remote gain contingency,* then, at most, a footnote could be included in the financial statements but is not required. In the case of a *remote loss contingency,* including a footnote in the financial statements is recommended.

Internal Controls

Okay, so why would you want to ensure that proper controls are in place for liabilities? You owe that money; if some amount doesn't get recorded, what's the big deal, right? It just makes your company look better. Wrong!

Besides being unethical and having the potential to anger creditors, especially if those debts that are unrecorded also go unpaid, failing to record all of a company's liabilities prevents the company from being able to assess its financial position adequately. In terms of current liabilities, there are three accounts that we will focus on—accounts payable, salaries payable, and warranty liabilities.

Establishment of Responsibility and Segregation of Duties

Establishment of responsibility and segregation of duties is especially relevant to the areas of accounts payable and salaries payable. In regard to accounts payable, when a purchase is made, the purchase order should be submitted to the accounting department. Once the associated goods arrive, the receiving report is also submitted to accounting so that the two documents can be matched, and a payable can be recorded on the books. You wouldn't want to pay for something that you never had possession of, right? The control just mentioned is designed to prevent such an incident. The last responsibility of accounting personnel is to look over the invoice when received and verify it with the other two documents, authorize the payable for payment, and finally record the payment after cash is disbursed. The accounting personnel who perform these functions should be separate from the individuals who make and authorize the purchases and those who take physical custody of the goods, as well as the treasurer who pays the debts.

There are also a number of requirements for proper control over payroll liabilities. In terms of responsibility and segregation of duties, the human resources department should be in charge of the hiring and firing of personnel, as well as the maintaining of employee records, including salary information. The accounting or payroll department should determine total pay using that information along with the hours worked by each employee. Those individuals also have the responsibility to issue checks for the treasurer to sign. Once the authorization and recordkeeping functions are complete, a different individual, the treasurer, should sign the checks and distribute them to the employees.

Documentation Procedures and Physical, Mechanical, and Electronic Controls

Aside from the three documents that we already mentioned that are associated with internal control over accounts payable—purchase orders, receiving reports, and invoices—a voucher also should be prepared verifying that the payable has been approved for payment. That voucher should be prenumbered, and once a check has been issued, the voucher should be canceled, preventing double payments.

In regard to payroll liabilities, whenever changes are made to any element that will affect the payroll, including the addition or elimination of employees or any alteration of hourly rates for one or multiple employees, an authorized document must be created to substantiate those changes. These documents, as well as time cards and the checks used to issue payroll payments, all should be prenumbered.

A company should document its warranty policies. Such documentation should include when warranties are established and how they should be valued on the books. With documentation, those responsible for recording related transactions will be better able to perform that function and be more consistent in their accounting.

Independent Internal Verification

For accounts payable, salaries payable, and warranty liabilities, the independent internal verifications that should be performed are very similar. They either involve matching subsidiary accounts with control or master accounts, performing recalculations, or both. First, the amount recorded for accounts payable should be verified against the subsidiary accounts payable ledger. Second, the payroll calculations should be verified for accuracy, and the total, recorded as a liability, should be matched with the payroll register. Finally, estimates for warranty liabilities should be reviewed periodically for adjustment. Certain conditions including product revisions or manufacturing changes that alter the quality of produced goods, changes in sales volume, and changes in normal repair costs signal that warranty valuations may need to be adjusted. Additionally, it is imperative from both a reporting and management standpoint to track the number of claims, and if an unusually large number are reported, actions should be taken to address the issue.

Do not be confused that we did not address every current liability discussed in this chapter in this section. It is not that internal control issues are not applicable to those accounts. In reality, many of the controls discussed here are equally valid and can be applied to the other accounts. The three accounts targeted are just the more prominent of the current liabilities and are often the areas discussed in auditing courses.

Well, by now, you should be able to easily identify a liability. Throughout this chapter we have listed and provided information regarding current liabilities derived from contracts, those based on operations, and even some linked to estimates. We also have offered some advice concerning contingencies and proper internal controls. Just like the bills that never end, though, liabilities do not stop with the current variety. In Chapter 8 we will discuss liabilities that are not expected to be paid within a year—long-term liabilities.

QUIZ

1. **Which of the following statements about current liabilities is *not* true?**
   A. Current liabilities have a normal credit balance and are presented on the balance sheet as a liability.
   B. Current liabilities can be satisfied with either current assets or the creation of other current liabilities.
   C. Current liabilities do not ever have to be paid.
   D. Current liabilities are created by past transactions.

2. **Which of the following statements is the correct definition of an accrued liability?**
   A. A liability that has been incurred but not yet paid nor recorded
   B. A revenue that has been earned but not yet paid nor recorded
   C. An expense that has been paid in advance
   D. A revenue that has been paid in advance

3. **The account unearned revenue is presented on the financial statements as**
   A. an asset.
   B. a liability.
   C. a stockholder's equity item.
   D. an expense.

4. **It is the responsibility of the _____ to collect the sales tax and remit it to the proper authority.**
   A. customer
   B. supplier of the goods
   C. supplier's chief financial officer
   D. seller of the goods

5. **An employee is responsible for paying all but**
   A. the employee's share of the FICA tax.
   B. the employer's share of the FICA tax.
   C. federal income tax on the employee's earnings.
   D. medical insurance authorized by the employee to be taken out of earnings.

6. **BLP, Inc., has net income of $200,000 and a tax rate of 30 percent. The company decided to pay its president a 10 percent bonus on net income after deducting both the bonus and taxes. How much is the bonus the president will receive?**
   A. $14,433
   B. $55,670
   C. $56,075
   D. $13,084

7. **Which of the following statements is *true*?**
   A. Property taxes should be recorded as a liability the day the bill is received.
   B. Property taxes should be recorded as a liability as of the lien date.
   C. Property taxes should be presented on the financial statements as an asset.
   D. Property taxes you owe should be presented on the financial statements as revenue.

8. **Which of the following methods for accounting for warranties is the theoretically best choice for the financial statements?**
   A. Expense warranty accrual method
   B. Sales warranty accrual method
   C. Modified cash basis method
   D. Both the expense warranty accrual method and the modified cash basis method

9. **Which of the following contingencies must be both disclosed and recorded?**
   A. Probable gain contingency
   B. Reasonably possible gain contingency
   C. Remote loss contingency
   D. Probable loss contingency

10. **If all the current liabilities are not recorded, the result would be**
    A. assets are understated.
    B. liabilities are overstated.
    C. liabilities are understated.
    D. stockholder's equity is neither understated nor overstated.

Long-Term Liabilities

CHAPTER OBJECTIVES

After completing this chapter, the student should

- Understand the financial statement presentation for long-term liabilities
- Understand the basics of bond selling prices
- Account for the issuance of bonds
- Account for amortization of bond premiums and discounts using both the straight-line method and the effective interest method
- Understand and account for bonds issued with detachable stock warrants
- Understand and account for the conversion of bonds into common stock using both the book value method and the market value method
- Understand internal controls over long-term liabilities

Overview

Think back a couple of chapters ago to when we introduced property, plant, and equipment. We explained how you record the high-priced assets on the books and then how you can slowly expense them through depreciation.

So how did you buy that computer desk for the top vice president of your company or that Mercedes used to chauffeur your clientele? Well, maybe it was with cash or a short-term liability, but more realistically, you relied on some type of long-term liability. That long-term liability may have been a note payable or perhaps a bond. Purchases encompassing large dollar amounts, construction and expansion of facilities, and many other transactions that do not fit properly within the scope of the day-to-day activities of an organization are financed through the incurrence of debt or, in this case, what accountants like to refer to as *long-term liabilities*.

Now here is one last real-world example before we let you jump right into the material. Are you in college? How about your kids, siblings, friends, or even just someone you know? Many universities have recreation centers, student unions, and many other projects that they have financed through the issuance of bonds. How do they pay the interest and principal on that debt? Yep, you got it! Their students help them through all those fees that are included with their tuition charges. We bet that if you think about it, you have been responsible for or otherwise have been exposed to long-term debt on many occasions. We hate to say it, but whether good or bad, debt is all around you!

Financial Statement Presentation

Long-term liabilities (LTL) have a normal credit balance and are reported on the face of the balance sheet. They represent the amount of money owed to long-term creditors. The most common LTL are long-term notes payable (LTNP) and bonds payable (BP). Because the accounting for long-term notes payable is so similar to the previously discussed short-term notes payable, we will omit that topic from our discussions in this chapter. Instead, we will focus our attention on bonds payable, a favorite intermediate accounting topic for at least one, if not both, of us. At first, BP may appear to be quite cumbersome to account for. However, once the insider tricks are revealed in the next few pages, you will be amazed at how simple accounting for them really is.

As you will see later in this chapter, BP can be issued at either a discount or a premium. For now, just understand that the discount on BP account has a normal debit balance and is deducted from the bonds payable credit balance on the face of the balance sheet. Likewise, the premium on BP account has a normal credit balance and is added to the bonds payable credit balance on the face of the balance sheet.

In this chapter we will discuss the following topics: bond selling prices, the issuance of bonds, the amortization of bond discounts and premiums, the issuance of bonds with detachable stock warrants, the conversion of bonds into common stock, and finally, internal controls over the instruments.

Bond Selling Prices

The first important element of bonds is their selling price. Bonds are sold at a percentage of their face value (FV). The face value of a bond can be $1,000, $5,000, or $10,000. For this book, we will assume the face value of *every* bond is $1,000.

When bonds are sold at *par*, they are sold at 100 percent of face value. Therefore, the proceeds from one bond sold at par would be exactly $1,000.

When bonds are sold at a *discount*, they are sold at an amount less than 100 percent of FV. For example, a bond may be sold at 97, which means that it is selling for 97 percent of FV. The proceeds from one bond sold at 97 would be $970 ($1,000 × 97%).

When bonds are sold at a *premium*, they are sold at an amount greater than 100 percent of FV. For example, a bond may be sold at 102, which means that it is sold for 102 percent of FV. The proceeds from one bond sold at 102 would be $1,020 ($1,000 × 102%).

So why aren't all bonds just sold at par? The answer is actually quite simple. First, all bonds have a stated interest rate that is likely different from the market rate of interest. For example, if a $1,000 bond has a stated interest rate of 5 percent, it will pay $50 ($1,000 × 5%) of interest each year to the bondholder. When the bonds are issued, the stated and market rates of interest may be equal. However, by the time the bonds are actually sold, the stated interest rate likely will *not* be equal to the market rate of interest. Who would purchase a bond offering a lower stated rate of interest than what otherwise could be obtained in the market? You're right, no one! How, then, does a company with such bonds entice buyers to purchase them? The answer can be found in adjustments to the selling price. Through the price adjustment, over the life of the bond, the stated interest rate will reflect the market rate of interest. This is a key point to understand. Another key point that *must* be understood is that the interest expense recorded by the issuing company must reflect the effective rate of interest. Let's delve a bit deeper into this issue.

When a bond is sold at *par*, the effective interest rate will equal the stated interest rate. Likewise, the interest expense will equal the interest paid, and the selling price will equal the face value.

Compare the preceding scenario with a bond that is sold at a discount. When a bond is sold at a *discount*, the effective interest rate is greater than the stated interest rate. The interest expense will be greater than the interest paid, and the selling price will be less than the face value.

Finally, compare those two situations with the final instance where a bond is sold at a premium. When a bond is sold at a *premium*, the effective interest rate is less than the stated interest rate. The interest expense will be less than the interest paid, and the selling price will be greater than the face value.

Issuing Bonds

Because there are three conditions under which bonds may be issued—at par, for a discount, or for a premium—you must be familiar with the related journal entries for each situation. The following three examples will illustrate such entries. These examples will continue through to the following sections and our discussion of the amortization of discounts and premiums. So pay attention!

 EXAMPLE 8-1

BLP, Inc., has decided to build a new facility and will acquire additional debt rather than equity to finance the expansion. On January 2, 2010, the company decided to issue 100 bonds. The bonds have a five-year life and a 5 percent stated rate of interest that will be paid semiannually on June 30 and December 31 of each year. The 100 bonds were issued at par. The journal entry to record the issuance would be

January 2, 2010:

Cash	100,000	
Bonds payable		100,000

 **EXAMPLE 8-2**

Take the same situation as in Example 8-1: BLP, Inc., will still issue 100 five-year bonds with a stated rate of interest of 5 percent on January 2, 2010. The interest will still be paid semiannually on June 30 and December 31 of each year. However, this time, let's assume that the bonds were issued at a discount—$87,883.64. The journal entry to record the issuance would be

January 2, 2010:

Cash	87,883.64	
Discount on BP	12,116.36	
Bonds payable		100,000

EXAMPLE 8-3

Let's revisit the issuance one last time. The same conditions apply as in the preceding two examples. This time, let's make the assumption that the bonds were issued at a premium—$108,110.88. The journal entry to record the issuance would be

January 2, 2010:

Cash	108,110.88	
Premium on BP		8,110.88
Bonds payable		100,000.00

Bond Discount Amortization

So what treatment must be applied to the discounts and premiums? There are two available amortization methods—the straight-line method and the effective interest method. However, only the effective interest method is accepted by generally accepted accounting principles (GAAP). While the straight-line method is not GAAP, it is allowed if the results are not materially different in amount from the effective interest method. In the next few pages we will provide you with examples of each method for both discounts and premiums.

One trick that may be used when preparing amortization schedules is to make the schedule's column headings the names of the accounts that will be used in the journal entries. Then all that is necessary is to transfer the already calculated amounts for each account to the entries. See, simple, right! Another trick is to remember that the first number in the book value of the BP column *always* will be the selling price of the bonds, and the final number in the book value of BP column *always* will be the face value of the bonds.

Straight-Line Discount Amortization

TABLE 8-1 Straight-Line Discount Amortization				
Date	Cr Cash Stated Rate[a]	Dr Interest Expense[b]	Cr Discount on BP[c]	Book Value of BP[d]
1/2/10				87,883.64
6/30/10	2,500.00	3,711.64	1,211.64	89,095.28
12/31/10	2,500.00	3,711.64	1,211.64	90,306.92
6/30/11	2,500.00	3,711.64	1,211.64	91,518.56
12/31/11	2,500.00	3,711.64	1,211.64	92,730.20
6/30/12	2,500.00	3,711.64	1,211.64	93,941.84
12/31/12	2,500.00	3,711.64	1,211.64	95,153.48
6/30/13	2,500.00	3,711.64	1,211.64	96,365.12
12/31/13	2,500.00	3,711.64	1,211.64	97,576.76
6/30/14	2,500.00	3,711.64	1,211.64	98,788.40
12/31/14	2,500.00	3,711.60	1,211.60	100,000.00
			12,116.36	

[a]Face value (100,000) times stated interest rate (5%) × 0.5.
[b]Sum of credit to cash and credit to discount on BP.
[c]Total discount of $12,116.36 divided by 10 periods.
[d]Previous BV plus credit to discount on BP.
Note: The 12/31/2014 credit to discount on BP was rounded by .04 to achieve an ending BV of 100,000.

Table 8-1, along with Example 8-4, will be used to illustrate the straight-line discount amortization for bonds payable.

EXAMPLE 8-4

Let's revisit the scenario we introduced in Example 8-2. Recall that BLP, Inc., has decided to build a new facility and has acquired additional debt rather than equity to finance the expansion through the issuance of 100 bonds. The five-year bonds with a stated interest rate of 5 percent paid semiannually on June 30 and December 31 were issued on January 2, 2010. The bonds were issued at $87,883.64, a discount. As shown previously, the journal entry to record the issuance would be

January 2, 2010:

Cash	87,883.64	
Discount on BP	12,116.36	
Bonds payable		100,000

The journal entry that will be made at *each* interest payment date (i.e., June 30 and December 31 of each year) will reflect the payment of the interest at the stated rate. It also will amortize the discount on BP and will record the interest expense. Notice in Table 8-1 that the amortization of the discount using the straight-line method reflects a *constant amount* of amortization each period. The journal entry for the first interest payment date would be

June 30, 2010:

Interest expense	3,711.64	
Discount on BP		1,211.64
Cash		2,500.00

Now *pay very close attention* to the following instructions regarding how to compute the numbers for each column in Table 8-1. As we explained earlier, the first number in the book value of BP column is the selling price of the bonds, which is the same as the present value (PV) of the bonds and also the same as the book value of the bonds. We have one final comment regarding the book value: It is computed as the face value of the BP plus the unamortized premium on BP or minus the unamortized discount on BP.

The column for credit to cash is computed as the face value of the BP times the stated interest rate. Remember, the interest payments occur semiannually. Therefore, the June 30, 2010, interest payment would be calculated as $2,500 ($100,000 × 5% × ½ year).

The column for credit to discount on BP is calculated by taking the total in the discount on BP account at the sale date and dividing by the life of the bonds [$12,116.36/10 periods (5 years × 2 periods each year)].

The column for debit to interest expense is computed as the sum of the cash paid and the discount amortization for the period. Thus the June 30, 2010, interest expense of $3,711.64 is calculated as the sum of $2,500.00 and $1,211.64.

The column for book value of BP is determined by adding the previous book value of BP to the amount of discount on BP that was amortized that period. The June 30, 2010, book value of BP amount of $89,095.28 thus is calculated as the sum of $87,883.64 and $1,211.64.

Effective Interest Discount Amortization

TABLE 8-2 Effective Interest Discount Amortization

Date	Cr Cash Stated Rate[a]	Dr Interest Expense Effective Rate[b]	Cr Discount on BP Difference[c]	Book Value of BP[d]
1/2/10				87,883.64
6/30/10	2,500.00	3,515.35	1,015.35	88,898.99
12/31/10	2,500.00	3,555.96	1,055.96	89,954.95
6/30/11	2,500.00	3,598.20	1,098.20	91,053.14
12/31/11	2,500.00	3,642.13	1,142.13	92,195.27
6/30/12	2,500.00	3,687.81	1,187.81	93,383.08
12/31/12	2,500.00	3,735.32	1,235.32	94,618.40
6/30/13	2,500.00	3,784.74	1,284.74	95,903.14
12/31/13	2,500.00	3,836.13	1,336.13	97,239.26
6/30/14	2,500.00	3,889.57	1,389.57	98,628.83
12/31/14	2,500.00	3,871.16	1,371.16	100,000.00
			12,116.36	

[a]Face value (100,000) times stated interest rate (5%) × 0.5.
[b]Previous BV (87,883.64) times effective interest rate (8%) × 0.5.
[c]Difference between credit to cash and debit to interest expense.
[d]Previous BV plus credit to discount on BP.
 Note: The 12/31/2014 debit to interest expense was rounded by 74.00 to achieve an ending BV of 100,000.

Table 8-2, along with Example 8-5, will be used to illustrate the effective interest discount amortization for bonds payable. As you will see, the process is very similar to amortization under the straight-line method with a few exceptions.

EXAMPLE **8-5**

Again, we have BLP, Inc., deciding to build a new facility and acquiring additional debt rather than equity as its financing source. The life of the bonds will still be five years, and the stated interest rate will be 5 percent paid semiannually. This time we also must keep in mind that the bonds were issued to reflect an effective interest rate of 8 percent. These bonds were issued at $87,883.64. Again, the journal entry to record the issuance would be

January 2, 2010:

Cash	87,883.64	
Discount on BP	12,116.36	
Bonds payable		100,000

The journal entry that will be made at *each* interest payment date (i.e., June 30 and December 31 of each year) will reflect the payment of the interest at the stated rate. It also will amortize the discount on BP and will record the interest expense. Notice in Table 8-2 that the interest expense using the effective interest method reflects a *constant rate* of interest expense each period. The journal entry for the first interest payment date would be

June 30, 2010:

Interest expense	3,515.35	
Discount on BP		1,015.35
Cash		2,500.00

In Table 8-2, the column for credit to cash is computed as the face value of the BP times the stated interest rate. Therefore, the June 30, 2010, interest payment is calculated as $2,500 ($100,000 × 5% × ½ year).

The column for debit to interest expense is computed as the previous book value of BP times the effective interest rate. Therefore, the June 30, 2010, interest expense of $3,515.35 is calculated as $87,883.64 times the effective interest rate of 8 percent for ½ year.

The column for credit to discount on BP is calculated as the difference between the interest expense and the cash payment. The $1,015.35 is the interest expense of $3,515.35 minus the cash payment of $2,500.00.

The column for book value of BP is determined by adding the previous book value of BP to the amount of discount on BP that was amortized that period. The June 30, 2010, book value of BP amount of $88,898.99 is calculated as the sum of $87,883.64 and $1,015.35.

Bond Premium Amortization

Just like discounts, there are two methods used to amortize bond premiums—the straight-line method and the effective interest method. Examples for each method are presented below.

Straight-Line Premium Amortization

TABLE 8-3 Straight-Line Premium Amortization

Date	Cr Cash Stated Rate[a]	Dr Interest Expense[b]	Dr Premium on BP[c]	Book Value of BP[d]
1/2/10				108,110.88
6/30/10	5,000.00	4,188.91	811.09	107,299.79
12/31/10	5,000.00	4,188.91	811.09	106,488.70
6/30/11	5,000.00	4,188.91	811.09	105,677.61
12/31/11	5,000.00	4,188.91	811.09	104,866.52
6/30/12	5,000.00	4,188.91	811.09	104,055.43
12/31/12	5,000.00	4,188.91	811.09	103,244.34
6/30/13	5,000.00	4,188.91	811.09	102,433.25
12/31/13	5,000.00	4,188.91	811.09	101,622.16
6/30/14	5,000.00	4,188.91	811.09	100,811.07
12/31/14	5,000.00	4,188.93	811.07	100,000.00
			8,110.88	

[a]Face value (100,000) times stated interest rate (10%) × 0.5.
[b]Difference between credit to cash and debit to premium on BP.
[c]Total premium of $8,110.88 divided by 10 periods.
[d]Previous BV minus debit to premium on BP.
 Note: The 12/31/2014 debit to premium on BP was rounded by 0.02 to achieve an ending
   BV of 100,000.

Table 8-3, along with Example 8-6, will be used to illustrate the straight-line premium amortization for bonds payable.

EXAMPLE 8-6

BLP, Inc., has decided to build a new facility and will issue additional debt instead of equity to finance the expansion. The company has decided to issue 100 bonds on January 2, 2010. The life of the bonds will be five years. The stated rate of interest will be 10 percent, and interest will be paid semi-annually on June 30 and December 31 of each year. The bonds were issued at $108,110.88. The journal entry to record the issuance would be

January 2, 2010:

Cash	108,110.88	
Premium on BP		8,110.88
Bonds payable		100,000.00

The journal entry that will be made at *each* interest payment date will reflect the payment of the interest at the stated rate. It also will amortize the premium on BP and will record the interest expense. Notice in Table 8-3 that the amortization of the premium on BP using the straight-line method reflects a *constant amount* of interest expense each period. The journal entry for the first interest payment date would be

June 30, 2010:

Interest expense	4,188.91	
Premium on BP	811.09	
Cash		5,000.00

The calculations for the amortization of premiums are very similar to those for discounts. Therefore, the same calculation rules apply.

In Table 8-3, the column for credit to cash is computed as the face value of the BP times the stated interest rate. Therefore, the June 30, 2010, interest payment is calculated as $5,000 ($100,000 × 10% × ½ year).

The column for debit to premium on BP is calculated by taking the total in the premium on BP account on the sale date and dividing by the life of the bonds ($8,110.88/10 periods).

The column for debit to interest expense is computed as the difference between the cash paid and the premium amortization for the period. Thus the June 30, 2010, interest expense of $4,188.91 is calculated as the difference between $5,000.00 and $811.09.

The column for book value of BP is determined by subtracting the amount of premium on BP that was amortized that period from the previous book value of BP. The June 30, 2010, book value of BP amount of $107,299.79 thus is calculated as the difference between $108,110.88 and $811.09.

Effective Interest Premium Amortization

TABLE 8-4 Effective Interest Premium Amortization				
Date	**Cr Cash Stated Rate[a]**	**Dr Interest Expense Effective Rate[b]**	**Dr Premium on BP Difference[c]**	**Book Value of BP[d]**
1/2/10				108,110.88
6/30/10	5,000.00	4,324.44	675.56	107,435.32
12/31/10	5,000.00	4,297.41	702.59	106,732.73
6/30/11	5,000.00	4,269.31	730.69	106,002.04
12/31/11	5,000.00	4,240.08	759.92	105,242.12
6/30/12	5,000.00	4,209.68	790.32	104,451.80
12/31/12	5,000.00	4,178.07	821.93	103,629.88
6/30/13	5,000.00	4,145.20	854.80	102,775.07
12/31/13	5,000.00	4,111.00	889.00	101,886.07
6/30/14	5,000.00	4,075.44	924.56	100,961.52
12/31/14	5,000.00	4,038.48	961.52	100,000.00
			8,110.88	

[a]Face value (100,000) times stated interest rate (10%) × 0.5.
[b]Previous BV (108,110.88) times effective interest rate (8%) × 0.5.
[c]Difference between credit to cash and debit to interest expense.
[d]Previous BV minus debit to premium on BP.
 Note: The 12/31/2014 debit to interest expense was rounded by 0.02 to achieve an ending
  BV of 100,000.

Table 8-4, along with Example 8-7, will be used to illustrate the effective interest method to account for the premium amortization on bonds payable.

EXAMPLE 8-7

Again, let's assume that BLP's bonds were issued at $108,110.88, which reflects an effective interest rate of 8 percent. The journal entry would be as follows:

January 2, 2010:

Cash	108,110.88	
Premium on BP		8,110.88
Bonds payable		100,000.00

Please note in Table 8-4 that the amortization of the premium on BP using the effective interest method reflects a *constant rate* of interest expense each period. The journal entry for the first interest payment date would be as follows:

June 30, 2010:

Interest expense	**4,324.44**	
Premium on BP	**675.56**	
Cash		**5,000.00**

In Table 8-4, the column for credit to cash is computed as the face value of the BP times the stated interest rate. Therefore, the June 30, 2010, interest payment is calculated as $5,000 ($100,000 × 10% × ½ year).

The column for debit to interest expense is computed as the previous balance in the book value of BP column times the effective interest rate. Therefore, the June 30, 2010, interest expense of $4,324.44 is calculated as $108,110.88 times 8% for ½ year.

The column for debit to premium on BP is calculated as the difference between the interest expense and the cash payment. The $675.56 is the cash payment of $5,000.00 minus the interest expense of $4,324.44.

The column for book value of BP is determined by subtracting the amount of premium on BP that was amortized during the period from the previous book value of BP. The June 30, 2010, book value of BP amount of $107,435.32 is calculated as the difference between $108,110.88 and $675.56.

Issuing Bonds with Detachable Stock Warrants

Sometimes a company does not want to issue plain bonds. Instead, it may want to offer an investor the opportunity to receive not only the right to receive interest income but also the right to obtain an equity interest in the company in the future. By offering what are known as *detachable stock warrants*, the company potentially can pay interest at a rate that is lower than the market rate of interest on the bonds or can more quickly obtain the money it needs for an important project.

In order to account for the warrants properly, we need to introduce a new account—*common stock warrants*. This account is reflected on the balance sheet in stockholders' equity as a part of additional paid-in capital. Thus common stock warrants will have a normal credit balance.

We will use Table 8-5, along with Example 8-8, to illustrate the issuance of bonds with detachable common stock warrants.

TABLE 8-5 Bonds Issued with Detachable Common Stock Warrants

Step 1: Determine proceeds from bond issue:

100 bonds issued at 103	$100,000 \times 1.03$		103,000.00

20 warrants are issued with each bond

Step 2: Determine book value to be assigned to bonds and warrants:

		FMV	BV
FMV of bonds	100 bonds × $1,000 × 0.98	98,000.00	(98,000/110,000) × 103,000	91,763.00
FMV of warrants	100 bonds × 20 warrants × $6	12,000.00	(12,000/110,000) × 103,000	11,237.00
		110,000.00		103,000.00

Step 3: Prepare journal entry:

Cash	103,000.00	
Discount on BP	8,237.00	
Bonds payable		100,000.00
Common stock warrants		11,237.00

EXAMPLE **8-8**

BLP, Inc., decided to issue 100 bonds at 103. The bonds will include 20 warrants with each bond. On the issue date, the fair market value (FMV) of each bond is 98, and the FMV of each warrant is $6. Each warrant allows the holder to purchase one share of $4 par stock for $30 per share. The bonds will pay interest at 9 percent.

The computations for this example are included in Table 8-5. The explanations for each computation are included below.

The first step is to determine the proceeds of the bond issue. In this example, the proceeds are $103,000 (100 bonds × $1,000 per bond × 1.03).

The second step is to determine the book value to be recorded for both the bonds and the common stock warrants. The book value is calculated by allocating the FMV of each item to the total proceeds. The mechanics of the computation is *exactly* like the allocation of a single purchase price to several items of property, plant, and equipment that we presented in Chapter 5. In this case, however, instead of acquiring assets, we are selling two items for one price and are simply allocating the cash we received to each item we sold based on its FMV. Please refer to Table 8-5 for the calculations of the book value of the bonds ($91,763) and the book value of the common stock warrants ($11,237).

The third step involves recording the sale of the bonds and common stock warrants. By the time we have finished the calculations in step 2, we already have the numbers for our journal entry. Please refer to Table 8-5 for the entry. Remember that the bonds payable account *always* reflects the *face value* of the bonds. Thus, in this case, for the BP to be reported at its book value, we also must record a discount on BP of $8,237 ($100,000 − $91,763).

EXAMPLE **8-9**

Let's continue Example 8-8 by assuming that 500 warrants are exercised. This means that 500 of the warrants are exchanged for 500 shares of $4 par stock for a price of $30 per share. The journal entry to record the event would be

Cash (500 × $30)	15,000	
Common stock warrants (500/2,000 × 11,237)	2,809	
Common stock (500 × $4)		2,000
Additional paid-in capital (plug)		15,809

EXAMPLE **8-10**

Let's continue Examples 8-8 and 8-9 by assuming that the remaining 1,500 warrants are allowed to expire. Notice in the journal entry below that we have labeled the additional paid-in capital account so that the reader knows where the money came from. The journal entry to record the expiration of the remaining warrants would be

Common stock warrants ($11,237 − $2,809)	8,428	
Additional paid-in capital from expired warrants		8,428

Converting Bonds into Common Stock

There are a number of reasons that could underlie a company's decision to issue bonds that can be converted into common stock. First, the company may not currently be ready to add additional equity owners in the company, but it may want to keep that option open in the future. Second, just like the bonds issued with the detachable common stock warrants, the company may want to pay a lower interest rate, and the only way to achieve this would be to include an equity feature with the bonds. Third, the company may want to issue equity but may not want to dilute the value of stock held by each shareholder, which typically occurs with the issuance of additional shares into the market. Finally, the company simply may perceive the current stock to be undervalued in the market and may not wish to issue additional stock at the present time.

There are two ways to account for convertible stock—the book value method and the market value method. Both will be discussed below. The initial journal entry to issue the convertible bonds is exactly like that presented earlier in this chapter in Examples 8-1 through 8-3. The book value or market value method is applied simply when the bonds are converted into common stock.

Book Value Method

The premise behind the book value method is that no gain or loss is recorded when the bonds are converted into common stock. The journal entry to record the conversion simply will remove the debt accounts and place the same total dollar amount in the new equity accounts.

 EXAMPLE 8-11

BLP, Inc., previously issued 100 bonds that will convert into 5,000 shares of $5 par common stock. The current book value of the bonds is $94,618. Therefore, we can infer that the books show a discount on BP of $5,382. Notice again that the additional paid-in capital account indicates where the money came from. The journal entry to record the conversion of the bonds into common stock would be

Bonds payable	100,000	
Discount on BP		5,382
Common stock (5,000 × $5)		25,000
Additional paid-in capital from bond conversion (plug)		69,618

Market Value Method

The premise behind the market value method is that the debt accounts are removed at their book values and the equity accounts are added at their FMVs. Because the BV of the debt will not equal the FMV of the equity, a gain or a loss must be recorded to make the journal entry balance.

EXAMPLE 8-12

BLP, Inc., previously issued 100 bonds that will convert into 5,000 shares of $5 par common stock. The current book value of the bonds is $94,618. Therefore, we can infer that the books show a discount on BP of $5,382. The common stock is currently selling for $18 per share. Notice again that the additional paid-in capital account indicates where the money came from. The journal entry to record the conversion of the bonds into common stock would be

Bonds payable	100,000	
Gain on conversion of BP		4,618
Discount on BP		5,382
Common stock (5,000 × $5)		25,000
Additional paid-in capital from bond conversion (5,000 × $13)		65,000

Internal Controls

Establishment of Responsibility and Segregation of Duties

While there is no clear segregation of duties for bonds as there is for inventory, accounts payable, accounts receivable, and so on, there are usually a number of individuals both inside and outside the organization who accept responsibility for various elements involved with the issuance and upkeep of bonds. First, it is normally the board of directors' responsibility to properly authorize the issuance and to create bond indentures, setting forth the protections granted to the holders of the instruments. Such protections may include the requirement that a minimum amount of retained earnings be kept rather than being distributed to shareholders in the form of dividends, as well as certain allowable ranges for various ratios pertaining to debt. The procedures for the retirement of the bonds are also included within the document. Second, an underwriter is usually enlisted to market the bonds. Finally, bond trustees are often hired to register and maintain lists of current bondholders and to issue the interest payments to those individuals after receiving the total interest obligation from the issuing organization. Such distribution of power both inside and outside the organization in regard to bonds helps to better prevent unauthorized acts or falsification of information in connection with bond issuances.

Documentation Procedures and Physical, Mechanical, and Electronic Controls

While physical controls are virtually nonexistent when dealing with bonds, there are a handful of documentation procedures and electronic controls that contribute to the oversight over the issuance and maintenance of bonds. As we just mentioned, each bond issuance must be accompanied by a bond indenture that not only outlines the specific promises of the issuer to creditors but also notifies the creditors of such promises. Although not kept with the issuer, registration lists must be created and maintained by the hired trustee. Additionally, policies describing proper amortization procedures must be established in writing and corresponding schedules kept to verify both the value of the bonds on the books and the amount of interest expense and cash payments recorded. Electronic controls such as access and edit restrictions on files containing such documents also may be necessary to prevent unauthorized changes.

Independent Internal Verification

Checks on both the reasonableness and accuracy of computations involved with the accounting for bonds are completed by both internal parties and external auditors. An individual otherwise not associated with the upkeep of the bonds should verify their valuation and the related amortization of their discounts or premiums, the calculation of the recorded interest expense, and any gains or losses that may result from refinancing initiatives. Verifying the issuance of a check to a trustee for the payment of interest to bondholders in accordance with the bonds' payment structure also may be completed by matching amortization schedules with canceled checks.

This chapter went crazy over bonds! Yep, their acquisition, amortization of premiums and discounts, special features, and the list goes on and on. Well, hopefully, after all your debts have been paid, you still will have at least a little left over. So what happens to the leftovers? Are they saved for tomorrow night's meal, or how about just a rainy day? Continue on to Chapter 9 to find out!

QUIZ

1. The account discount on bonds payable is presented on the financial statements
   A. on the income statement as an addition to revenues.
   B. on the balance sheet as a deduction from bonds payable.
   C. on the income statement as an addition to expenses.
   D. on the balance sheet as an addition to bonds payable.

2. Which of the following statements is *false*?
   A. When bonds are sold at a discount, the effective rate of interest is greater than the stated rate of interest.
   B. When bonds are sold at a premium, the effective rate of interest is greater than the stated rate of interest.
   C. When bonds are sold at par, the effective rate of interest is equal to the stated rate of interest.
   D. When bonds are sold at a discount, the selling price is less than the face value.

3. Which method of amortization of bond discounts and premiums is GAAP?
   A. Straight-line method
   B. Declining-balance method
   C. Effective interest method
   D. Sum of the years' digits method

   Questions 4 through 7 are based on the following data:

   BLP, Inc., decided to issue 100 bonds on January 2, 2010. The life of the bonds will be three years. The stated rate of interest will be 8 percent, and interest will be paid annually on December 31 of each year. These bonds were issued at $95,027, which reflects an effective interest rate of 10 percent. (*Hint:* Prepare an amortization table and journal entries prior to answering the following questions.)

4. The journal entry to issue the bonds includes a
   A. debit to cash of $100,000.
   B. debit to premium on bonds payable of $4,973.
   C. credit to bonds payable of $95,027.
   D. debit to discount on bonds payable of $4,973.

5. At the first interest payment date of December 31, 2010, the journal entry will include a
   A. credit to discount on bonds payable of $1,503.
   B. debit to premium on bonds payable of $1,503.
   C. credit to interest expense of $9,503.
   D. debit to cash of $8,000.

6. What is the book value of the bonds payable on December 31, 2011?

 A. $95,027
 B. $96,530
 C. $98,183
 D. $100,000

7. On the third interest payment date of December 31, 2013, the journal entry will include a

 A. debit to cash of $8,000.
 B. credit to cash of $8,000.
 C. credit to interest expense of $9,817.
 D. debit to discount on bonds payable of $1,817.

8. The account common stock warrants is reflected on the financial statements as

 A. an asset.
 B. a liability.
 C. an expense.
 D. additional paid-in capital.

9. BLP, Inc., has decided to issue 100 bonds at 102. The bonds will include 10 warrants with each bond. On the issue date, the FMV of each bond is 98, and the FMV of each warrant is $7. Each warrant allows the holder to purchase one share of $5 par stock for $25 per share. The company will pay interest of 8 percent. On the date of issue, the journal entry will include a

 A. debit to cash of $102,000.
 B. credit to cash of $100,000.
 C. credit to premium on bonds payable of $4,800.
 D. debit to common stock warrants of $6,800.

10. BLP, Inc., previously issued 100 bonds that will convert into 10,000 shares of $5 par common stock. The current book value of the bonds is $104,618. The common stock is currently selling for $9 per share. The journal entry to record the conversion of the bonds, using the market value method, into common stock includes a

 A. debit to discount on bonds payable of $4,618.
 B. debit to premium on bonds payable of $4,618.
 C. credit to bonds payable of $100,000.
 D. debit to loss on conversion of bonds payable of $14,618.

Part III

The Balance Sheet: Stockholders' Equity—What Is Left Over?

chapter **9**

Contributed Capital

CHAPTER OBJECTIVES

After completing this chapter, the student should

- Understand the financial statement presentation for contributed capital
- Understand and account for stock issued for cash
- Account for stock subscriptions
- Account for combined sales of stock
- Understand and account for stock splits
- Understand and account for stock options
- Understand the preference features of preferred stock
- Account for the issuance of preferred stock with common stock warrants attached
- Account for treasury stock using both the cost and par value methods
- Understand the internal controls over contributed capital

Overview

Have you ever wanted to do something but didn't have the funds? Maybe you wanted to go on a trip to the Arctic or buy a new musical instrument so that you could fulfill your dream of learning to play. You really wanted to go or do such grand things but didn't think that a bank would take you seriously enough to lend you some cash for your off-the-wall pursuits. Corporations and organizations have the same issue. They may have great plans for future growth and see wonderful opportunities, but they may not have the funds to get there. Sometimes they may rely on borrowing from financial institutions or issuing debt to other creditors in the form of bonds to provide them with the needed resources to carry out their activities. No company wants too much debt and related interest, however. There is a delicate balance that must be achieved between debt and equity when it comes to financial structure.

If you were like most kids growing up, you had to partake in a few fundraisers (alright, probably a few more than you ever cared to) for your school, your sports team, your religious group, and so on. Did you have to give that money back? Well, unless it was some unusual fundraiser, probably not. Usually, however, your kind benefactor received something in return, a product, some coupons or special deals, and so on. Stock works in much the same way. The money does not need to be paid back by the company. However, the purchaser receives something in return, either dividends or increases in stock prices making each share more valuable. Now, don't get us wrong, the fund-raising example does not mimic this process exactly because it is more of a donation from others than an investment, but still, hopefully, it helps make our point about the uses and benefits of stock issuances at a very basic level a bit clearer.

Financial Statement Presentation

Like other stockholders' equity accounts, the accounts that comprise the contributed capital section of stockholders' equity (SE) on the balance sheet all have normal credit balances. Table 9-1 provides a list of all such accounts that will be introduced in this chapter. As is customary for the other components of a balance sheet—assets and liabilities—these accounts follow a standard order that normally should not be altered to meet specific company desires. That order is presented in Table 9-1 and should be followed when preparing the financial statement.

There are five terms associated with stock transactions that you must be familiar with in order to establish the basic foundation of your contributed capital knowledge. *Authorized stock* refers to the number of shares that a corporation *may issue*. *Issued stock* consists of the number of shares that a corporation *actually has issued* (from these two definitions, you can see that the number of shares issued always must be equal to or less than the number authorized). *Outstanding stock* is the number of shares that are *still held* by stockholders. Okay, so based on these definitions, shouldn't the number of shares issued and outstanding always be the same? Well, not exactly. Sometimes, for a variety of reasons ranging from a desire to have extra shares available to issue as stock options to executives or wishing to hold a larger ownership interest in the company to ward off takeover attempts to attempting to improve earnings per share, a company will repurchase some of its own stock. *Treasury stock* consists of the shares that are bought back and is the difference between the number of shares issued and the number of shares outstanding. Finally, *subscribed stock* refers to the number of shares that will be issued in the future based on purchase agreements that already have been established.

So why must you know such definitions? Okay, besides the fact that your professor or boss has just asked you about them. The answer is that generally accepted accounting principles (GAAP) require the number of shares authorized, issued, and outstanding all to be presented in the financial statements. Parenthetical notation on the face of the balance sheet in the contributed capital section is a common presentation method. An acceptable alternative is to prepare a footnote disclosure and include it with the financial statements.

TABLE 9-1 Contributed Capital Section of the Balance Sheet
Par value (or stated value) of preferred stock
Par value (or stated value) of common stock
Common (or preferred) stock subscribed
Common stock warrants
Stock dividends to be distributed
Additional paid–in capital on preferred stock
Additional paid–in capital on common stock
Additional paid–in capital from other sources

Throughout this chapter we will discuss the journal entries related to the issuance of stock for cash, stock subscriptions, combined sales of stock, nonmonetary issuances of stock, stock splits, stock options, preferred stock, and finally, treasury stock.

Stock Issuances Involving Cash

Par value is an important concept related to stock transactions. The *par value* of a particular class of stock represents the legal capital associated with that class. *Legal capital*, in essence, is the portion of the proceeds from the issuance that cannot be distributed to stockholders as dividends. The par value usually is set at a very small amount and is established at the time of corporate formation or on the authorization of a new class of stock. Stock may or may not be issued with a par value. When a par value is not established, a stated value may be present instead. A *stated value* will represent the legal capital, just as the par value does. When neither a par nor a stated value is present, all the proceeds represent the legal capital and are restricted from being distributed.

Once the monetary value for legal capital has been calculated, that value can be credited to the common stock or preferred stock account. As part of most issuances, the cash collected per share will exceed the par amount. Such additional proceeds thus are credited to the additional paid-in capital (PIC) account for the respective stock that was sold.

EXAMPLE 9-1

BLP, Inc., sold 1,000 shares of $10 par common stock for $35 each. The journal entry associated with that transaction is presented in Table 9-2.

TABLE 9-2 Example 9-1

Cash	1,000 × $35	35,000	
Common stock	1,000 × $10		10,000
PIC—CS plug ($35 – $10 = $25)	1,000 × $25		25,000

EXAMPLE 9-2

BLP, Inc., sold 1,000 shares of no par common stock for $35 each. The stock has a stated value of $5 each. The journal entry is presented in Table 9-3.

TABLE 9-3 Example 9-2

Cash	1,000 × $35	35,000	
Common stock	1,000 × $5		5,000
PIC—CS	1,000 × $30		30,000

EXAMPLE 9-3

BLP, Inc., sold 1,000 shares of no par common stock with no stated value for $35 each. The journal entry that would be recorded is presented in Table 9-4.

TABLE 9-4 Example 9-3

Cash	1,000 × $35	35,000	
Common stock	1,000 × $35		35,000

Stock Subscriptions

A *stock subscription* is another form of a stock sale. The concept is very similar to a payment plan for an asset, so, in that respect, it can be considered a stock payment plan. The contract provisions dictate the specific accounting treatment for the stock subscription. For instance, the contract may state that none of the stock is to be distributed until full payment is made, or the contract may state that when half the payment is satisfied, half the stock issue can be distributed.

Another contract element might describe the treatment for payment defaults. One possibility is that the money that has already been paid be retained by the company, with the subscriber receiving no stock in return for the underpayment. Another possibility is that some shares be issued relative to the amount already paid. If the contract does not specify how the default is accounted for, then state law governs, and the related rules must be followed.

**EXAMPLE 9-4**

BLP, Inc., entered into a stock subscription contract with Jones Company. Jones agreed to purchase 1,000 shares of $10 par common stock for $35 each by paying 10 percent down on February 1, 45 percent on March 1, and 45 percent on April 1. The contract stated that no stock is to be issued until the subscription is paid in full. The journal entries that would be made on the respective dates are illustrated in Table 9-5.

TABLE 9-5 Example 9-4			
1–Feb Cash	1,000 × $35 × 10%	3,500	
Subscriptions receivable	1,000 × $35 × 90%	31,500	
CS subscribed	1,000 × $10		10,000
PIC—CS	1,000 × $25		25,000
1–Mar Cash	1,000 × $35 × 45%	15,750	
Subscriptions receivable			15,750
1–Apr Cash	1,000 × $35 × 45%	15,750	
Subscriptions receivable			15,750
CS subscribed		10,000	
CS			10,000

Combined Sales of Stock

In an effort to entice investors to provide funds, a company sometimes will sell both common and preferred stocks together at less than full fair market value (FMV). In such an instance, the actual purchase price must be allocated to each type of stock based on the FMVs of each class. The par or stated values must be credited to the common and preferred stock accounts, and any additional proceeds must be credited to the PIC accounts for the common and preferred stock, respectively. Remember, because they are reported separately in the contributed capital section of the balance sheet, there is a separate PIC account for both common and preferred stock.

 EXAMPLE 9-5

BLP, Inc., sold 1,000 shares of $10 par common stock along with 50 shares of $5 par preferred stock for a total of $34,000. At the time of sale, the FMV of the common stock was $35 per share, and the FMV of the preferred stock was $50 per share. The computation to allocate the proceeds to each type of stock is shown in Table 9-6, along with the journal entry to record the combined sale.

Note that the book value of the common stock totals $31,733. The sum of the common stock account and the PIC—CS account must equal $31,733. Therefore, the PIC—CS account is credited for the proceeds that exceed the common stock par value. Likewise, the preferred stock book value total must equal $2,267. Therefore, the sum of the preferred stock account and the PIC—PS account must equal $2,267. Any proceeds above the preferred stock par amount thus are credited to the PIC—PS account.

TABLE 9-6 Example 9-5

				FMV		
Common stock	1,000	×	35	35,000	(35,000/37,500) × 34,000	31,733
Preferred stock	50	×	50	2,500	(2,500/37,500) × 34,000	2,267
				37,500		34,000
Cash			34,000			
Common stock	1,000 × $10			10,000		
PIC—CS	31,733 – 10,000			21,733		
Preferred stock	50 × $5			250		
PIC—PS	2,267 – 250			2,017		

Nonmonetary Issuance of Stock

Sometimes money is not received when stock is issued. Instead, the stock is issued in exchange for property or services. When this happens, the stock should be recorded at the FMV of the stock or property (or services), whichever is more reliable. If the stock is traded on a national stock exchange, the price of the stock is usually considered the most reliable value. What if the stock is not publicly traded and the FMV of the property is considered to be more reliable, though? Is any person's judgment just as good as anyone else's? Are you more likely to believe someone within the company or someone outside it? With ethics becoming so prominent in business and especially the accounting profession these days, we would hope the involved parties would be fair in their valuations. However, self-interest or, in this case, company interest tends to dominate, and one can never be completely certain that valuations are accurate unless an independent third party is used. Thus, when the FMV of the property is to be used, an "outside" appraisal of the property should be obtained. If using the FMV of the services rendered, the normal billing rate would be an acceptable FMV.

EXAMPLE 9-6

BLP, Inc., acquired a piece of land in exchange for 1,000 shares of $10 par common stock. The stock is all privately held, and the last sale was made two months ago for $35 per share. The owner of the land thinks that the land is worth $50,000. BLP decided to obtain an independent appraisal of the land, and the appraised value was determined to be $40,000. Because the independent appraisal is the most reliable FMV, the land and stock issue will be recorded at $40,000, as illustrated in Table 9-7.

TABLE 9-7 Example 9-6		
Land		40,000
Common stock	1,000 × $10	10,000
PIC—CS	Plug	30,000

Stock Splits

The first point to remember about stock splits is that they have absolutely no effect on total stockholders' equity. The distribution of funds may differ following a stock split, but the total always will remain the same. So what, then, is the purpose of such splits? Does a company executive or board member just wake up one day and randomly decide to propose a stock split? Well, no, not exactly.

Stock splits can be desired for a number of reasons. One of the main reasons, though, is that the company may think that the market price of the stock is too high, and it wants to drive the price down to make the stock more afford-able for investors. In this chapter we will cover three types of stock splits—proportionate, disproportionate, and reverse.

Proportionate Stock Split

Let's start with a *proportionate stock split*. With this type of split, the par value of the stock is decreased in direct proportion to the increase in the number of shares. A journal entry is *not* required because the final amount in the common stock (or preferred stock) account is the same as before the proportionate stock split. The same is true for the PIC—CS (or PIC—PS) account. Because the amounts are the same, we can deduce that the total SE and the individual com-ponents of SE *do not change*. Even though a journal entry is not required, the company still must make a memorandum entry to note that the proportionate stock split has occurred.

EXAMPLE 9-7

BLP, Inc., has 10,000 shares of $10 par common stock issued and outstand-ing. The company has 100,000 shares authorized. Effective January 1, the stock will split two for one. Based on such parameters, immediately after the stock split, the authorized number of shares will double to 200,000, and the issued and outstanding number of shares likewise will increase by the same proportion, becoming 20,000, whereas the par value will be cut in half to $5. BLP only needs to prepare a memorandum entry to record the proportionate stock split. While every company will have its preferred method of recording this event, for teaching and learning purposes, we will record the memo entry as follows:

Authorized	Old	100,000	New	200,000
Issued	Old	10,000	New	20,000
Par value	Old	$10	New	$5

Disproportionate Stock Split

In a *disproportionate stock split*, the reduction in par value is not proportionate to the increase in the number of shares. As a result, a journal entry is required to remove the old legal capital and put on the new legal capital in the common stock (or preferred stock) account. The difference in the legal capital is credited to a new account called *PIC from stock split*. In a disproportionate stock split, the individual components of contributed capital *do* change, but the total SE *does not* change.

EXAMPLE 9-8

BLP, Inc., has 10,000 shares of $10 par common stock issued and outstanding. The company has 100,000 shares authorized. Effective January 1, the stock will split, and there will be 150,000 shares authorized, 15,000 shares issued and outstanding, and the par value will become $4. Because the stock split is disproportionate, a journal entry must be prepared to change the amount of legal capital. The journal entry is illustrated in Table 9-8.

TABLE 9-8 Example 9-8			
Common stock	10,000 × $10	100,000	
Common stock	15,000 × $4		60,000
PIC—stock split	Plug		40,000

Reverse Stock Splits

A *reverse stock split* will reduce the number of shares while increasing the par value per share. A reverse stock split can be either proportionate or disproportionate and is handled in the same manner as was discussed earlier. A proportionate reverse stock split will require only a memorandum entry, whereas a disproportionate reverse stock split will require a journal entry to change the stock's legal capital.

Stock Options

Stock options (warrants) may be issued to employees. Such warrants allow employees to purchase company stock at less than the market rate. There are two main reasons that a company may be interested in becoming involved in such activities. First, in an effort to more directly link the interests of employees with the company's performance, the company may wish to encourage increased employee ownership in the company. Second, a company may want to provide additional compensation to employees but without spending any cash, its most liquid asset. In this section we will briefly cover both types of stock option plans.

Noncompensatory Stock Option Plans

A *noncompensatory stock option plan* is used to encourage increased employee ownership in the company. There is no additional compensation included in these types of plans. Additionally, to be labeled *noncompensatory*, the plan must allow most of the employees in the company to participate, and the purchase price of the stock usually must be greater than or equal to 95 percent of the market price of the stock. When the stock options are granted, a memorandum entry is made, and on issuance, a normal stock issuance journal entry is recorded. If any of the stock options expire before being exercised, another memorandum entry is made to note the expiration.

Compensatory Stock Option Plans

A *compensatory stock option plan* is used to provide additional compensation to employees without spending any cash. The GAAP rules for compensatory stock option plans are extremely complex, and for simplicity, we will cover only a very basic example of how these plans work.

Before we begin our discussion, let's introduce you to a few definitions that will help you to better understand compensatory plans and the accounting for the associated options. On the *grant date*, the employee and the company agree on the stock option plan, and the contract is signed. *Vesting* refers to fulfillment of all the requirements for the employee to be eligible to purchase the stock at a reduced rate. Finally, the *exercise price* is simply an alternative name for the option price and is the amount the employee will pay for the stock after vesting occurs.

In regard to the accounting for compensatory stock options, there are three items that must be considered. First, the FMV of the stock options must be determined at the grant date. The models used in determining the FMV of options are quite complex, and we do not intend to present them in this book (such models may be covered in an advanced accounting or finance course). Instead, we will always provide you with the appropriate FMV. The FMV at the grant date represents the total amount that will be recognized as compensation expense. Second, journal entries must be made to recognize the compensation expense that is incurred. The plans usually require an employee to stay with the company for a certain amount of time before being vested in the plan. This length of time is called the *service period*. The compensation expense thus is recognized over the service period in order to properly match expenses to the period incurred. The journal entry includes a debit to compensation expense and a credit to an account called *common stock option warrants* (CSOW). As you observed in Table 9-1, CSOW is a stockholders' equity account presented in the contributed capital section of the balance sheet.

Finally, the actual stock must be issued. The company debits cash for the actual amount of cash received as well as debits CSOW to eliminate the options (warrants) that are exercised. The balancing credits consist of the normal credits for a stock issuance (CS and PIC—CS).

EXAMPLE 9-9

On January 1, 2010, BLP, Inc., adopted a compensatory stock option plan for its key employees. The plan allowed one option to be used to purchase one share of stock for $25 at the time of exercise. The company granted 10,000 options related to 10,000 shares of $10 par common stock.

The market price and exercise price of the stock on the grant date were both $25. On the grant date, the FMV of the options was determined to be $15 each. The options will fully vest at the end of two years, December 31, 2011. Any unexercised options will expire at the end of four years. The key employees exercised all options on December 31, 2011, and none were allowed to expire. Please refer to Table 9-9 for the journal entries associated with these events. Note that the total fair value of the options is multiplied by ½ or divided by 2 because the service period over which the compensation expense must be recognized is two years.

TABLE 9-9 Example 9-9				
1–Jan	Memo entry only to record details of compensatory stock option plan.			
31–Dec–10	Compensation expense	10,000 × $15 × ½	75,000	
	CSOW			75,000
31–Dec–11	Compensation expense	10,000 × $15 × ½	75,000	
	CSOW			75,000
31–Dec–11	Cash	10,000 × $25	250,000	
	CSOW		150,000	
	Common stock	10,000 × $10		100,000
	PIC—CS	Plug to balance		300,000

Preferred Stock

Preferred stock is usually stated as a certain percentage, such as 7 *percent preferred stock*. The 7 percent (or whatever percentage) indicates that 7 percent (that percentage) of the par value of the preferred stock will be paid as a dividend anytime dividends are actually paid.

There are five additional items that we will discuss in relation to preferred stock—preferences, cumulative versus noncumulative, participating versus non-participating, a convertible feature, and the issuance of preferred stock with common stock warrants attached.

Preferences

Preferred stock isn't called preferred stock for nothing! Just as the name of the game Monopoly makes the objective self-explanatory, preferred stock is also defined by its name. Preferred stock takes preference over common stock in many situations, including the payment of dividends. Whereas common stock normally is voting stock by default, preferred stock can be either voting or nonvoting.

Cumulative versus Noncumulative

If preferred stock is issued with a cumulative feature, a dividend not paid in a prior year (a *dividend in arrears*) must be paid in the current year before the current year's preferred dividend and before common stockholders can receive any dividends. We will provide an example of this in Chapter 10. With noncumulative stock, when a year passes without a dividend declaration, no dividends accumulate, and on the next declaration, only the current year's preferred dividend must be paid before common stockholders can be issued any dividends.

Participating versus Nonparticipating

When preferred stock is *participating*, it gets the same percentage of par value as the common stock when dividends are paid. When preferred stock is *nonparticipating*, however, preferred stockholders receive only their respective percentage of par value in dividends, and common stockholders receive all the remaining dividends. An example of this also will be provided in Chapter 10, where dividends are described in greater depth.

Convertible Preferred Stock

Convertible preferred stock is a special type of preferred stock that can be converted into common stock at the discretion of either the stockholder or the company. Companies often issue this type of preferred stock because it is easier to sell with the convertible feature attached. When convertible preferred stock is issued, a traditional journal entry is made. When it is converted into common stock, the book value method must be used. The book value method requires the removal of the preferred stock accounts and the addition of the common stock accounts to the books. A new account likely will be credited; it is PIC from converting PS into CS.

EXAMPLE 9-10

BLP, Inc., issued 1,000 shares of 10 percent, $15 par convertible preferred stock on February 1, 2010, for $50 each. One share of PS is convertible into five shares of CS. On November 30, 2010, 500 of these shares were converted into $5 par common stock. Refer to Table 9-10 for the related journal entries. Note that the PS and the PIC—PS are taken off the books at the same amount for which they were originally put on the books.

TABLE 9-10	Example 9-10			
1–Feb–10	Cash	1,000 × $50	50,000	
	PS	1,000 × $15		15,000
	PIC—PS	1,000 × $35		35,000
30–Nov–10	PS	500 × $15	7,500	
	PIC—PS	500 × $35	17,500	
	CS	500 × 5 × $5		12,500
	PIC conversion of PS into CS	Plug to balance		12,500

Preferred Stock with Common Stock Warrants Attached

Instead of issuing convertible preferred stock, companies may issue preferred stock with warrants (options) attached that allow the stockholders to purchase common stock at a reduced price. As with convertible preferred stock, having this feature makes the preferred stock easier to sell. When this type of preferred stock is sold initially, the proceeds must be allocated to the preferred stock and the common stock warrants based on the FMV of both on the date of sale. A new account is credited for the FMV of the common stock warrants and is appropriately named *common stock warrants*. This account is reported in the contributed capital section of the balance sheet.

EXAMPLE 9-11

On February 1, 2010, BLP, Inc., sold 1,000 shares of 7 percent, $20 par preferred stock with 1,000 common stock warrants (CSW) attached for $45,000. Each warrant allows the holder to purchase one share of $10 par common stock for $30. On the date of sale, the FMV of the PS was $50 per share, and the FMV of the CSW was $5.

On March 1, 2010, 600 of the common stock warrants were exercised. As of March 31, 2010, the remaining 400 common stock warrants expired. Refer to Table 9-11 for the computations and journal entries.

TABLE 9-11 Example 9-11

					FMV		
1-Feb-10	Preferred stock	1,000	×	50	50,000	50,000/55,000 × 45,000	40,909
	Common stock warrants (CSW)	1,000	×	5	5,000	5,000/55,000 × 45,000	4,091
					55,000		45,000
1-Feb-10	Cash	1,000 × $45	45,000				
	PS	1,000 × $20			20,000		
	PIC—PS	40,909 − 20,000			20,909		
	CSW	FMV of CSW			4,091		
1-Mar-10	Cash	600 × $30	18,000				
	CSW	600/1,000 × 4,091	2,455				
	CS	600 × $10			6,000		
	PIC—CS	Plug to balance			14,455		
31-Mar-10	CSW	4,091 − 2,455	1,636				
	PIC expired CSW				1,636		

Treasury Stock

When the corporation purchases either its own CS or PS from a stockholder, that stock becomes *treasury stock* (TS). Treasury stock is considered issued but not outstanding and is reported in the stockholders' equity section of the balance sheet. However, unlike other stockholders' equity accounts, treasury stock has a normal *debit* balance. Therefore, TS is subtracted from the total of the other account balances in that section. Two methods are available for accounting for TS—the cost method and the par value method. TS is presented in a different place under each method, but the total stockholders' equity will be the same, no matter which method is used.

It is important to remember that even though TS has a debit balance, it is *not* an asset. Additionally, a company *cannot* recognize any gains or losses on treasury stock transactions.

One helpful hint to assist you in making the correct treasury stock entries is to write out the journal entry that would have been made when the stock was originally issued. Another thing that we suggest is to keep the journal entries posted to T-accounts so that you can track the balances in the related accounts continuously. You will need these balances to determine accounts to be debited on some of the journal entries.

Cost Method

The cost method assumes that the stockholders are the same individuals both before and after the treasury stock transactions. Remembering this assumption may help you to better visualize the reasoning behind the journal entries.

Treasury stock is presented on the financial statements as a deduction from total stockholders' equity on the balance sheet. A footnote is also required noting that retained earnings are restricted in the amount of the cost of the TS. Now that we have our trusted road map in front of us, let's make the journal entries to get there.

First, journalize the original stock transaction. Then make the journal entry to reacquire the treasury shares. Under the cost method, TS is debited for the *cost* to repurchase the TS.

At some point in time the TS may be reissued. The TS likely will be reissued either above or below the price at which the company repurchased the shares. If TS is reissued at a price *above cost*, then cash is debited for the proceeds, TS is credited for the cost (if it goes in at cost, it comes out at cost), and PIC—TS is credited for the difference.

If TS is reissued at a price *below cost*, then cash is debited for the proceeds, TS is credited for the cost (if it goes in at cost, it comes out at cost), and you will need another debit to balance the journal entry. If there is a balance in PIC—TS, that account is debited. If the balance in PIC—TS is not large enough, then you will debit retained earnings for any additional amount needed.

Par Value Method

The par value method assumes that the corporate relationship with the original stockholder has completely ended. Again, remembering this assumption hopefully will help you to better visualize the reasoning behind the journal entries. Under the par value method, TS is presented as a deduction from the capital stock account in the stockholders' equity section of the balance sheet. A footnote is also required noting that retained earnings is restricted in the amount of the *cost* of the TS. Thus, even though we are using the par value method, we still must keep up with the cost of the TS for disclosure purposes.

First, journalize the original stock transaction. Then make the journal entry to reacquire the treasury shares. Under the par value method, TS is debited for the *par value* of the TS, and PIC—CS (or PIC—PS) is debited for the average price per share in the account.

Under the par value method, it does not matter if the shares are reissued above or below cost. The reissuance journal entry will be the same either way; Cash is debited for the proceeds, TS is credited for the par value (if it goes in at par value, it comes out at par value), and PIC—CS (or PIC—PS) is credited for the difference. Note that we increase the original PIC account and not PIC—TS.

Okay, we have explained the basic differences in each method. Let's do an example that demonstrates the journal entries for each method. The facts in the example will apply to both methods. Table 9-12 will show the journal entries and financial statement presentation for each method. Note that the total stockholders' equity is the same, but the presentation of TS is different.

EXAMPLE 9-12

We will not prepare the T-accounts for you, but you *must* prepare T-accounts so that you can follow the journal entries. Post each entry to the T-accounts before you make the next entry.

1. BLP, Inc., initially issued 1,000 shares of $10 par value common stock for $35 per share.

2. BLP, Inc., reacquired 600 common stock shares at $37 per share.

3. BLP, Inc., reissued 400 common stock shares at $40 per share (above cost).

4. BLP, Inc., reissued 100 common stock shares at $27 per share (below cost).

5. BLP, Inc., reissued 75 common stock shares at $32 per share (below cost).

6. BLP, Inc., still has 25 shares of TS as of the balance sheet date. (*Note:* 25 TS shares × $37 per share = $925 restriction on retained earnings.)

TABLE 9-12 Example 9-12

TS—Cost Method

1 Initial sale

Cash	1,000 × $35	35,000	
CS	1,000 × $10		10,000
PIC—CS	1,000 × $25		25,000

2 Reacquire 600 shares at $37 each

TS	600 × $37	22,200	
Cash	600 × $37		22,200

3 Reissue 400 shares at $40 each (above cost)

Cash	400 × $40	16,000	
TS	400 × $37		14,800
PIC—TS	400 × $3		1,200

4 Reissue 100 shares at $27 each (below cost)

Cash	100 × $27	2,700	
PIC—TS	100 × $10	1,000	
TS	100 × $37		3,700

5 Reissue 75 shares at $32 (below cost)

Cash	75 × $32	2,400	
PIC—TS	Remaining balance	200	
Retained earnings	Plug to balance	175	
TS	75 × $37		2,775

Stockholdes' equity section of the balance sheet

Common stock	10,000
PIC—CS	25,000
PIC—TS	—
Retained earnings	(175)
Subtotal	34,825
Less: Treasury stock	(925)
Total stockholders' equity	33,900

Note: Retained earnings is restricted to the cost of treasury stock—$925.

TABLE 9-12 Example 9-12 (*Continued*)

TS—Par-Value Method

1 Initial sale

Cash	1,000 × $35	35,000	
CS	1,000 × $10		10,000
PIC—CS	1,000 × $25		25,000

2 Reacquire 600 shares at $37 each

TS	600 × $10	6,000	
PIC—CS	600 × $25	15,000	
Retained earnings	Plug to balance	1,200	
Cash	600 × $37		22,200

3 Reissue 400 shares at $40 each (above cost)

Cash	400 × $40	16,000	
TS	400 × $10		4,000
PIC—CS	400 × $30		12,000

4 Reissue 100 shares at $27 each (below cost)

Cash	100 × $27	2,700	
TS	100 × $10		1,000
PIC—CS	100 × $17		1,700

5 Reissue 75 shares at $32 (below cost)

Cash	75 × $32	2,400	
TS	75 × $10		750
PIC—CS	75 × $22		1,650

Stockholders' equity section of the balance sheet

Common stock	10,000
Less: Treasury stock	(250)
Subtotal	9,750
PIC—CS	25,350
Retained earnings	(1,200)
Total stockholders' equity	33,900

Note: Retained earnings is restricted to the cost of treasury stock—$925.

Internal Controls

Establishment of Responsibility and Segregation of Duties

Stock, for the most part, serves the same purpose as bonds. That purpose—financing the company—is especially important. A company does not want to be in a predicament in which the numbers in the books state that a certain amount of money has been provided by stockholders when, in reality, the money is not available or actually has been received from creditors and has a significant amount of interest that must be paid along with principal. Additionally, because the financial structure of an organization affects so many areas, including available future funding, a company needs to have proper authorizations for the issuance of stock, just as it does for debt acquisition. As a result, internal controls are required for the various capital accounts.

The proper procedures for the issuance of shares normally are outlined from the moment of an organization's inception within the articles of incorporation. Usually, the articles of incorporation indicate the initial number of shares that are authorized to be issued. Using the articles as a guideline, the board of directors is responsible for voting on all such issuances, authorizations of additional shares if appropriate, declarations of dividends, and approvals of all purchases of the company's own stock, which, as you recently learned, is known as *treasury stock*. Sometimes a company will choose to employ a third-party stock transfer agent that is responsible for selling shares and recording all stock dealings. Otherwise, an individual within the organization should be given the task of keeping the stock certificate book up to date.

Documentation Procedures and Physical, Mechanical, and Electronic Controls

As you might expect, physical and mechanical controls over stock transactions are virtually nonexistent simply because there is no physical object that requires protection. However, there are some documentation, and potentially electronic, controls that must be addressed. First, the minutes of board meetings should note the authorizations of stock, the declarations of stock dividends, the authorizations of treasury stock purchases, and any other items, including shares issued with special features discussed during such meetings as they pertain to the capital accounts. There are also a number of disclosure requirements that must accompany the financial statements to be in accordance with GAAP. Such disclosures include the number of shares that are authorized, issued, and outstanding. Additionally, any stock options that may be outstanding, convertible features with which shares may be issued, and stock warrants that may be present also must be disclosed along with their dilutive effects, which will all be covered more fully in Chapter 10. If part of retained earnings is appropriated or otherwise restricted, this fact must be noted as well. Finally, any electronic access to such information and the ability to add, edit, or delete data should be restricted through the use of passwords and other controls, as it is with other areas of the business.

Independent Internal Verification

An individual or group of individuals who are not responsible for authorizing or recording transactions and events related to the stockholders' equity accounts should be designated within the organization to perform internal verification. As part of those duties, supporting documentation, including minutes from board meetings, receipts, and entries in the stock certificate book, should be used to verify the existence and magnitude of stock transactions. Ensuring the proper valuation of stock issuances and repurchases of stock is also a task designated for the independent party. Such a check is especially crucial when stock is issued for assets other than cash and choices must be made to determine whether the market value of the stock or the market value of the asset is a better representation of the economic reality of the transaction. Recording the stock at an amount greater than actual market value results in *watered stock*, whereas recording the stock at an amount less than actual market value results in *secret reserves*. Thus auditors particularly remain on the lookout for such over- or undervaluations of assets and equity. Similar checks are required for treasury stock transactions. Additionally, because the proceeds from stock issuances are to be distributed between two accounts—common or preferred stock and a related additional paid-in-capital account—verification that the proper amounts have been recorded in each of those accounts based on par or stated value is essential.

Now you know a lot about stock, including issuances, subscriptions, combined sales, splits, options, preferences, warrants, and values. In Chapter 10 you will get a glimpse of another component of stockholders' equity; it includes everything that is not distributed outside the organization and is known as *retained earnings*.

QUIZ

1. **Which of the following is *not* a true statement?**

   A. Common stock must have a par value.
   B. Common stock can be authorized with or without a par value.
   C. Preferred stock can be authorized with a stated value.
   D. Common stock can be issued in exchange for property.

2. **The journal entry for issuing common stock that was purchased on a subscription basis would include**

   A. a credit to cash.
   B. a debit to common stock subscribed.
   C. a debit to common stock.
   D. a debit to subscriptions receivable.

3. **BLP, Inc., sold 500 shares of $10 par common stock along with 100 shares of $5 par preferred stock for a total of $23,000. At the time of sale, the FMV of the common stock was $40 per share and the FMV of the preferred stock was $50 per share. Which of the following would be included in the journal entry to record this sale?**

   A. A credit to common stock for $18,400
   B. A credit to preferred stock for $4,600
   C. A credit to PIC—CS for $13,400
   D. A credit to cash for $23,000

4. **BLP, Inc., sold 500 shares of 7 percent, $10 par preferred stock with 500 common stock warrants (CSW) attached for $60,000. Each warrant allows the holder to purchase one share of common stock for $30. On the date of sale, the FMV of the PS was $100 per share, and the FMV of the CSW was $40 each. Which of the following would be included in the journal entry to record this sale?**

   A. A debit to preferred stock for $5,000
   B. A credit to cash for $60,000
   C. A debit to PIC—PS for $37,857
   D. A credit to CSW for $17,143

5. **Which of the following is a *true* statement?**

   A. Cumulative preferred stock means that any dividends in arrears must be paid before any current year dividends can be paid.
   B. Cumulative preferred stock means that the common stock and the preferred stock each will be paid the same amount of dividends.
   C. Cumulative preferred stock means that the common stock and the preferred stock each will be paid the same percentage of par value in dividends.
   D. None of the above are true statements.

6. GBW, Inc., acquired a piece of equipment in exchange for 10 shares of $10 par common stock. The stock is currently traded on a public market at $25 per share. The company's executive, believing that the stock was worth more than that, enlisted one of its top financial experts to determine the fair value. The financial expert returned a value of $35 per share. The owner of the equipment, LC Enterprises, believes that the equipment is worth $450. For what amount should the equipment be recorded on the company's books?

   A. $100
   B. $450
   C. $250
   D. $350

7. On January 1, 2012, LC Enterprises adopted a compensatory stock option plan for its key employees. The plan enabled eligible employees to purchase 10 shares of $5 par common stock for each option granted to them. The exercise price would be $10. The number of eligible employees totaled 20, and each of those employees was granted 20 options. On the grant date, the FMV of the options was determined to be $15. The options will fully vest at the end of four years, December 31, 2015. What amount should be recorded as compensation expense on December 31, 2012?

   A. $15,000
   B. $60,000
   C. $750
   D. $10,000

8. Which of the following is true of treasury stock recorded under the par value method but not under the cost method?

   A. The initial journal entry consists of a debit to cash for the total proceeds amount and a credit to common stock, with any additional amount of proceeds over par being credited to PIC—CS.
   B. The reacquisition of shares is recorded at cost with a debit to treasury stock and a credit to cash for the repurchase price.
   C. A reissuance above cost is recorded as a debit to cash for the reissuance price along with a credit to treasury stock for the reacquisition cost and a credit to PIC—TS for the portion of the reissuance price that exceeds the reacquisition cost.
   D. A reissuance above cost is recorded as a debit to cash for the reissuance price along with a credit to treasury stock for the par value of the common stock and a credit to PIC—CS for the portion of the reissuance price that exceeds the par value.

9. Amethyst, Inc., originally issued 2,000 shares of $15 par value common stock for $30 each on February 25, 2010. On August 31, 2010, the company reacquired 500 of these shares at a cost of $20 per share. On October 19, 2010, the company reissued 300 of these shares at a price of $22 per share. Two days later, on October 21, 2010, the company reissued 100 of the shares at a price of

$18 per share. As a result of all these events, and assuming that these are the only events that affect PIC—TS, what should be the balance of PIC—TS on December 31, 2010, using the cost treasury stock method?

A. $0

B. $400

C. $29,900

D. $30,400

10. **GAAP disclosures for stock transactions include all the following *except***

A. the number of shares authorized, issued, and outstanding.

B. any stock options, warrants, and convertible features that may be outstanding and/or available along with their dilution effects.

C. the additional number of shares that the company intends to authorize within the next 10 years.

D. the amount of retained earnings that is appropriated or restricted.

chapter 10

Retained Earnings

CHAPTER OBJECTIVES

After completing this chapter, the student should

- Understand the financial statement presentation for retained earnings
- Account for cash dividends
- Account for property dividends
- Understand the accounting for script dividends
- Account for both small and large stock dividends
- Understand liquidating dividends

Overview

Why would you offer your money to a company if you expected to receive nothing in return? Well, you wouldn't! If you had no chance of receiving dividends or an increase in stock price, you would have absolutely no reason to purchase stock. Instead, you would simply place those funds in a bank account or purchase some asset that you expected to be able to provide a stream of benefits in the future. Lucky for you, though, a good number of companies declare dividends on a quarterly, annual, or at least a somewhat frequent basis.

Of course, not all classes of stock are the same, and sometimes one class receives greater benefits than another. As a freshman in high school, you might remember being looked down on by the upperclassmen. Maybe you had to wait until last to eat lunch, had to lug the equipment bags around during sporting trips, and even had to accept using the lockers farthest from the classrooms. All that changed when you became a senior, though. You ruled the school, or so you thought, right? Let's expand this to an even more relevant example. Many restaurants offer senior citizens a discount. Those who qualify may have a small selection of menu items from which to choose. By reaching a certain age, individuals receive a benefit—a reduced price—but they may have to settle for a certain entrée. They, like the high school seniors, would be the preferred stock. They receive extra benefits but may lack voting rights.

Financial Statement Presentation

The account retained earnings is reported in the stockholders' equity section of the balance sheet. Often it is also presented as a separate financial statement. Please refer to Table 10-1 for the proper format for a statement of retained earnings.

TABLE 10-1 BLP, Inc., Statement of Retained Earnings, FYE December 31, 2010
Retained earnings, beginning balance
Plus/minus: Prior–period adjustments
Plus: Net income
Less: Dividends
Retained earnings, ending balance

Prior-period adjustments will be covered in Chapter 17. Throughout this chapter we will restrict our discussion to the various types of dividends—cash, property, scrip, and stock.

Cash Dividends

Cash dividends usually are paid on both common and preferred stock. When cash dividends are paid on common stock, they are usually stated as a certain dollar amount per share. When dividends are paid on both common and preferred stock, the computations become a bit more complex. Don't worry, though, after a little bit of help from us, you will be able to handle them easily! Each computation is different depending on the particular characteristics the preferred stock possesses. In the following sections we have prepared detailed instructions for each type of scenario.

Important Dates

When dealing with dividends, there are four important dates that you must be able to recognize. First, the *date of declaration* is the date the board of directors actually declares that a dividend will be paid in the future. The dividend becomes a legal liability on the date of declaration. On that date, a journal entry should be made with a debit to retained earnings and a credit to dividends payable.

 EXAMPLE 10-1

The board of directors of BLP, Inc., declared a 1 cent dividend on December 1, 2010. There were 10,000 shares of common stock issued and outstanding on the date of declaration. The journal entry would be

December 1, 2010:

Retained earnings	100	
Dividends payable		100

Second, the *ex-dividend date* is the date that the stock stops selling with the dividend attached. No journal entry is required. Note, however, that the ex-dividend date is before the date of record.

Third, the *date of record* represents the date that determines which stockholders will receive the dividend. Only the investors listed in the stockholders' ledger on the date of record will receive the dividends. Remember, the stock would have stopped selling with the dividend attached by this date. Any stock sales after this date will be sold without the dividend attached. Only a memorandum entry is required for the date of record.

Finally, the *date of payment* is the date that the dividend is actually paid and is distributed to the eligible stockholders. The journal entry to record the payment is a debit to dividends payable and a credit to cash for the amount of the dividend.

 EXAMPLE 10-2

Continuing Example 10-1, BLP, Inc., paid the dividend on December 31, 2010. The following journal entry is required on the date of payment:

December 31, 2010:

Dividends payable	100	
Cash		100

Cumulative Preferred Stock

Remember that we discussed in Chapter 9 that there are reasons why preferred stock has been dubbed with its name: It gets certain preferences over common stock, especially when it comes to dividends. To refresh your memory, recall that preferred stock is usually stated as a certain percentage, such as 7 percent preferred stock. The 7 percent means that 7 percent of the par value of the preferred stock will be distributed as a dividend anytime dividends are actually paid.

When preferred stock is cumulative, if a dividend is not paid in a prior year, that prior-year dividend, along with the current-year dividend, must be paid in the current year before common stock can receive any dividends.

There is a particular order in which dividends are to be paid. That order is as follows:

1. Dividends in arrears
2. Current-year preferred stock dividends
3. Current-year common stock dividends
4. Common and preferred stock participating dividends

EXAMPLE 10-3

BLP, Inc., has been retaining cash for the past couple of years. The last year that the company paid a dividend was 2007. BLP has decided that this year it will pay a dividend. The total amount declared for 2010 is $100,000. The company has issued and outstanding 10,000 shares of $10 par common stock for a total par value of $100,000. BLP also has issued and outstanding 15,000 shares of 5 percent, $20 par cumulative preferred stock for a total par value of $300,000. The computation to determine the amount of dividends received by the common and preferred shareholders is presented in Table 10-2.

TABLE 10-2 Example 10-3

		Par Value		
Common stock	10,000 × $10	100,000		
5% Preferred stock	15,000 × $20	300,000		
		400,000		
		Preferred Stock	**Common Stock**	**Total**
1. Dividend for 2008	300,000 × 5%	15,000		
1. Dividend for 2009	300,000 × 5%	15,000		
2. Dividend for 2010	300,000 × 5%	15,000		
3. Remaining amount goes to common			55,000	
Total		**45,000**	**55,000**	**100,000**

Participating Preferred Stock

If preferred stock is *fully participating*, the preferred stock receives the same percentage of par value as the common stock when dividends are paid. If preferred stock is only *partially participating*, the preferred stock will participate fully with common stock up to a certain percentage of par value, and any remaining dividend will be paid to common shareholders. If preferred stock is *nonparticipating*, the preferred stock will receive only its respective percentage of par value in dividends, and common stock will receive all the remaining dividends.

 **EXAMPLE 10-4**

NONPARTICIPATING PS

BLP, Inc., has been retaining cash for the past couple of years. The last year that the company paid a dividend was 2007. BLP has decided that this year it will pay a dividend. The total amount declared for 2010 is $100,000. The company has issued and outstanding 10,000 shares of $10 par common stock for a total par value of $100,000. BLP also has issued and outstanding 15,000 shares of 5 percent, $20 par cumulative preferred stock for a total par value of $300,000. The computation to determine the amount of dividends received by the common and preferred shareholders is identical to that presented in Table 10-2, so it will not be presented again.

 **EXAMPLE 10-5**

PARTIALLY PARTICIPATING PS

BLP, Inc., has been retaining cash for the past couple of years. The last year that the company paid a dividend was 2007. BLP has decided that this year it will pay a dividend. The total amount declared for 2010 is $100,000. The company has issued and outstanding 10,000 shares of $10 par common stock for a total par value of $100,000. BLP also has issued and outstanding 15,000 shares of 5 percent, $20 par cumulative preferred stock for a total par value of $300,000. The preferred stock is partially participating up to 10 percent of the par value. The computation to determine the amount of dividends received by the common and preferred shareholders is presented in Table 10-3. Two different computational methods are presented. Please note that the same answer is obtained regardless of the method used.

TABLE 10-3 Example 10-5

	Par Value
Common stock	10,000 × $10	100,000
5% Preferred stock	15,000 × $20	300,000
		400,000

		Preferred Stock	Common Stock	Total
1. Dividend for 2008	300,000 × 5%	15,000		
1. Dividend for 2009	300,000 × 5%	15,000		
2. Dividend for 2010	300,000 × 5%	15,000		
3. Equal participation for CS	100,000 × 5%		5,000	
4. 5% participation for PS	300,000 × 5%	15,000		
4. 5% participation for CS	100,000 × 5%		5,000	
Remaining dividend to CS			30,000	
Total		60,000	40,000	100,000

Alternative Computation:

		Preferred Stock	Common Stock	Total
1. Dividend for 2008	300,000 × 5%	15,000		
1. Dividend for 2009	300,000 × 5%	15,000		
2. 10% to PS for 2010	300,000 × 10%	30,000		
3. 10% to CS for 2010	100,000 × 10%		10,000	
Remaining dividend to CS			30,000	
Total		60,000	40,000	100,000

EXAMPLE 10-6

FULLY PARTICIPATING PS

BLP, Inc., has been retaining cash for the past couple of years. The last year that the company paid a dividend was 2007. BLP has decided that this year it will pay a dividend. The total amount declared for 2010 is $100,000. The company has issued and outstanding 10,000 shares of $10 par common stock for a total par value of $100,000. BLP also has issued and outstanding 15,000 shares of 5 percent, $20 par cumulative preferred stock for a total par value of $300,000. The preferred stock fully participates with the common stock.

Notice that in this example the par values of the common stock and preferred stock are 25 and 75 percent, respectively, of the total par values for both classes of stock. The computation to determine the amount of dividends received by the common and preferred shareholders is presented in Table 10-4. Two different computational methods are presented. Please note that the same answer is obtained regardless of the method used.

Property Dividends

When a corporation declares a property dividend, some of its assets other than cash will be distributed to stockholders. This situation is much more common among closely held corporations than publicly held ones. The property dividend is recorded at fair market value (FMV) on the date of declaration. There are two journal entries made on the date of declaration. The first journal entry is to write the asset up or down to FMV and record the corresponding gain or loss. The second journal entry's purpose is to actually record the dividend on the books with a debit to retained earnings for the FMV of the property and a credit to property dividends payable for the same amount. On the payment date, the journal entry made is a debit to property dividends payable and a credit to the asset account.

EXAMPLE 10-7

BLP, Inc., has decided to issue a parcel of land to one of its shareholders as a property dividend. The board of directors declared the dividend on December 1 when the land was recorded on the books at $10,000 and the FMV was $15,000. The dividend is payable on December 31. The following journal entries would be recorded for this transaction:

December 1:

Land	5,000	
Gain on disposal of land		5,000

TABLE 10-4 Example 10-6

	Par Value	
Common stock	10,000 × $10	100,000	25%
5% Preferred stock	15,000 × $20	300,000	75%
		400,000	100%

		Preferred Stock	Common Stock	Total
1. Dividend for 2008	300,000 × 5%	15,000		
1. Dividend for 2009	300,000 × 5%	15,000		
2. Dividend for 2010	300,000 × 5%	15,000		
3. Equal participation for CS	100,000 × 5%		5,000	
25% of remaining dividend to CS	50,000 × 25%		12,500	
75% of remaining dividend to PS	50,000 × 75%	37,500		
Total		82,500	17,500	100,000

Alternative Computation:

		Preferred Stock	Common Stock	Total
1. Dividend for 2008	300,000 × 5%	15,000		
1. Dividend for 2009	300,000 × 5%	15,000		
25% of remaining dividend to CS	70,000 × 25%		17,500	
75% of remaining dividend to PS	70,000 × 75%	52,500		
Total		82,500	17,500	100,000

December 1:

Retained earnings	15,000	
Property dividend payable		15,000

December 31:

Property dividend payable	15,000	
Land		15,000

Scrip Dividends

Scrip dividends are used when a corporation has ample retained earnings but lacks cash. The simplest way to describe a scrip dividend is by comparing it to an IOU. The IOU is accounted for as a note that carries with it interest expense. The interest will be accrued at each balance sheet date until the dividend is paid. Because we covered notes and interest in a previous chapter, we will not provide an example here.

Stock Dividends

Stock dividends will decrease retained earnings and increase contributed capital but will not change total stockholders' equity. There are two types of stock dividends—small and large. The accounting for each is different.

Small Stock Dividends

A *small stock dividend* is defined as a dividend disbursement of less than 20 to 25 percent of the previously outstanding shares of stock. Such a dividend is recorded at FMV. The journal entry to record a small stock dividend includes a debit to retained earnings for the FMV of the dividend, a credit to CS (or PS) for the par value, and a credit to PIC—CS (or PS) for the difference.

EXAMPLE 10-8

BLP, Inc., has 10,000 shares of $10 par common stock issued and outstanding when the board of directors declares a 10 percent stock dividend. The FMV of the common stock on the declaration date is $15 per share. Because a 10 percent stock dividend is below the 20 to 25 percent threshold, the stock dividend is considered small and will be recorded at FMV. The following journal entry will be used to record this dividend:

Retained earnings (10,000 × 10% × $15)	15,000	
CS (10,000 × 10% × $10)		10,000
PIC—CS (10,000 × 10% × $5)		5,000

Large Stock Dividends

A *large stock dividend* is defined as a dividend disbursement of more than 25 percent of the previously outstanding shares of stock. A large stock dividend more closely resembles a stock split and therefore is recorded at par value. The journal entry to record a large stock dividend includes a debit to retained earnings for the par value and a credit to common stock (or preferred stock) for the same amount.

EXAMPLE 10-9

BLP, Inc., has 10,000 shares of $10 par common stock issued and outstanding when the board of directors declares a 30 percent stock dividend. The FMV of the common stock on the declaration date is $15 per share. Because a 30 percent stock dividend is above the 25 percent threshold, the stock dividend is considered large and will be recorded at par value. The following journal entry will be used to record this dividend:

Retained earnings (10,000 × 30% × $10)	30,000	
CS (10,000 × 30% × $10)		30,000

Liquidating Dividends

When a company is nearing the end of its operations, it still may want to appear to be paying dividends. At that time, a *liquidating dividend* often arises. Treatment of such dividends is governed by state law. Normally, any regular portion of the dividend is recorded in the usual manner with a debit to retained earnings. The liquidating portion, however, is essentially a return of capital and thus is recorded as such. A debit entry is made either to PIC—CS, PIC—PS, or a new account that may have various names including *liquidating dividend*. The amount of any liquidating dividend is required by GAAP to be disclosed.

Did you ever think there were as many types of dividends as we introduced in this chapter—cash, property stock, script, and liquidating? No, we didn't think so! In Chapter 11 we will combine some of the knowledge that we have presented in the previous chapters regarding currently outstanding and potentially new outstanding shares of stock with information from the income statement to obtain a measure of profitability that is useful to both creditors and investors.

QUIZ

1. The date of declaration is
   A. the date the board of directors determines that a dividend will be paid.
   B. the date the stock stops selling with the dividend attached.
   C. the same as the date of record.
   D. the date the dividend is paid.

2. Which of the following is a *true* statement?
   A. Prior-year dividends must be paid prior to paying any dividends in arrears.
   B. Dividends in arrears on cumulative preferred stock must be paid prior to paying any current-year dividends.
   C. Cumulative preferred stock is not eligible to receive any dividends in arrears.
   D. Fully participating preferred stock is eligible to receive dividends in arrears.

3. Which of the following is a *false* statement?
   A. Cumulative preferred stock does not share an equal percentage of par value with common stock when dividends are paid.
   B. Fully participating preferred stock shares an equal percentage of par value with common stock when dividends are paid.
   C. Partially participating preferred stock shares an equal percentage of par value with common stock when dividends are paid.
   D. Cumulative preferred stock is entitled to dividends in arrears.

4. BLP, Inc., has been retaining cash for the past couple of years. The last year that the company paid a dividend was 2007. BLP has decided that this year it will pay a dividend. The total amount declared for 2010 is $150,000. The company has issued and has outstanding 30,000 shares of $10 par common stock. BLP also has issued and outstanding 10,000 shares of 5 percent, $20 par cumulative preferred stock. The preferred stock fully participates with the common stock. What amount of dividends will the preferred stock receive in 2010?
   A. $30,000
   B. $90,000
   C. $60,000
   D. $72,000

5. BLP, Inc., has 20,000 shares of $10 par common stock issued and outstanding when the board of directors declares a 30 percent stock dividend. The FMV of the common stock on the declaration date is $15 per share. The journal entry to record this dividend will include
   A. a credit to PIC—CS of $30,000.
   B. a credit to common stock of $90,000.
   C. a debit to retained earnings of $90,000.
   D. a debit to retained earnings of $60,000.

6. GBW, Inc., has decided to issue a garage to a shareholder as a property dividend. When the board of directors declared the dividend, the garage was listed on the books at $30,000, and the fair market value was $50,000. The dividend will be paid before the end of the year. Based on this information, which of the following entries will be made to record the declaration?

A. A credit to garage for $20,000
B. A debit to property dividend payable for $50,000
C. A credit to gain on disposal of garage of $20,000
D. A debit to loss on disposal of garage of $20,000

7. Which of the following is *not* a characteristic of a small stock dividend?

A. The percentage of the dividend distribution is 20 to 25 percent of the currently outstanding shares of stock.
B. The dividend distribution is recorded at the FMV of the stock on the date of the dividend declaration.
C. The entry to record the dividend declaration may include a credit to PIC—CS or PIC—PS.
D. The dividend distribution is recorded at the FMV of the stock on the date of the dividend payment.

8. BLP, Inc., has been retaining cash for the past couple of years. The last year that the company paid a dividend was 2006. BLP has decided that this year it will pay a dividend. The total amount declared for 2010 is $150,000. The company has issued and outstanding 30,000 shares of $10 par common stock. BLP also has issued and outstanding 10,000 shares of 5 percent, $20 par cumulative preferred stock. The preferred stock is partially participating up to 15 percent of the par value. What amount of dividends will the preferred stock receive in 2010?

A. $30,000
B. $90,000
C. $60,000
D. $72,000

9. BLP, Inc., has 20,000 shares of $10 par common stock issued and outstanding when the board of directors declares a 10 percent stock dividend. The FMV of the common stock on the declaration date is $15 per share. The journal entry to record this dividend will include

A. a debit to retained earnings of $30,000.
B. a credit to common stock of $60,000.
C. a credit to common stock of $30,000.
D. a debit to retained earnings of $60,000.

10. All the following types of dividends include a debit to retained earnings at the date of declaration *except*

A. a cash dividend.
B. a liquidating dividend.
C. a property dividend.
D. stock dividend.

chapter 11

Earnings per Share

CHAPTER OBJECTIVES

After completing this chapter, the student should

- Understand the financial statement presentation for earnings per share
- Understand the difference between a basic and a complex capital structure
- Compute basic earnings per share
- Compute diluted earnings per share
- Determine if securities are dilutive or antidilutive

Overview

Earnings per share (EPS) is an important measure of profitability for users of the financial statements, especially stockholders. However, as with everything else, there is more than one way to look at EPS. One of the key items that must be known to calculate EPS properly is the number of shares outstanding. In fact, diluted EPS, which we will discuss in this chapter, is affected directly by the number of shares.

Let's forget about numbers for a moment. We think that it is safe to assume that everyone reading this book has purchased a soda from a fast-food restaurant. Sometimes the restaurant gives the customer a cup, and the customer is directed to the soda fountain. The soda is dispensed from the fountain, where a limited amount of the product is being stored. Regardless of how many customers there are, no more product than is currently being stored in the fountain can be dispensed. The customer is the stockholder and thus receives a portion of the total product. While at the fountain and before placing the product in his or her cup, the customer must make the decision of how much ice, if any, to add. The customer might decide on a drink without ice, one with half a cup of ice, or even one with a full cup of ice. The ice represents the number of possible shares outstanding. Now everybody knows that a drink with more ice will taste more watered down or what is more properly defined as *diluted*. By choosing to add ice to the cup, the customer is allowing the total soda product to be spread out for more customers to enjoy but is making his or her share more diluted. A similar phenomenon occurs with stock, and we will highlight such effects in this chapter.

Financial Statement Presentation

EPS must be shown on the face of the income statement for four items—income from continuing operations, discontinued operations, extraordinary items, and net income. In addition to disclosure on the face of the income statement, a footnote disclosure is also required. The footnote needs to have enough information in it so that an intelligent reader of the financial statements can reconstruct the computations for both basic and diluted EPS.

Capital Structures

There are two types of capital structures. A *basic* capital structure consists of only common stock. A *complex* capital structure, however, consists of common stock as well as other types of stock. Such other types may include preferred stock, convertible preferred stock, or even stock options.

In addition to two capital structures, there are also two types of computations for EPS—basic and diluted.

Basic EPS

Let's start with the formula for basic EPS. As its name suggests, basic EPS is very basic and is also where we want to begin our computations. Therefore, it is the perfect place to start this discussion. The EPS formula is net income less preferred dividends divided by the weighted-average number of common shares outstanding (WACSO). From experience, we have determined that it is easier to deal with the numerator and denominator separately, and thus we will provide the information that you will need to work these problems in that manner.

First, we will tackle the numerator. Net income is the net income shown on the income statement. Since we want to compute the earnings available to common stockholders only, we must subtract the dividends that will be paid to the preferred stockholders. Remember that preferred stock can be cumulative or noncumulative. Those characteristics thus have a bearing on the monetary amount that must be deducted for preferred dividends. If the preferred stock is noncumulative, then you will deduct only dividends declared for the current year. If the preferred stock is cumulative, you will deduct the dividends for the current year whether they have been declared or not.

Now that we have a handle on the numerator, let's move on to the denominator. We want to use the weighted-average number of common shares outstanding. Make sure that your reading and comprehension skills are operating at 100 percent accuracy for this one! We like to think in terms of *layers* of shares or in *equivalent whole* shares. You will see what we mean when we go through an example. There is one important point you need to remember: If there has been a stock dividend or a stock split, you *must* assume that they occurred at the beginning of the earliest period presented on the financial statements. Additionally, if a company has a contingent issue in which it may be obligated to issue shares in the future and all the conditions for that issuance have been met, the contingent shares are considered to be outstanding for basic EPS computations.

In all EPS computations, you should concentrate on calculating one item at a time. First, calculate the numerator, and then calculate the denominator. Let's try an example for basic EPS. Please follow this example carefully. We suggest that you use the format shown in Table 11-1 for all EPS problems.

EXAMPLE 11-1

BLP, Inc., wants to compute basic EPS for 2010. It has provided the following information relevant to this computation:

1. Net income for 2010 is $200,000.

2. $100,000 of noncumulative 5 percent preferred stock is issued and outstanding. No dividends have been declared for 2010.

3. $120,000 of cumulative 8 percent preferred stock is issued and outstanding. No dividends have been declared for 2010.

4. As of January 1, 2009, 10,000 shares of common stock were issued and outstanding.

5. On December 31, 2009, a two-for-one stock split occurred on the common stock.

6. On March 1, 2010, another 2,000 shares of common stock were issued.

7. On September 1, 2010, a 10 percent stock dividend was issued.

Refer to Table 11-1 for the calculations. Remember to calculate the numerator first and then perform the calculations for the denominator.

TABLE 11-1 Basic EPS

Numerator:

Net income		200,000
Noncumulative 5% PS, no dividend declared		—
Cumulative 8% PS, no dividend declared	120,000 × 8%	(9,600)
		190,400

Denominator:

Date	No. of Shares before Stock Split before Stock Dividend		No. of Shares after Stock Split before Stock Dividend		No. of Shares after Stock Split after Stock Dividend	No. of Months Outstanding	No. of Shares for EPS
January–December 2009	10,000	2	20,000	1.1	22,000	12/12	22,000
January–February 2010	20,000		20,000	1.1	22,000	2/12	3,667
March–August 2010	22,000		22,000	1.1	24,200	6/12	12,100
September–December 2010	22,000		22,000	1.1	24,200	4/12	8,067
							23,833

	Numerator	Denominator	EPS
Basic	190,400	23,833	7.99

Diluted EPS

Do you remember when you were young and you played "pretend"? We bet you never thought you would do that again. Life is life, no pretending about it, right? Well, not exactly! In fact, we will do a lot of "pretending" when calculating diluted EPS. The premise behind diluted EPS is that every single financial instrument that can be converted into common shares is assumed to be converted whether or not it is actually converted. As for the conversion date, it is either the first day of the earliest period presented in the financial statements or the date the financial instrument actually was issued, whichever is earlier.

Now, let's talk about what kind of instruments can be converted into common stock. We will discuss convertible preferred stock, convertible bonds issued at a discount, convertible bonds issued at a premium, and stock options and warrants. We will present each one separately and will work an example for each to determine the changes in the numerator and the denominator. We then will put it all together in one big computation for EPS. In order to make things a bit easier, we will continue with Example 11-1.

Convertible Preferred Stock

When dealing with convertible preferred stock, the change in the numerator represents the dividend that would not be paid *if* the PS were converted into common stock at the beginning of the period. The change in the denominator represents the additional shares of common stock that would have been outstanding *if* the PS had been converted into common stock at the beginning of the period. You likely have noticed that we have highlighted the word *if*. Convertible preferred stock as well as convertible bonds, which will be presented in the next section, follow the "if-converted" method. Now that we have the rules, let's continue with another example that builds on the preceding one.

EXAMPLE 11-2

The 8 percent cumulative preferred stock introduced in Example 11-1 also has a convertible feature in which one share of preferred stock may be converted into five shares of common stock. Remember that the total par value was $120,000. Let's assume that the par value per share is $10, resulting in there being 12,000 shares of preferred stock issued and outstanding. Let's also assume that the issuance occurred in 2007. Therefore, the converted common stock thus would be issued and outstanding for all of 2010. Refer to Table 11-2 for the computations related to the changes in the numerator and denominator.

TABLE 11-2 Convertible Preferred Stock		
Numerator: Dividend not paid	120,000 × 8%	9,600
Denominator: Additional common shares assumed issued	12,000 × 5	60,000

Convertible Bonds Issued at a Discount

When dealing with convertible bonds, the change in the numerator represents the interest that would not have been paid *if* the bonds had been converted into common stock at the beginning of the earliest period presented. Not only do we have a change in the numerator for interest that we assume is not paid, but we also have to take into account any discount amortization and related tax effects.

Let's discuss the discount amortization first. We believe that it is beneficial to always recreate the journal entries that gave rise to the discount. Remember, when a bond is issued at a discount, the journal entry would be

Cash

Discount on bonds payable

Bonds payable

Then, when the discount is amortized, the journal entry would be

Interest expense

Discount on bonds payable

When a period ends with interest being accrued but not paid, the journal entry would be

Interest expense

Interest payable

From studying these journal entries, we can see that when the bond discount is amortized, interest expense is increased. Therefore, when we compute the interest that we assumed we did not pay as a result of the bonds' conversion to shares of stock, an expense that would have been incurred is no longer present (the bond discount amortization) and is thus added back to the interest that was not paid.

Now let's talk about the tax effects. Recall that dividends are not tax deductible and that interest expense is tax deductible. Because the dividends are not tax deductible, we did not have to consider the tax effects in Example 11-2.

However, because interest is tax deductible, we have to consider its effects here. The easiest way to do this is to take the amount of interest expense plus any discount amortization and multiply that total by 1 minus the tax rate. The result will be the change in the numerator. (An alternative method is to take the interest expense plus any discount amortization and multiply that total by the tax rate and subtract the result from the previous total.) When interest expense was paid out, a tax benefit was obtained. Without the payment of interest, that tax benefit is lost, resulting in the increase in the numerator being less than what one would hypothesize originally.

The change in the denominator represents the additional shares of common stock that would have been outstanding *if* the bonds had been converted into common stock at the beginning of the period. Now that we have the rules, let's continue with another example that builds on the first two.

EXAMPLE 11-3

BLP, Inc., has $100,000 of 9 percent convertible bonds payable that were issued in 2008 and mature in 2013. Each bond has a face value of $1,000. The appropriate tax rate is 30 percent. The discount amortization is $450 per year. Each bond is convertible into 50 shares of common stock. Refer to Table 11-3 for the computations for the changes in the numerator and denominator.

TABLE 11-3 Convertible Bonds Payable Issued at a Discount

Numerator:	Interest not paid	100,000 × 9%	9,000
	Add: Discount amortization		450
	Total		9,450
	Times 1 minus the tax rate		70%
	Change in numerator		6,615
Denominator:	Additional common shares assumed issued	100 × 50	5,000

Convertible Bonds Issued at a Premium

When dealing with convertible bonds, the change in the numerator represents the interest that would not have been paid *if* the bonds had been converted into common stock at the beginning of the earliest period presented. Not only do we have a change in the numerator for interest that we assume is not paid, but we also have to take into account any premium amortization and related tax effects.

Let's discuss the premium amortization first. We believe that it is beneficial to always recreate the journal entries that gave rise to the premium. Remember, when a bond is issued at a premium, the journal entry would be

Cash

    Premium on bonds payable

    Bonds payable

Then, when the premium is amortized, the journal entry would be

Premium on bonds payable

    Interest expense

When a period ends with interest being accrued but not paid, the journal entry would be

Interest expense

    Interest payable

From these journal entries, we can see that when the bond premium is amortized, interest expense is decreased. Therefore, when we compute the interest that we assumed we did not pay, we will subtract the bond premium amortization from it.

Remember to calculate the tax effect because interest is a tax-deductible item. It works the same as it did for bond discounts.

Now let's add another complicating factor that must be examined when working with any convertible security. It is imperative to look at the date that the convertible security was issued to determine how long it actually has been outstanding and thus the appropriate amount of interest for the year. Recall that we want to assume that all securities are converted at the beginning of the first period presented. However, if the securities had not even been issued as of that date, it must be assumed that conversion occurs as of the date of actual issuance.

Therefore, if a convertible bond is not issued until October 1, you would consider the interest for only 3 of the 12 months. The same rules apply for any bond discount or premium amortization. In regard to dividends, the rules are the same if the security is convertible preferred stock.

Let's now return to our premium amortization problem. We have completed our discussion regarding the numerator, so let's move on to the denominator.

The change in the denominator represents the additional shares of common stock that would have been outstanding *if* the bonds had been converted into common stock at the beginning of the period. Now that we have the rules, let's continue with another example that builds on the first three.

 **EXAMPLE 11-4**

BLP, Inc., has $200,000 of 10 percent convertible bonds payable that were issued on June 30, 2010. These bonds mature in 2018. Each bond has a face value of $1,000. The appropriate tax rate is 30 percent. The premium amortization is $500 per year. Each bond is convertible into 20 shares of common stock. Refer to Table 11-4 for the computations for the changes in the numerator and denominator.

TABLE 11-4	Convertible Bonds Payable Issued at a Premium		
Numerator:	Interest not paid	200,000 × 10% × ½ year	10,000
	Less: Premium amortization	500 × ½ year	(250)
	Total		9,750
	Times 1 minus the tax rate		70%
	Change in numerator		6,825
Denominator:	Additional common shares assumed issued	200 × 20 × ½ year	2,000

Stock Options and Warrants

Do you recall the concept of and calculations for compensatory stock options that we presented in Chapter 9? We know that this is going to excite all of you. You get to work with them again in this chapter! Because we are "pretending" to convert every financial security possible to common stock, we must assume that these stock options (and warrants) are converted as well.

A unique feature of stock options is that there is *never* a numerator change. Therefore, we will always use –0– as the change in the numerator. This fact will be very important in the next section on ranking—remember it for later!

To compute the change in the denominator, we must make additional assumptions that are unique to stock options and warrants. We will be using the *treasury stock method*. First, we must assume that all the options are exercised and that we receive the appropriate amount of proceeds from the exercise of the options. Then we must pretend to go out into the market and repurchase as many shares as we can at the average market price. We then divide the proceeds by the average market price. Next, we must compare the number of shares issued (with the exercise of the stock options) with the number of shares that can be repurchased in the market.

We need to take a break here and talk about dilutive versus antidilutive securities. Let's back up to the very beginning of our EPS discussion. The idea of pretending to convert all these securities into common stock is to increase the denominator as much as possible. The higher the denominator, the lower the EPS number will be. The lower the EPS number, the more conservatively it is presented on the financial statements. And, of course, being conservative is one of those guiding principles (one of those financial commandments, if you will) of accountants!

Back to dilutive versus antidilutive securities. *If* a security is dilutive, it is adding to the number of shares in the denominator and thus is attaining a more conservative EPS number. On the other hand, *if* a security is antidilutive, it is decreasing the number of shares in the denominator and thus is attaining a less conservative EPS number. We *never* want to include any security that is antidilutive in a diluted EPS calculation. We will discuss this topic again in the section on ranking. Again, remember it for later!

Now let's go back to our treasury stock method. *If* the number of shares assumed to be issued is greater than the number of shares assumed to be repurchased, the options are dilutive and will be included in the EPS computations. This always occurs when the average market price is greater than the option price. However, *if* the number of shares assumed to be issued is less than the number of shares assumed to be repurchased, the options are antidilutive and will *not* be included in the EPS computations. This always occurs when the average market price is less than the option price. Now that we have the rules, let's continue with another example that builds on the others.

EXAMPLE 11-5

BLP, Inc., had stock options A outstanding for all of 2010 that allow for the purchase of 2,000 shares at $30 per share. The average market price for 2010 was $35. The company also had stock options B outstanding for all of 2010 that allow for the purchase of 2,000 shares at $40 per share. Refer to Table 11-5 for the computations of the denominator change related to these stock options.

TABLE 11-5 Stock Options

Stock Options A

Numerator:	There is never a change in the numerator.		0.00	
			$	**Shares**
Denominator:	Compute proceeds received	2,000 × $30	60,000	2,000
	Divide by average market price		35	
	Equals: Assumed shares reacquired		1,714	(1,714)
	Additional shares in marketplace: Dilutive			286

Stock Options B

Numerator:	There is never a change in the numerator		0.00	
			$	**Shares**
Denominator:	Compute proceeds received	2,000 × $40	80,000	2,000
	Divide by average market price		35	
	Equals: Assumed shares reacquired		2,286	(2,286)
	Less shares in marketplace: Antidilutive			(286)

Ranking

Before we can perform the EPS computations, we must rank all the convertible securities. To understand the ranking, think back to our discussion on dilutive versus antidilutive securities. We only want to include in the EPS computations the dilutive securities. Therefore, there is a specific order in which we must include the securities in the EPS computations. We will determine the impact on the EPS by taking, for each security, the change in the numerator divided by the change in the denominator. Then we will rank the results from lowest to highest. Because stock options and warrants have no effect on the numerator, the impact always will be zero, thus making them the first securities to be included in the EPS computation. Now that we have the rules, let's continue with another example building on the preceding ones.

**EXAMPLE 11-6**

There is really no new information to introduce for this example. You will, however, need to pull the numbers from the preceding examples for the changes in the numerators and denominators for each convertible security. In this example it happened that the ranking was in the same order as each security was introduced (except, of course, for the stock options). This is simply a coincidence and will not occur very often! Refer to Table 11-6 for the impact and ranking of each convertible security.

TABLE 11-6 Ranking

	Change in Numerator	Change in Denominator	Impact	Ranking
Stock options A	0.00	286	0.00	1
Stock options B				"Antidilutive"
8% PS	9,600	60,000	0.16	2
9% Bonds	6,615	5,000	1.32	3
10% Bonds	6,825	2,000	3.41	4

Diluted EPS Computation

Whew! After all that, we are finally ready to make the actual diluted EPS computations. The starting point is the basic EPS we computed in Example 11-1. From there, we add the dilutive securities one at a time. We compute a new EPS number after the addition of each security. If at any point the newest EPS is higher than the previous EPS, the previous EPS is the diluted EPS, and no further calculations are necessary. Remember, we want to be as conservative as possible, so we must report the lowest EPS number. Refer to Table 11-7 for the EPS computations. Notice that the diluted EPS is $2.32 per share.

This chapter concludes our discussion on stockholders' equity as well as the balance sheet. Now that you know about capital structure, basic and diluted earnings per share, and dilutive and antidilutive securities, we feel confident that you are prepared to tackle a new financial statement. In Chapter 12 we will move on to the income statement and will present various revenue recognition topics.

TABLE 11-7 EPS

		Numerator	Denominator	EPS	Still Dilutive?	
Basic	Example 11–1	190,400	23,833	7.99		
Ranking 1	Example 11–5	0.00	286			
		190,400	24,119	7.89	Yes	
Ranking 2	Example 11–2	9,600	60,000			
		200,000	84,119	2.38	Yes	
Ranking 3	Example 11–3	6,615	5,000			
		206,615	89,119	2.32	Yes	This is diluted EPS
Ranking 4	Example 11–4	6,825	2,000			
		213,440	91,119	2.34	No	

QUIZ

1. Which of the following is a *false* statement?

   A. For noncumulative preferred stock, all dividends, whether declared or not, should be considered in the numerator change.

   B. For noncumulative preferred stock, only declared dividends should be considered in the numerator change.

   C. For cumulative preferred stock, all dividends, whether declared or not, should be considered in the numerator change.

   D. All the above statements are true.

2. BLP, Inc., has $300,000 of 10 percent bonds payable that were issued at a discount in 2007. These bonds mature in 2027. The discount is amortized at $1,000 per year. Each $1,000 bond is convertible into 40 shares of common stock. The tax rate is 30 percent. What is the change in the numerator for these convertible securities?

   A. $12,000

   B. $20,300

   C. $21,700

   D. $31,000

3. BLP, Inc., has $150,000 of 6 percent bonds payable that were issued on April 1, 2010. Each $1,000 bond is convertible into 20 shares of common stock. The tax rate is 30 percent. What is the change in the numerator for these convertible securities?

   A. $3.000

   B. $3,150

   C. $4,725

   D. $9,000

4. Which is a *true* statement regarding stock options and warrants?

   A. Stock options and warrants are always ranked last.

   B. Stock options and warrants never use the treasury stock method.

   C. Stock options and warrants always use the treasury stock method.

   D. Stock options and warrants do not affect EPS.

5. The impact of each dilutive security should be ranked

   A. from highest to lowest.

   B. from lowest to highest.

   C. There is no need to rank the impact of each dilutive security.

   D. None of these answers is correct.

6. In 2010, GBW, Inc., had net income of $250,000. The company had 10,000 shares of $1 par value, 10 percent cumulative preferred stock outstanding but had not declared a dividend as of the end of the year. On January 1, 2010, GBW had 5,000 shares of common stock outstanding. On June 1, the company's board of directors declared a two-for-one stock split. Additionally, on August 31, the company repurchased 2,000 shares. For purposes of a basic EPS calculation, what is the weighted-average number of shares outstanding for 2010?

   A. 5,000
   B. 10,000
   C. 8,667
   D. 9,334

7. Using the same facts as in question 6, what amount should be used in the numerator of GBW's basic EPS calculation?

   A. $250,000
   B. $249,000
   C. $251,000
   D. $225,000

8. Using the same facts as in question 6, what is GBW's basic EPS for 2010?

   A. $26.68
   B. $26.78
   C. $24.90
   D. $25.10

9. All the following convertible securities follow what is known as the "if-converted" method for diluted EPS calculations *except*

   A. convertible preferred stock.
   B. options and warrants.
   C. convertible bonds issued at a discount.
   D. convertible bonds issued at a premium.

10. Which of the following statements is *false* regarding convertible preferred stock as it pertains to diluted EPS computations?

   A. The amount of preferred dividends is subtracted from net income to determine the basic EPS numerator.
   B. The number of new shares of common stock that the preferred stock would be converted into is added to the basic EPS denominator.
   C. The amount of preferred dividends is multiplied by the reciprocal of the tax rate before being added back to the basic EPS numerator.
   D. No tax effects are taken into consideration.

Part IV

The Income Statement—How Much Have I Earned?

chapter **12**

Income Measurement

CHAPTER OBJECTIVES

After completing this chapter, the student should

- Understand the financial statement presentation for income
- Understand the differences between the cash basis and accrual basis of accounting
- Account for long-term construction projects using both the percentage-of-completion method and the completed contract method
- Account for income recognized under the installment method and the cost recovery method
- Understand internal controls over income measurement

Overview

Revenue, it's the life of any business, right? No business, even a nonprofit one, can survive very long without a steady revenue stream. But how exactly does a business know when it can recognize revenue? We have learned from many of the recent financial scandals that knowing when and how much revenue to recognize often can be considered tricky business. Recognize too much revenue, and investors are provided with a false sense of security, but recognize too little, and the company might miss out on opportunities for additional financial backing and much more.

209

The process of recognizing just the right amount of revenue is further complicated by self-interests. If you were among the top executives at a firm, would you work hard and exert your creative abilities at the maximum possible every day if you weren't rewarded for your efforts? If you are like most people, probably not! Companies have realized this and, as a result, have altered compensation plans. Today, earnings often drive compensation in one form or another. Unfortunately, while providing the incentive for employees to do their best every day, such plans also have resulted in income manipulation. Time and time again, earnings targets are not met, and some accounting trick is used to make the books look better than they actually are. Move a few numbers here, use an aggressive policy there, and poof, the earnings target is suddenly met. While such practices are common, they are both improper and unethical. In this chapter we will present some acceptable revenue recognition techniques as they relate to long-term contracts and both the uncertain and extremely doubtful collectibility of accounts receivable.

Financial Statement Presentation

Income, as you would suspect, is reported on the income statement. But how does it actually get recognized? You mean you don't know! Don't worry, this chapter will tell you all about it.

Cash versus Accrual Basis

Recall from earlier chapters that there are two ways of recognizing revenue. However, only one method follows the generally accepted accounting principles (GAAP). The cash basis method recognizes revenue when cash is received. Because the cash basis does not match revenues and expenses, this technique cannot be considered GAAP. The accrual basis method, though, recognizes revenue when earned, just as expenses are recognized when incurred, and thus is considered GAAP. So the question becomes, When exactly is revenue earned? The *general rule* is that revenue is earned at the point of sale. By now, you probably have realized that, as we pointed out in Chapter 1, for every general rule, there are several exceptions. Such is the case here. Revenue can be recognized at the point of sale (the general rule) or either before or after the point of sale (the exceptions). In this chapter we will explore the accounting rules for the exceptions.

Recognize Revenue *prior to* Sale

When revenue is recognized prior to the point of sale, economic substance over legal form is reflected. The economic substance of the transaction consists of the sale that has been made. Legally, however, title has not been officially transferred. The most common situation for recognizing revenue prior to the point of sale is with long-term construction projects. There are two ways to account for such projects—the completed contract method and the percentage-of-completion method. We will illustrate both approaches with examples.

Completed Contract

The completed contract method follows the general rule of recognizing revenue at the point of sale, when title has changed hands. There are two new accounts that we need to introduce at this point. The first account is called *construction in progress.* Construction in progress is an inventory account for long-term construction projects. As an inventory account, it has a normal debit balance and is reported on the balance sheet as an asset. The second account is called *partial billings.* The easiest way to understand how partial billings works is to view it as a holding account for sales revenue. For financial statement presentation, the partial billings account is netted with the construction in progress account each year. When the balance in the construction in progress account is larger than the balance in the partial billings account, the net amount is reported as a current asset. In essence, more work has been done than has been billed for, and the company expects to receive monetary benefits from such extra work in the future. When the balance in the construction in progress account is smaller than the balance in the partial billings account, however, the net amount is reported as a current liability. More has been billed for than actually has been worked or completed, and thus the construction company owes the client more hours of service.

Think about how money flows in and out when you are working on a project. The related journal entries will follow that flow. First, a contract is signed with the customer for the construction of some structure large enough to be deemed a project. Once the contract is signed, money begins to be spent and charged to the project.

Journal entry 1: To record construction costs:

Construction in progress

        Cash (or accounts payable)

After a portion of the construction has been completed on the project, a bill will be sent to the customer so that there will be some cash inflow to help pay for the remaining construction costs. As soon as a bill is sent, journal entry 2 will be made.

Journal entry 2: To record partial billings:

Accounts receivable

        Partial billings

After a customer receives the bill, at least a portion of the billed total usually will be paid. The cash flowing in thus must be recorded using journal entry 3.

Journal entry 3: To record cash collections:

Cash

        Accounts receivable

The same set of journal entries will continue to be recorded until the project is completed. After title has changed hands, journal entry 4, as shown below, will then be made. The inventory represented as the construction in progress account will need to be removed from the books. The debit side of the entry will be to record the total expense of the project. Additionally, the partial billings account will need to be eliminated while simultaneously recognizing the revenue. The net result will be the recognition of gross profit as the difference between the revenue and expense.

Journal entry 4: Record revenue and expenses:

Construction expense

        Construction in progress

Partial billings

        Construction revenue

Because the project may take several years to complete, balance sheets and income statements will need to be prepared for each of those years. Based on experience, we believe that it is much easier to prepare each year's respective financial statements as work is being completed on the project. Additionally, preparing T-accounts and posting the journal entries as the various transactions or events are occurring is also beneficial.

Now on to one more item that we need to discuss before you will be fully prepared to work out an example. It is imperative that you know how to report the partial billings account on the financials each year. *If* construction in progress is greater than partial billings at year end, a net asset results, and both construction in progress and partial billings are itemized in the current assets section of the balance sheet, with partial billings subtracted from construction in progress. However, *if* construction in progress is less than partial billings at year end, a net liability results, and again, both partial billings and construction in progress are itemized in the current liabilities section of the balance sheet, with construction in progress subtracted from partial billings. Now that we have covered the basics of the completed contract method, let's try an example.

EXAMPLE 12-1

BLP, Inc., has entered into a contract to build a large yacht for Ocean Adventures, Inc. The sales price is $1 million, and work will begin in 2009, with the yacht scheduled to be completed in 2011. At the time the contract was signed, BLP estimated that the total cost would be $700,000. At the end of 2010, the estimated total cost had increased to $750,000. By the time the yacht was complete in 2011, the total cost had accumulated to $800,000. The actual costs

TABLE 12-1 Construction Costs	2009	2010	2011
Billed each year	400,000	275,000	325,000
Collected each year	350,000	280,000	370,000
Cost incurred each year	300,000	275,000	225,000
Cost incurred to date	300,000	575,000	800,000
Estimated cost to complete	400,000	175,000	0
Total estimated cost of yacht	700,000	750,000	800,000

incurred each year were $300,000 in 2009, $275,000 in 2010, and $225,000 in 2011. The amount billed in 2009 was $400,000; in 2010, $275,000; and in 2011, $325,000. The amount collected in 2009 was $350,000; in 2010, $280,000; and in 2011, $370,000. Refer to Table 12-1 for a chart related to the estimated and actual costs incurred, along with the amounts billed and collected.

Once the chart is prepared, you then can prepare the journal entries for each year. Refer to Table 12-2 for those entries. We also have prepared a partial balance sheet and income statement for each year. Refer to Table 12-3 for these financial statements.

Percentage of Completion

The percentage-of-completion method is an exception to the general rule because revenue is recognized each year based on the percent of the project that

TABLE 12-2 Journal Entries—Completed Contract		
2009		
1. Record construction cost		
Construction in progress	300,000	
Cash (AP)		300,000
2. Record partial billings		
Accounts receivable	400,000	
Partial billings		400,000
3. Record cash collections		
Cash	350,000	
Accounts receivable		350,000
		(Continued)

TABLE 12-2 (Continued)

2010

1. Record construction cost

Construction in progress	275,000	
Cash (AP)		275,000

2. Record partial billings

Accounts receivable	275,000	
Partial billings		275,000

3. Record cash collections

Cash	280,000	
Accounts receivable		280,000

2011

1. Record construction cost

Construction in progress	225,000	
Cash (AP)		225,000

2. Record partial billings

Accounts receivable	325,000	
Partial billings		325,000

3. Record cash collections

Cash	370,000	
Accounts receivable		370,000

4. Record expense and eliminate inventory

Construction expense	800,000	
Construction in progress		800,000

5. Record revenue and eliminate partial billings

Partial billings	1,000,000	
Construction revenue		1,000,000

TABLE 12-3 Partial Balance Sheet and Partial Income Statement—Completed Contract Method

Partial Balance Sheet		Partial Income Statement	
2009			
Current assets:		Revenues	0.00
Accounts receivable	50,000	Expenses	0.00
		Gross profit	0.00
Current liabilities:			
Construction in progress	300,000		
Less: Partial billings	(400,000)		
Excess of billings over costs	(100,000)		
2010			
Current assets:		Revenues	0.00
Accounts receivable	45,000	Expenses	0.00
		Gross profit	0.00
Construction in progress	675,000		
Less: Partial billings	(575,000)		
Excess of costs over billings	100,000		
2011			
Current assets:		Revenues	1,000,000
		Expenses	(800,000)
		Gross profit	200,000

is complete. The accounting for the percentage-of-completion method is very similar to the accounting for the completed contract method. However, there are two important differences.

The first difference is that gross profit is recognized every year, not just in the year of completion, as it is under the completed contract method. The gross profit that is recognized is based on, yes, you guessed it, the percentage of completion! We have prepared a chart that simplifies the computations related to calculating the percentage of completion for each year. The same numbers from Example 12-1 are used in this percentage-of-completion example, and the related chart is presented in Table 12-4.

TABLE 12-4 Percentage of Completion

	2009	2010	2011
Billed each year	400,000	275,000	325,000
Collected each year	350,000	280,000	370,000
Cost incurred each year	300,000	275,000	225,000
Cost incurred to date	300,000	575,000	800,000
Estimated cost to complete	400,000	175,000	0
Total estimated cost of yacht	700,000	750,000	800,000
Percent complete to date	43%	77%	100%
Less: Percent complete in previous years	0%	-43%	-77%
Percent of revenue to be recognized each year	43%	34%	23%
Times: Total revenue	1,000,000	1,000,000	1,000,000
Equals: Revenue recognized each year	430,000	340,000	230,000
Less: Cost each year	(300,000)	(275,000)	(225,000)
Equals: Gross profit recognized each year	130,000	65,000	5,000

Now it is time to discuss the journal entries for the percentage-of-completion method. Unlike the completed contract method, which has three entries each year, there are four entries for the percentage-of-completion method. The first three are identical to those prepared under the completed contract method because the transactions that the company is involved in are still the same; the company spends money on the project and bills and collects money from the client. The additional journal entry is necessary to recognize the gross profit earned each year rather than recognizing the total amount at completion of the project. To recognize the gross profit, a debit entry is made to construction expense for the cost incurred in the current year, a credit entry is made to construction revenue for the amount of revenue recognized in the current year (the number will come from Table 12-4), and another debit entry is made to balance the journal entry. That debit is to the construction in progress (inventory) account.

Notice that under the completed contract method, the construction in progress account includes only the cost of construction. However, under the percentage-of-completion method, construction in progress includes the cost of construction *and* the gross profit recognized each year.

We are now ready to prepare the journal entries for the percentage-of-completion method. Refer to Table 12-5 for these entries. We also will prepare partial balance sheets and income statements for each year. Refer to Table 12-6 for those financial statements.

TABLE 12-5 Journal Entries—Percentage of Completion

2009

1. Record construction cost

Construction in progress	300,000	
Cash (AP)		300,000

2. Record partial billings

Accounts receivable	400,000	
Partial billings		400,000

3. Record cash collections

Cash	350,000	
Accounts receivable		350,000

4. Record gross profit

Construction expense	300,000	
Construction in progress	130,000	
Construction revenue		430,000

2010

1. Record construction cost

Construction in progress	275,000	
Cash (AP)		275,000

2. Record partial billings

Accounts receivable	275,000	
Partial billings		275,000

3. Record cash collections

Cash	280,000	
Accounts receivable		280,000

4. Record gross profit

Construction expense	275,000	
Construction in progress	65,000	
Construction revenue		340,000

2011

1. Record construction cost

Construction in progress	225,000	
Cash (AP)		225,000

2. Record partial billings

Accounts receivable	325,000	
Partial billings		325,000

(Continued)

TABLE 12-5 (*Continued*)

3. Record cash collections		
Cash	370,000	
Accounts receivable		370,000
4. Record gross profit		
Construction expense	225,000	
Construction in progress	5,000	
Construction revenue		230,000
5. Remove inventory and partial billings		
Partial billings	1,000,000	
Construction in progress		1,000,000

TABLE 12-6 Partial Balance Sheet and Partial Income Statement—Percentage-of-Completion Method

Partial Balance Sheet		Partial Income Statement	
2009			
Current assets:		Revenues	430,000
Accounts receivable	50,000	Expenses	(300,000)
		Gross profit	130,000
Construction in progress	430,000		
Less: Partial billings	(400,000)		
Costs and recognized profit not billed	30,000		
2010			
Current assets:		Revenues	340,000
Accounts receivable	45,000	Expenses	(275,000)
		Gross profit	65,000
Construction in progress	770,000		
Less: Partial billings	(675,000)		
Costs and recognized profit not billed	95,000		
2011			
Current assets:		Revenues	230,000
		Expenses	(225,000)
		Gross profit	5,000

Recognize Revenue *after* Sale

It's now time to turn our attention to two other exceptions to the general rule for recognizing revenue—the installment method and the cost recovery method. Both methods recognize revenue after the point of sale.

Installment Method

Revenue is recognized after the point of sale under the installment method because the collectibility of the receivable is not reasonably assured. In other words, there is some doubt as to whether money from the purchaser will be received. Therefore, only as money (cash) is received is revenue recognized.

It's again time to add to your list of friends with two new accounts. The first account is *deferred gross profit*. Deferred gross profit is kept as a separate account for each year (e.g., deferred gross profit for 2009 and deferred gross profit for 2010). This account is reported on the balance sheet as a contra account to accounts receivable from installment sales. The second account is *gross profit realized on installment sales*. Gross profit realized on installment sales is reported on the income statement as an addition to gross profit. Unlike deferred gross profit, the gross profit realized on installment sales account is not kept separately for each year.

As a side note, deferred gross profit is a balance sheet account, and gross profit realized on installment sales is an income statement account. Because we have a balance sheet account and an income statement account, you likely can deduce that it takes an adjusting journal entry to get these accounts recorded. You are correct!

We have developed a step-by-step process for making the required computations and journal entries for the installment method. We will illustrate those steps with an example.

EXAMPLE 12-2

BLP, Inc., makes all its sales on credit. There are some customers who are considered to be a higher credit risk. Therefore, sales to those customers, along with the corresponding cost of goods sold (COGS), are reported separately from regular sales and are denoted as installment sales and installment COGS. The information needed for this example is illustrated in Table 12-7. Please carefully examine that information now.

The journal entries for both 2009 and 2010 are presented in Table 12-8.

A partial balance sheet and a partial income statement for both 2009 and 2010 are presented in Table 12-9. To determine the appropriate numbers for the financial statements, it is helpful if you prepare T-accounts and post the journal entries as they are prepared.

TABLE 12-7 Installment Method

	2009		2010	
Total credit sales	200,000		300,000	
Total COGS	150,000		200,000	
Installment sales	50,000	100%	100,000	100%
Installment COGS	(37,500)	−75%	(70,000)	−70%
Installment gross profit	12,500	25%	30,000	30%
Gross profit rate on installment sales	25%		30%	
Cash receipts on installment method sales				
2009 sales	30,000		20,000	
2010 sales			60,000	
Cash receipts on other credit sales	100,000		200,000	

TABLE 12-8 Journal Entries—Installment Method

2009		
1. Record sales and COGS in normal manner		
Accounts receivable	200,000	
Sales		200,000
COGS	150,000	
Inventory		150,000
2. Record cash collections on all sales in normal manner		
Cash	130,000	
Accounts receivable		130,000
3. Reverse installment sales and related COGS		
Sales	50,000	
Deferred gross profit 2009 Plug to balance		12,500
COGS		37,500
4. Recognize gross profit on cash collected		
Deferred gross profit 2009 30,000 × 25%	7,500	
Gross profit recognized on installment sales		7,500
5. Prepare year-end closing entry		
Gross profit recognized on installment sales	7,500	
Income summary		7,500

TABLE 12-8 *(Continued)*			
2010			
1. Record sales and COGS in normal manner			
Accounts receivable		300,000	
Sales			300,000
COGS		200,000	
Inventory			200,000
2. Record cash collections on all sales in normal manner			
Cash		280,000	
Accounts receivable			280,000
3. Reverse installment sales and related COGS			
Sales		100,000	
Deferred gross profit 2010	Plug to balance		30,000
COGS			70,000
4. Recognize gross profit on cash collected			
Deferred gross profit 2009	20,000 × 25%	5,000	
Deferred gross profit 2010	60,000 × 30%	18,000	
Gross profit recognized on installment sales			23,000
5. Prepare year-end closing entry			
Gross profit recognized on installment sales		23,000	
Income summary			23,000

Cost Recovery Method

Revenue is also recognized after the point of sale under the cost recovery method. This time such a practice is followed because the collectibility of the receivable is extremely uncertain. In other words, there is *much* doubt as to whether money from the customer will be received. As a result, no gross profit is recognized until all the cost has been recovered. The deferred gross profit and the gross profit realized accounts introduced in the preceding section will be used again here. However, there are two differences. First, there is no need to keep track of the deferred gross profit by year. Second, the realized gross profit account is renamed *gross profit realized on cost recovery transactions*, even though its function remains the same.

EXAMPLE 12-3

BLP, Inc., purchased a piece of land as an investment in 2007 at a cost of $100,000. Just as the company suspected, the land has increased in value rapidly. In 2009, BLP sold the land to BRB, Inc., for $150,000. Unfortunately, BLP has many doubts as to whether BRB will make all the required payments because the company could not obtain a bank loan. BLP thus has agreed to carry a three-year note for BRB. BLP decided it was best to account for the

TABLE 12-9 Partial Balance Sheet and Partial Income Statement—Installment Method

2009

Balance Sheet

Computation for B/S presentation	Total	Installment	Noninstallment
Credit sales	200,000	50,000	150,000
Less: Cash receipts	(130,000)	(30,000)	(100,000)
AR at end of year	70,000	20,000	50,000
Current assets:			
Accounts receivable		50,000	
Installment accounts receivable	20,000		
Less: Deferred gross profit 2009	(5,000)	15,000	

2009 Income Statement

Sales		150,000
Less: COGS		(112,500)
Gross profit		37,500
Gross profit realized on installment sales		7,500
Total gross profit		45,000

2010

Balance Sheet

Computation for B/S presentation	Total	Installment	Noninstallment
Credit sales	500,000	150,000	350,000
Less: Cash receipts	(410,000)	(110,000)	(300,000)
AR at end of year	90,000	40,000	50,000
Current assets:			
Accounts receivable		50,000	
Installment accounts receivable	40,000		
Less: Deferred gross profit 2009	0		
Less: Deferred gross profit 2010	(12,000)	28,000	

2010 Income Statement

Sales		200,000
Less: COGS		(130,000)
Gross profit		70,000
Gross profit realized on installment sales		23,000
Total gross profit		93,000

sale of the land as a cost recovery transaction and not to record any gross profit until the cost is fully recovered. Lucky for BLP, BRB was able to make all the required payments. BLP received $50,000 in 2009, $60,000 in 2010, and $40,000 in 2011. For a chart of the amount of gross profit realized each year and the corresponding journal entries, refer to Table 12-10.

TABLE 12-10 Cost-Recovery Method

		Cash Collected	Gross Profit Realized
Selling price of land	150,000		
Cost of land	(100,000)		
Gross profit	50,000		
Collections:		**Cash Collected**	**Gross Profit Realized**
2009		50,000	0
2010		60,000	10,000
2011		40,000	40,000
Year 2007			
Land	100,000		
Cash		100,000	
Year 2009			
AR	150,000		
Deferred gross profit		50,000	
Land		100,000	
Cash	50,000		
AR		50,000	
Year 2010			
Cash	60,000		
AR		60,000	
Deferred gross profit	10,000		
Gross profit realized on cost–recovery transactions		10,000	
Year 2011			
Cash	40,000		
AR		40,000	
Deferred gross profit	40,000		
Gross profit realized on cost–recovery transactions		40,000	

Internal Controls

Establishment of Responsibility and Segregation of Duties

For a typical retail and similar business, many of the internal control measures for revenue were covered in Chapter 1 when we introduced accounts receivable. Remember, the individual who checks the customer's credit eligibility and authorizes the sale should not be the same individual who actually waits on the customer, and neither of those two individuals should be responsible for recording the sale in the books. For revenue recognition on construction contracts, as was discussed in this chapter, a member of top management should be responsible for making the decision regarding how revenue and profits will be recognized (i.e., either at completion of the contract or in annual portions based on the progress of the project). Likewise, there needs to be a designated party within the organization who determines when collectibility of receivables is not reasonably assured or is extremely uncertain so that revenue recognition after the point of sale can be authorized.

Documentation Procedures and Physical, Mechanical, and Electronic Controls

For typical businesses, sales orders, receipts, and checks from customers could serve as documentation that a sale has taken place and that revenue should be recognized. With regard to construction contracts, as highlighted in this chapter, records should be kept indicating the costs that were incurred in each period as well as some type of documentation indicating completion of the project. For receivables where the collectibility is questionable, evidence to prove that belief should be documented. Electronic controls should be implemented to protect records from being tampered with and better ensure against income manipulation or earnings management via changes to the accounting records.

Independent Internal Verification

Price checks are important to the independent internal verification of recognized revenue. Additionally, verifying that there is evidence of a sale arrangement, that either the service has been rendered or the product has been delivered, that the purchase price is determinable, and that collectibility is reasonably assured before revenue is recognized is an important internal check. Finally, determining the true substance of the transaction (e.g., arm's length transaction versus related party transaction) is imperative to ensuring that the proper amount of revenue is recorded on the books.

Cash and accrual basis, it's something that you will hear all the time throughout your accounting career, and we would like to think that in this chapter we helped you to learn the differences because we focused on construction contracts under the percentage-of-completion and completed contract methods and the installment and cost recovery methods for receivables. In Chapter 13 we will continue to look at issues affecting the income statement while focusing on the differences between two types of accounting—financial and tax.

QUIZ

1. **Which of the following statements is _true_?**
   A. Construction in progress under the completed contract method includes both the construction costs and the gross profit.
   B. Construction in progress under the percentage-of-completion method includes both the construction costs and the gross profit.
   C. Construction in progress is not an inventory account.
   D. None of these statements are true.

2. **When is revenue recognized under the completed contract method?**
   A. At the point of sale
   B. Incrementally over the life of the project
   C. When the project is completed
   D. The year after the project is completed

   Questions 3, 4, and 5 are based on the following information:

   BLP, Inc., agreed to construct a boathouse for a company at a price of $400,000. The costs incurred and estimated to complete the project are presented below:

	2009	2010	2011
Cost incurred each year	100,000	150,000	75,000
Cost incurred to date	100,000	250,000	325,000
Estimated cost to complete	225,000	75,000	0
Total estimated cost	325,000	325,000	325,000

3. **How much revenue is recognized in 2009 under the completed contract method (round any percentages used to the nearest whole number)?**
   A. $0
   B. $124,000
   C. $184,000
   D. $400,000

4. **How much revenue is recognized in 2009 under the percentage-of-completion method (round any percentages used to the nearest whole number)?**
   A. $24,000
   B. $124,000
   C. $184,000
   D. $92,000

5. How much gross profit is recognized in 2011 under the percentage-of-completion method (round any percentages used to the nearest whole number)?

   A. $0
   B. $17,000
   C. $24,000
   D. $34,000

6. Which of the following statements is *true*?

   A. The installment method for accounts receivable is always used when a customer agrees to pay the total bill in predetermined portions.
   B. The cost recovery method for accounts receivable uses a partial billings account.
   C. The installment method for accounts receivable is used when collection is not reasonably assured.
   D. The cost recovery method for accounts receivable is used when collection is absolutely assured.

The table below represents the information for GBW, Inc., for 2009. Use the information to answer questions 7, 8, and 9.

Total credit sales	$200,000
Total COGS	$160,000
Installment sales	$100,000
Installment COGS	$ 70,000
Cash receipts on installment sales, 2009	$ 60,000
Cash receipts on other credit sales	$ 80,000

7. What is the gross profit rate on installment sales for 2009?

   A. 70 percent
   B. 30 percent
   C. 40 percent
   D. 80 percent

8. What amount of gross profit should be recognized on installment sales in 2009?

   A. $18,000
   B. $30,000
   C. $24,000
   D. $42,000

9. What total amount of gross profit should be presented on GBW's income statement for 2009?

   A. $10,000
   B. $58,000
   C. $70,000
   D. $28,000

10. In 2010, PJC Unlimited sold a building to a customer. PJC fears that it is extremely doubtful that the customer will make all the required payments. The original cost of the building (net) was $50,000, and PJC resold the structure to the customer for $75,000. Cash collections for 2010, 2011, and 2012 were $25,000, $35,000, and $15,000, respectively. Based on these facts, how much gross profit on the sale would PJC have recognized in 2011?

    A. $15,000
    B. $10,000
    C. $35,000
    D. $25,000

chapter **13**

Income Taxes

CHAPTER OBJECTIVES

After completing this chapter, the student should

- Understand the financial statement presentation for income taxes
- Understand what is considered a permanent difference between book and taxable income
- Understand what is considered a temporary difference between book and taxable income
- Understand the terms *future deductible* and *future taxable*
- Account for deferred tax assets and deferred tax liabilities
- Reconcile book income to taxable income and taxable income to book income

Overview

If you have never studied tax law, then this chapter likely will be a bit fuzzy to you. Don't worry, though, we are not big tax fans ourselves and have presented the material as though you, the reader, are in that fuzzy position. So why exactly are tax rules important in financial accounting? They are two separate branches of accounting, right? There is one accountant that takes care of your business's books and another who you take your taxes, and those two individuals may not even know each other. How, then, could there possibly be any connection between the federal and state taxes that you pay and your income statement? Well, your income statement shows revenues, expenses (yes, tax expense is included), and net income, whereas your tax return lists your taxable income and tax liability. Both the tax liability, when paid, and the income tax expense must be recorded in the accounting system. However, rarely will those two numbers be equal. Hence there is a need for a chapter on reconciling those two amounts or what we will call *accounting for income taxes*. Depending on type and geographic location, some businesses will prepare federal, state, and local income tax returns. In this chapter we will limit our discussion simply to federal taxes.

So what are the main differences between the financial income statement and the federal income tax return? The objective of financial accounting is primarily to provide useful information to external users about the balance sheet, income statement, and company's cash flows. The objective of tax accounting, on the other hand, is to provide revenue for the federal government. Essentially, tax accounting allows Uncle Sam to receive his fair share of your earnings. The Financial Accounting Standards Board (FASB) is responsible primarily for creating financial accounting rules, whereas Congress is responsible for passing tax laws, and the Internal Revenue Service (IRS) has the authority to enforce those laws. Because the objectives and rule making bodies for each are different, it is logical to assume that revenues and expenses are often treated differently on an income statement versus a tax return.

Financial Statement Presentation

In this chapter we will introduce three new accounts—*deferred tax asset* (DTA), *deferred tax liability* (DTL), and *allowance to reduce deferred tax asset to net realizable value* (allowance account). All three accounts are reported on the balance sheet. Current and noncurrent classifications usually depend on the origination of the DTA or DTL. For example, a DTA will be reported as a current asset if the temporary difference relates to a current account. Otherwise, it will be reported as a noncurrent asset. The allowance account is a contra account to the DTA, and we will discuss its use later in this chapter. Likewise, a DTL will be reported as a current liability if the temporary difference relates to a current account. Otherwise, it will be reported as a noncurrent liability. The current deferred tax accounts then are netted together and reported as either a current asset or current liability, and the noncurrent deferred tax accounts are also netted together separately and reported as either a noncurrent asset or a noncurrent liability.

Permanent Differences

Permanent differences are differences between financial income and taxable income that will *never* reverse. We will cover six of the most common permanent differences, which, by any means, is not an exhaustive list. We will break the six differences into three categories—nontaxable revenues, nondeductible expenses, and allowable deductions.

Nontaxable Revenues

Nontaxable revenue is revenue that is included on an income statement but is *never* included on a tax return. There are two common nontaxable revenues—interest on municipal bonds and life insurance proceeds payable to the business.

Nondeductible Expenses

Nondeductible expenses are expenses that can be expensed on an income statement but are *never* deductible on a tax return. There are two common nondeductible expenses—life insurance premiums on officers and fines and penalties.

Allowable Deductions

Allowable deductions are deductions that can be taken on an income tax return but are not recorded as expenses on the income statement. There are two common allowable deductions. The first is *depletion*. On the books (income statement), depletion expense can be taken in an amount equal to the cost of the asset being depleted. On the tax return, however, an amount equal to a percentage of the gross income generated by the asset being depleted can be expensed. In other words, the amount of depletion expense for the tax return is *not* limited to the cost of the asset. Yes, you are interpreting this correctly. You actually can deduct a higher amount of depletion expense on the tax return than was paid for the asset! Who do you think lobbied Congress to get that law passed?

The second allowable deduction concerns *dividends received*. While both the books and tax return will report income for the dividend received, the difference will appear on the expense/deduction side. There is no expense on the books when a dividend is received. However, there is one related to dividends on the tax return. When a corporation receives a dividend from another corporation, the receiving corporation is allowed a deduction for a certain percentage of the dividends received. The actual percentage depends on the amount of stock owned by the corporation. Why would such a deduction be allowed? Well, you have all heard about double taxation, right? While there is nothing to prevent that, the corporate deduction has been instituted to mitigate triple taxation. Without the deduction, the dividends would be taxed once when the corporation distributing the dividend earned the money, again when the receiving corporation included the dividend in its revenues, and finally when the receiving corporation paid out a dividend of its own.

We have prepared Table 13-1 to summarize these common permanent differences.

TABLE 13-1 Permanent Differences

	Book	Tax
Interest on municipal bonds	Recognize as revenue	Nontaxable
Life insurance proceeds payable to the business	Recognize as revenue	Nontaxable
Life insurance premiums on officers	Recognize as an expense	Nondeductible
Fines and penalties	Recognize as an expense	Nondeductible
Percentage depletion in excess of cost depletion	Recognize only cost depletion	Deduct percentage depletion
Dividend received deduction	No expense recognized when dividends are received	Deduct a percentage of dividends received

Temporary Differences

Temporary differences are differences between financial income and taxable income that *will reverse* at some future time. We will cover 10 of the most common temporary differences, which, again, is by no means an exhaustive list. We will break the 10 differences into two categories—future taxable and future deductible.

Future Taxable

There are two instances in which a temporary difference could be taxable in the future. First, revenue could be included in book income before it is included on the tax return. We will discuss three examples to demonstrate that process. Second, an expense could be deducted on the tax return before it is recognized as an expense on the books. For this case, we will present two examples.

Let's start with the first situation, where revenue is included on the books before it is placed on the tax return.

Gross Profit on Installment Sales

For book purposes, the entire amount of gross profit normally is included in income at the point of sale. However, tax accounting focuses on cash flows, and thus gross profit is recognized as cash is collected.

Gross Profit on Long-Term Construction Contracts

For book purposes, revenue may be recognized under the percentage-of-completion method, in which a percentage of profit is recognized each year.

For tax purposes, however, the completed contract method likely would be adopted, in which no profit is recognized until the project is complete.

Investment Income

When one company has a 20 to 50 percent ownership interest in another company, the company that owns the other is required to use the equity method to account for the investment on the books. Recall that the equity method records income for the percentage ownership in the investment company, and any dividends received are considered a return of capital. Therefore, on the books, income is recognized whether received or not. On the tax return, however, only dividends received are taxed. Earnings may not be distributed in the form of dividends for many years into the future and thus will not be taxed until then.

Now, let's move to the second situation, where expenses are deducted on the tax return before they are expensed on the books.

Depreciation

For book purposes, assets must be depreciated using straight-line, declining balance, sum of the years' digits, or units of output depreciation. Useful lives are determined by the company and normally are set for a long period of time. However, for tax return purposes, the modified accelerated cost recovery system (MACRS) is the required depreciation method. The primary characteristic of MACRS is relatively short useful lives for the assets being depreciated. Therefore, assets normally will be depreciated much more quickly on the tax return than on the books. Stated a different way, depreciation expense will be higher under MACRS on the tax return during an asset's early years.

Interest and Taxes on Self-Construction Projects

For book purposes, interest and taxes on self-constructed projects must be capitalized and depreciated. However, for tax purposes, the interest and taxes may be deducted as incurred.

Future Deductible

There are two instances in which a temporary difference could be deductible in the future. First, revenue could be included on the tax return before it is included on the books. We will present two examples in which this is the case. Second, an expense could be recognized on the books before it is deducted on the tax return. For this case, we will present three examples.

Let's start with the first situation, in which revenue is included on the tax return before it is included on the books.

Prepaid Revenues

There are three prepaid revenues that are quite common—prepaid rent, prepaid interest, and prepaid royalties. For book purposes, those prepaid revenues follow the general rule for accrual basis income recognition and are recognized as income when earned. For tax purposes, however, those same prepaid revenues follow the *wherewithal to pay principle*, which means that they are taxed as soon as they are received. It is at this point that the taxpayer has money in his, her, or its pocket to pay the taxes.

Gains on Sales and Leasebacks

For book purposes, such gains are recognized as earned over the life of the lease contract. For tax purposes, however, they are taxed in the year of sale.

Now let's move to the second situation, in which expenses are recognized on the books prior to being deducted on the tax return.

Estimated Expenses

There are four common expenses that, for book purposes, are based on estimates—product warranties, bad debts, compensatory stock options, and inventory losses. For book purposes, such expenses are estimated and recognized at those estimated amounts as an expense on the books. Strange as this many seem, however, the federal government does not usually condone basing a deduction on any type of estimate. Therefore, for tax purposes, such expenses may be deducted only when actually paid or incurred.

Indirect Costs of Producing Inventory

For book purposes, indirect costs of producing inventory may be recognized as expenses immediately. However, for tax purposes, such indirect costs must be capitalized and may be deducted only as costs of goods sold (COGS) when inventory actually is sold.

Contingent Liabilities

For book purposes, following the conservatism principle, contingent liabilities may be expensed provided that the loss is both probable and measurable. Again, the federal government does not want taxpayers to base any deduction on an estimate. Therefore, for tax purposes, a contingent liability (loss) may be deducted only when it is actually paid.

We have prepared Table 13-2 to summarize these common temporary differences.

TABLE 13-2 Temporary Differences

	Book	Tax
Gross profit on installment sales	Income at point of sale	Income as cash is collected
Gross profit on long-term construction contracts	Income under percentage-of-completion method	Income under completed-contract method
Investment income	Income under equity method	Income as dividends are received
Depreciation	Expense over a longer time period	Deducted over a shorter time period
Interest and taxes on self-construction projects	Capitalized and depreciated	Deducted as incurred
Prepaid revenues	Income when earned	Income when received
Gains on sales and leasebacks	Revenue over life of lease contract	Revenue on date of sale
Estimated expenses	Expenses can be estimated and expensed	Deducted when actually incurred
Indirect costs of producing inventory	Expensed immediately	Capitalized and expensed to COGS as inventory is sold
Contingent liabilites (losses)	Expensed if loss is probable and measureable	Deducted when actually paid

Deferred Tax Assets

Any future deductible temporary difference will result in a deferred tax asset. As we discussed earlier, tax expense (a debit) is based on book income, whereas tax liability (a credit) is based on taxable income. Therefore, a balancing entry is needed. In the case of future deductible temporary differences, the account charged is a deferred tax asset.

There are four basic principles that must be applied to the area of deferred tax assets and liabilities. They are

1. A current tax liability or asset is recognized for the current year.

2. A deferred tax liability or asset is recognized for each temporary difference.

3. The enacted tax rates must be used to measure any deferred tax asset or liability.

4. A valuation allowance account may be needed to reduce a deferred tax asset so that it is reported at net realizable value (NRV).

Okay, now that you have enough background information, let's try to work some examples.

EXAMPLE 13-1

BLP, Inc., had $10,000 in income for both 2009 and 2010 for both book and tax return purposes. That total was calculated before taking into consideration $1,000 in prepaid rent that was received in December 2009 but that will not be earned until January 2010. The enacted tax rate for both years is 30 percent. The 2009 journal entry showing the originating deferral and the 2010 journal entry showing the reversal are both presented in Table 13-3. In the table, note that the tax liability account represents the *current* tax obligation, whereas the tax expense account represents the sum of both the current and deferred tax obligations. Additionally, the tax liability account may be referred to by alternative names, including *income taxes payable*.

TABLE 13-3 Deferred Tax Asset (Example 13-1)

	2009	2010	Difference	
Book income	10,000	11,000	1,000	
Taxable income	11,000	10,000	1,000	
2009: Originating difference				
Tax expense		10,000 × 30%	3,000	
Deferred tax asset		1,000 × 30%	300	
Tax liability		11,000 × 30%		3,300
2010: Reversing difference				
Tax expense		11,000 × 30%	3,300	
Deferred tax asset		1,000 × 30%		300
Tax liability		10,000 × 30%		3,000

If the company does not expect to have enough taxable income in the future to be able to take advantage of a future deductible amount, it then will need to create a valuation allowance account to offset the deferred tax asset. Again, such a practice follows the conservatism principle. Let's look at an example.

EXAMPLE 13-2

Over the past several years, BLP, Inc., sold products that carried warranties. In 2010, BLP had book income and taxable income of $10,000 before considering any warranty expenses. The 2010 estimated warranty expense for book purposes was $8,000. The actual amount spent on warranties, however, was only $3,000. The enacted tax rate for 2010 was 30 percent. BLP has some concerns related to future taxable income and has determined that only half the deferred tax asset created by the temporary future deductible item will be realized. The 2010 journal entries to account for those events are presented in Table 13-4.

TABLE 13-4 Deferred Tax Asset with Allowance (Example 13-2)

	Book Income	Taxable Income	Difference	
2010	2,000	7,000	5,000	
2010	Tax expense	2,000 × 30%	600	
	Deferred tax asset	5,000 × 30%	1,500	
	Tax liability	7,000 × 30%		2,100
2010	Tax expense	1,500 × 0.50	750	
	Allowance to reduce DTA to NRV	1,500 × 0.50		750

Deferred Tax Liabilities

Any future taxable temporary difference will result in a deferred tax liability. As we discussed earlier and highlighted with some examples in the last section, tax expense (a debit) is based on book income, and tax liability (a credit) is based on taxable income. Therefore, a balancing entry is needed. In the case of future taxable temporary differences, the account charged is a deferred tax liability. Let's work a simple example to demonstrate.

 **EXAMPLE 13-3**

BLP, Inc., has $20,000 of income for 2010 that has been included on its books and income tax return for the year. The income was calculated before considering depreciation. For book purposes, assets are depreciated using the straight-line method, and the total amount that should be recognized is $5,000. For tax purposes, though, $9,000 of depreciation should be recognized under MACRS. The enacted tax rate is 30 percent. The related journal entry that would be recorded is shown in Table 13-5.

TABLE 13-5 Deferred Tax Liability (Example 13-3)

		Book Income / Taxable Income	Difference	
	Book Income	**Taxable Income**	**Difference**	
2010	15,000	11,000	4,000	
2010	Tax expense	15,000 × 30%	4,500	
	Deferred tax liability	4,000 × 30%		1,200
	Tax liability	11,000 × 30%		3,300

Complex Examples

Now that you understand the basics of accounting for income taxes, let's try a few examples that are a bit more complicated.

EXAMPLE 13-4

Let's attempt an example that has both a future taxable item and a future deductible item along with beginning balances in both the deferred tax asset account and the deferred tax liability account.

The beginning balance in the deferred tax asset account is a $500 debit. The beginning balance in the deferred tax liability account is a $700 credit. The enacted tax rate for 2010 is 30 percent. The taxable income for 2010 is $20,000. There is a future taxable difference of $4,000 in 2010 and a future deductible difference of $3,000.

The starting point for working this example is to set up T-accounts for both deferred tax accounts and to insert the beginning balances in each. When you calculate the tax effect of the future taxable difference, the result represents the *required* ending balance in the deferred tax liability account. So the difference between the beginning and ending balances will represent the necessary adjustment to the deferred tax liability account.

When you calculate the tax effect of the future deductible difference, the result represents the *required* ending balance in the deferred tax asset account. Therefore, the difference between the beginning and ending balances will represent the necessary adjustment to the deferred tax asset account.

The credit to tax liability is the taxable income times the tax rate. This just leaves the debit to tax expense, which will be a plug to balance the journal entry.

The T-accounts and the journal entry are shown in Table 13-6.

TABLE 13-6 DTA and DTL (Example 13-4)

Differences		Deferred Tax Asset		Deferred Tax Liability	
4,000	Future taxable – DTL	500	Beg bal	Beg bal	700
3,000	Future deductible – DTA	400			500
		900	End bal	End bal	1,200
2010 Tax expense	Plug to balance	6,100			
Deferred tax asset	Plug from T–account	400			
Deferred tax liability	Plug from T–account		500		
Tax liability	20,000 × 30%		6,000		

EXAMPLE 13-5

Up to this point, the enacted tax rate has been the same for all future years. In this example, we will demonstrate what happens when this is not the case. Let's assume that book and tax depreciation amounts are different for 2010, 2011, and 2012, as shown in Table 13-7. The enacted tax rates are 30, 35, and 40 percent for the three years, respectively. The taxable income for 2010 is $20,000. To determine the credit to deferred tax liability, you must take the difference in depreciation expense for each year and multiply that amount times the appropriate enacted tax rate. Those products then are added, and the corresponding journal entry is recorded for that amount. Refer to Table 13-7 for the computations.

The tax liability is based on taxable income times the enacted tax rate for the current year. This leaves only the debit to tax expense, which, in this case, will be a plug to balance the journal entry, as shown in Table 13-7.

TABLE 13-7 Different Enacted Tax Rates (Example 13-5)

	2010	2011	2012	Total
Tax depreciation	2,000	3,000	4,000	
Book depreciation	(1,500)	(1,800)	(2,500)	
Difference	500	1,200	1,500	
Times: Enacted tax rate	30%	35%	40%	
Deferred tax	150	420	600	1,170
2010 Tax expense		Plug to balance	7,170	
Deferred tax liability		Total from table above		1,170
Tax liability		20,000 × 30%		6,000

Reconciliation of Book and Taxable Income

Now that you have a good understanding of permanent and temporary differences, it is important to ensure that you can reconcile book income with taxable income and vice versa. Let's test your knowledge with an example.

EXAMPLE 13-6

BLP, Inc., had book income of $100,000 in 2010. However, the following permanent and temporary differences exist between its book and taxable income. BLP received $5,000 of municipal bond income. The company also paid $500 in life insurance premiums for the officers of the company. The company recorded $2,000 of cost depletion on the books, whereas percentage depletion for tax purposes was calculated as $3,000. BLP had an estimated warranty expense valued at $2,000 but paid out only $500 in actual warranty costs. The reconciliation of book income to taxable income is presented in Table 13-8.

TABLE 13-8 Reconciliation of Book Income to Taxable Income	
Book income	100,000
Municipal bond income	(5,000)
Included in book income	
Not taxable	
Life insurance premiums	500
Expensed on the books	
Nondeductible on the tax return	
Excess depletion	(1,000)
Cost depletion of $2,000 expensed on books	
% depletion of $3,000 deducted on tax return	
Warranty expense	1,500
Estimated $2,000 warranty expensed on books	
Actual $500 warranty cost deducted on tax return	
Taxable income	96,000

Well, that's all we have for you in the areas of permanent and temporary differences, deferred tax assets, deferred tax liabilities, and related reconciliations. Now that all this is complete, we have a question for you. Are any of you close to retirement? Even if you find yourself in the large class of people who probably are not, you will be one day. In Chapter 14 we will present information regarding accounting for pension plans of your company's employees.

QUIZ

1. **Which of the following is an example of a future taxable item?**
   A. Warranty expense when book expense is more than the tax deduction
   B. Contingent liability when book expense is more than the tax deduction
   C. Prepaid rent when book income is less than taxable income
   D. Depreciation expense when book expense is less than the tax deduction

2. **Which of the following is an example of a temporary difference?**
   A. Municipal bond interest
   B. Life insurance proceeds payable to a corporation
   C. Warranty expense
   D. Fines and penalties

Questions 3, 4, and 5 are based on the following information:

BLP, Inc., determined that the enacted tax rates are 30, 35, and 40 percent for 2009, 2010, and 2011 respectively. The taxable income for 2009 is $120,000. The book and tax depreciation for each year is shown in the table below:

	2009	2010	2011
Book depreciation	100,000	150,000	75,000
Tax depreciation	75,000	125,000	55,000

3. **In 2009, the deferred tax asset account should be**
   A. credited for $7,500.
   B. debited for $8,000.
   C. debited for $8,750.
   D. debited for $24,250.

4. **The current-year tax obligation is**
   A. $11,750.
   B. $28,500.
   C. $36,000.
   D. $43,500.

5. **The tax expense account should be credited for**
   A. $0.
   B. $11,750.
   C. $24,250.
   D. $36,000.

The following information is to be used to answer questions 6, 7, and 8:

On its December 31, 2009, balance sheet LJC, Inc., reported a deferred tax asset of $5,000. For 2010, financial income before taxes of $120,000 was reported.

As part of that income, the company had included municipal bond interest of $15,000. Additionally, the company had straight-line depreciation of $10,000 for the year recorded on its books, where as MACRS tax depreciation totaled $25,000 for the year. No other temporary or permanent differences existed on December 31, 2010. LJC's enacted tax rate for the current and future years is 20 percent.

6. **What is LJC's taxable income for 2010?**

   A. $90,000
   B. $105,000
   C. $120,000
   D. $95,000

7. **LJC's 2010 current year tax obligation is**

   A. $19,000.
   B. $18,000.
   C. $24,000.
   D. $21,000.

8. **Which of the following is a *true* statement?**

   A. $15,000 is a permanent difference.
   B. $25,000 is a permanent difference.
   C. $15,000 is a future deductible temporary difference.
   D. $15,000 is a future taxable temporary difference.

9. **On December 31, 2010, PJB, Inc., had the following deferred tax items:**
   - A deferred tax asset of $16,000 related to prepaid rent
   - A deferred tax liability of $10,000 related to long-term construction contracts
   - A deferred tax liability of $5,000 related to installment sales for 2011

   Which of the following, should be reported on PJB's balance sheet for 2010?

   A. A noncurrent deferred liability of $1,000
   B. A current deferred asset of $16,000 and a current deferred liability of $15,000
   C. A current deferred asset of $11,000 and a noncurrent deferred liability of $10,000
   D. A noncurrent deferred asset of $16,000 and a noncurrent deferred liability of $15,000

10. **J Unlimited had book income of $200,000 in 2010. Included within that income was $26,000 related to life insurance proceeds on its key officers. Additionally, the company had incurred $12,000 in fines related to illegal gambling activities. Rent on one of the company's buildings had been collected in the amount of $20,000, which constituted the outstanding rent payments for 2010. Based on this information, how many temporary differences must J Unlimited account for at the end of 2010?**

    A. One
    B. Two
    C. Three
    D. Zero

chapter 14

Pensions

CHAPTER OBJECTIVES

After completing this chapter, the student should

- Understand the financial statement presentation for pensions
- Understand definitions related to pension accounting
- Account for defined benefit pension plans
- Compute pension expense

Overview

Ah, retirement! It's the day that most people look forward to from the day they start working. Regardless of one's feelings toward the event, though, being prepared is still a wise choice. Luckily for many employees, after many years of dedicated service to their company or organization, their employers have their financial stability taken care of or at least partially so. While we are sure that you all want to know the best saving techniques to ensure that your little nest egg turns into a million or more dollars, providing you with a comfortable life throughout your days of relaxation, unfortunately, we will be disappointing you in that area. If only we knew ourselves! All we can help you with is the accounting, the accounting on the employer's side, that is.

Maybe you're an employer and realize how important determining and actually putting money away for your employees' pensions is. Even if you're not an owner or a top manager, though, someday you might be. Without the proper amount of funding and a good idea of when employees will be retiring, your organization could be in quite a pickle! Imagine arriving at the office one morning with a couple of notices of retirement from employees awaiting you. Not a big deal, you think, we should have enough money stashed away to cover those employees' pensions. Then a few months pass, and you receive a few more retirement notices. It doesn't even take a call to your financial expert to realize that you now have a problem.

Planning for pensions involves risk taking, but some of that risk can be mitigated with a good foundation in statistical, mainly probability theory and good decision making based on the results obtained from the application of such theory. Now, as accountants, we are not officially trained in this area. Some accountants could be, but it is more likely that an individual who specializes in actuarial science will develop the models. Then, once the modeling and funding rules have been established, that's when we enter the picture. Let's journey to that point now.

Financial Statement Presentation

Unlike in previous chapters where we have presented the proper financial statement presentation at the beginning, we believe that, because of the nature of this topic, it is better suited to one of our final discussions. We know you can hardly wait!

Definitions

A *defined benefit pension plan* is a plan that specifically states the actual benefits to be received by employees when they retire or the method of determining such benefits. A *defined contribution pension plan*, on the other hand, is a plan in which the employer's contribution to the employee's retirement is based on a formula. The benefits received by the employee on retirement are based on the amount of cash in the retirement account at that point.

Aside from having a defined benefit or a defined contribution, a plan also may be either funded or unfunded. A *funded pension plan* is a plan in which money (funds) is set up in a special account from which retirement payments are distributed. An *unfunded pension plan*, however, is a plan in which no funds are set aside, and retirement payments are made from existing resources.

A final question that must be asked in regard to the classification of plans is who exactly provides the retirement funds. In a *contributory pension plan*, both the employee and the employer make contributions. In a *noncontributory pension plan*, though, only the employee makes contributions.

Defined Benefit Pension Plans

Because of the poor economy and other changing societal and corporate conditions, defined benefit pension plans are not as prevalent today as they used to be. However, many such plans are still in existence. The Certified Public Accountant (CPA) exam focuses its pension related questions on defined benefit plans, and intermediate textbooks tend to devote the majority of their pension coverage to those plans as well. For these reasons, our focus in this chapter also will be on that area.

Just as tax expense does not usually equal tax liability because two sets of rules are in play, pensions are prone to such problems as well. The Financial Accounting Standards Board (FASB) has created rules concerning the amount that is to be debited to pension expense. The Employee Retirement Income Security Act (ERISA), however, has created mandates for the actual funding of plans that, in accounting, translates into a credit to cash. As you probably have already suspected, there must be another account to balance the entry. The balancer is *prepaid/accrued pension cost* or a similarly named account. If, at the end of the reporting period, the prepaid/accrued pension cost account has a debit balance, it will be reported as an asset. If, however, at the end of the reporting period, it has a credit balance, it will be reported as a liability.

Journal Entries

Let's stop here and go over the basic journal entries that are used for pension accounting. If pension expense equals pension funding, the journal entry (using assumed numbers) would be as follows:

Pension expense	200	
Cash		200

If pension expense is greater than pension funding, the journal entry (using assumed numbers) would be as follows:

Pension expense	200	
Prepaid/accrued pension cost		20
Cash		180

If pension expense is less than pension funding, the journal entry (using assumed numbers) would be as follows:

Pension expense	180	
Prepaid/accrued pension cost	20	
Cash		200

Obligation and Assets

Again, because of the different rule systems and companies not always setting aside enough money to satisfy their pension obligations, a plan may be either over- or underfunded. An *underfunded plan* surfaces when the projected benefit obligation is greater than the fair value of the plan assets. In other words, the company owes (obligation) more than it has funds set aside (plan assets) to cover. An *overfunded plan*, on the other hand, occurs when the fair value of the plan assets is greater than the projected benefit obligation. In this case, the company has more funds than liabilities, and this is a great position to be in!

Now, *pay attention*! You must understand this next concept. At the end of the year, the difference between the projected benefit obligation and the fair value of the plan assets must be calculated. The result represents the *required* ending balance in the prepaid/accrued pension cost account. If the value of the plan assets is greater than the obligation (overfunded), then the difference represents the required *debit* balance in the prepaid/accrued account. If, however, the obligation is greater than the plan assets (underfunded), the difference represents the required *credit* balance in the prepaid/accrued account.

Pension Expense

There are five components of pension expense. These components either will be provided in problems or you must be able to compute them. (In the real world, you will need to know where to find these items and/or how to calculate them.) Remember, pension expense is a debit in the journal entry.

Service cost is the first of the five components of pension expense. Service cost represents the pension benefits employees have earned in the current period. It is an amount determined through present value techniques and is computed by an actuary.

The second component is *interest cost*. Interest cost represents the interest that a company owes to its employees for benefits obtained while the employees are still working. It is computed by taking the beginning of the year balance in the projected benefit obligation and multiplying it by the discount rate used by the company. The interest cost then is added to service cost when computing pension expense.

The next component in the calculation of pension expense is the *expected return on plan assets*. The expected return equals the interest that the company expects to earn on the plan assets in the coming year. It is computed by multiplying the beginning of the year balance in the plan asset account by the long-term rate of return. Because the earnings on the plan assets ultimately will reduce the pension obligation (the interest earned is applied to the obligation to satisfy a portion of the total amount owed), the expected interest is subtracted in the computation of pension expense.

Amortization of any unrecognized prior service cost makes up the fourth component. Prior service cost represents the amount of any retroactive pension benefits granted to employees when either the pension plan is adopted or when it is amended. Because the retroactive benefits are often of a large magnitude, they are amortized to pension expense over several years. The amortization amount then is added to pension expense.

The amount of amortization to be recognized in a year may be determined on either a straight-line or what some intermediate textbooks refer to as *years-of-future-service basis*. Under the latter option, an equal amount of prior service cost is assigned to each qualifying employee for each future service period.

EXAMPLE 14-1

The easiest way to present this concept is with an example. Please refer to Table 14-1 for the related information. Note that the amortization listed in the amortization schedule for each year is added as a part of pension expense for the year.

The final item factored into pension expense is *any gain or loss*. Because the expected results are, as implied, estimates, they normally will not equal the actual results. Therefore, a gain or loss will occur.

To determine the gain or loss, the cumulative net loss or gain first must be obtained from the company's actuary. A corridor amount then must be calculated as either 10 percent of the actual projected benefit obligation (PBO) at the beginning of the year or 10 percent of the fair value of the plan assets at the beginning of the year, whichever is greater. The corridor is compared with the absolute value of the cumulative net loss or gain for the year. Whenever the absolute value of the cumulative amount exceeds the corridor, a net loss or gain (depending on if the cumulative amount is a gain or loss) results. The excess then is amortized over the average remaining service life of employees to determine the amount to be added to pension expense (a loss) or subtracted from pension expense (a gain).

TABLE 14-1 Years-of-Future-Service Method (Example 14-1)

Total prior service cost: $250,000

Employees	Expected Years of Future Service for Each Employee	Years Over Which Service Will Be Rendered					
		2010	2011	2012	2013	2014	Total
John, Sarah	3	2	2	2			
Jackie, Alex, Naomi	4	3	3	3	3		
Brenda, Tom, Kevin, Brandon	2	4	4				
Buck	5	1	1	1	1	1	
Total		10	10	6	4	1	31
Fraction		10/31	10/31	6/31	4/31	1/31	31/31

Amortization schedule:

Year	Total Prior Service Cost	Fraction	Amortization	Balance in Prior Service Cost
2010	250,000	10/31	80,645	169,355
2011	250,000	10/31	80,645	88,710
2012	250,000	6/31	48,387	40,323
2013	250,000	4/31	32,258	8,065
2014	250,000	1/31	8,065	0
			250,000	

EXAMPLE 14-2

Let's refer to Table 14-2 for this example.

TABLE 14-2	Net Gain/Loss Calculations					
Average remaining service life of employees: 10 years						
Year	Cumulative Net Loss (Gain)	PBO	FV Plan Assets	Corridor	Excess Net Loss (Gain)	Amortized Excess
2010	10,000	100,000	150,000	15,000	–	–
2011	20,000	125,000	120,000	12,500	7,500	750
2012	(18,000)	145,000	110,000	14,500	(3,500)	(350)
2013	(5,000)	130,000	115,000	13,000	–	–

Step-By-Step Procedure

As with many topics in this book, we have developed a step-by-step process for working out defined benefit pension problems. It is *imperative* that these steps be completed in their entirety before proceeding to the next step. If you follow these steps exactly, you should have no problem understanding and working defined benefit pension problems. Please refer to Table 14-3 for the suggested procedure.

TABLE 14-3	Step-by-Step Procedure
1.	Set up T–accounts for plan assets, projected benefit obligation, and prepaid/accrued pension cost.
2.	Post interest incurred on the beginning balance of projected benefit obligation.
3.	Post actual interest earned on the beginning balance of plan assets.
4.	Post payments to retirees.
	Debit projected benefit obligation
	Credit plan assets
5.	Compute pension expense.
6.	Make the journal entry to record pension expense.
7.	Post amount funded as a debit to plan assets.
	Post service cost as a credit to projected benefit obligation.
	Post amount from step 6 to prepaid/accrued pension cost account.
8.	Calculate the ending balances of plan assets, projected benefit obligation, and prepaid/accrued.
9.	Determine if there is underfunding or overfunding and if an entry needs to be made to prepaid/accrued to reflect the required balance.
	Underfunding = obligation > plan assets; prepaid/accrued must have a credit balance equal to the difference
	Overfunding = plan assets > obligation; prepaid/accrued must have a debit balance equal to the difference

EXAMPLE 14-3

We will use the step-by-step procedure to illustrate how to work out a sample problem. The data for the example is presented in Table 14-4. You must pay attention to each step and read each word carefully. We suggest that, using the procedure, you work the problem out on your own before looking at the solution.

TABLE 14-4   Data for Example 14-3

	Year 1	Year 2	Year 3
Service cost	200,000	230,000	250,000
Interest cost	10%	10%	10%
Actual interest earned	14%	14%	14%
Expected interest earned	12%	12%	12%
Amount funded	225,000	250,000	275,000
Payments to retirees	0.00	10,000	10,000

For each year, follow each step presented in Table 14-3, and use the data from Table 14-4. We have provided the resulting T-accounts in Table 14-5, the computation for pension expense in Table 14-6, and the journal entries in Table 14-7.

TABLE 14-5 T-Accounts for Example 14-3

Plan Assets

Debit		Credit	
Beg bal	0	0	
Yr 1 actual interest earned	0	0	Yr 1 payments to retirees
Yr 1 funding	225,000		
Yr 2 beg bal	225,000		
Yr 2 actual interest earned	31,500	10,000	Yr 2 payments to retirees
Yr 2 funding	250,000		
Yr 3 beg bal	496,500		
Yr 3 actual interest earned	69,510	10,000	Yr 3 payments to retirees
Yr 3 funding	275,000		
Yr 4 beg bal	831,010		

Projected Benefit Obligation

Debit		Credit	
		Beg bal	0
		Yr 1 interest incurred	0
		Yr 1 service cost	200,000
Yr 1 payments to retirees	0		
		Yr 2 beg bal	200,000
		Yr 2 interest incurred	20,000
		Yr 2 service cost	230,000
Yr 2 payments to retirees	10,000		
		Yr 3 beg bal	440,000
		Yr 3 interest incurred	44,000
		Yr 3 service cost	250,000
Yr 3 payments to retirees	10,000		
		Yr 4 beg bal	724,000

Prepaid/Accrued Pension Cost

Yr 1	25,000
Yr 2	27,000
Balance	52,000
Yr 2 additional entry	4,500
Balance	56,500
Yr 3	40,580
Balance	97,080
Yr 3 additional entry	9,930
Balance	107,010

TABLE 14-6 Computation of Pension Expense for Example 14-3

		Year 1
1. Service cost		200,000
2. Interest incurred	0.00 × 10%	0
3. Expected interest earned	0.00 × 12%	0
4. Amortization of PSC		0
5. Gain/loss		0
Pension expense		200,000
		Year 2
1. Service cost		230,000
2. Interest incurred	200,000 × 10%	20,000
3. Expected interest earned	225,000 × 12%	(27,000)
4. Amortization of PSC		–
5. Gain/loss		–
Pension expense		223,000
		Year 3
1. Service cost		250,000
2. Interest incurred	440,000 × 10%	44,000
3. Expected interest earned	496,500 × 12%	(59,580)
4. Amortization of PSC		–
5. Gain/loss		–
Pension expense		234,420

For year 1, please notice that an additional adjustment is not needed for the prepaid/accrued pension cost account. However, adjustments are needed for years 2 and 3. When an adjustment is needed, the offsetting account is other comprehensive income, which is reported in stockholders' equity on the balance sheet.

TABLE 14-7 Journal Entries for Example 14-3

Year 1	Pension expense		200,000	
	Prepaid/accrued pension cost		25,000	
	Cash			225,000
	Plan assets balance	225,000		
	Obligation balance	(200,000)		
	Required balance in prepd/acc.	25,000		
	Prepaid/accrued balance	25,000		
	No adjustment necessary	0		
Year 2	Pension expense		223,000	
	Prepaid/accrued pension cost		27,000	
	Cash			250,000
	Plan assets balance	496,500		
	Obligation balance	(440,000)		
	Required balance in prepd/acc.	56,500		
	Prepaid/accrued balance	(52,000)		
	Adjustment needed	4,500		
	Prepaid/accrued pension cost		4,500	
	Other comprehensive income			4,500
Year 3	Pension expense		234,420	
	Prepaid/accrued pension cost		40,580	
	Cash			275,000
	Plan assets balance	831,010		
	Obligation balance	(724,000)		
	Required balance in prepd/acc.	107,010		
	Prepaid/accrued balance	(97,080)		
	Adjustment needed	9,930		
	Prepaid/accrued pension cost		9,930	
	Other comprehensive income			9,930

Financial Statement Presentation—For Real This Time

Okay, so now you know that a pension plan can be either overfunded, in which the plan assets are greater than the projected benefit obligation and you have an asset, or underfunded, in which the projected benefit obligation is greater than the plan assets and you have a liability. From early chapters and your basic accounting knowledge, you know where assets and liabilities are found in the financial statements, the balance sheet, right? The only question left unanswered is whether that asset or liability is current or noncurrent. Whenever you have an overfunded plan, it is *always* reported as a noncurrent asset. When you have an underfunded plan, though, there is a comparison or two that need to be made to determine the proper reporting status. For such comparisons, one additional fact beyond what has already been covered will need to be known. This piece of information is how much of the projected benefit obligation is expected to be paid within the next 12 months. This "current" expected payment then is compared with the fair value of the plan assets. If the current expected payment exceeds the plan asset value, the plan liability will be reported as a current liability to the extent of that excess, with any remaining portion of the full liability reported as a noncurrent liability. For an example of this, please see Table 14-8. Note that when a company has multiple pension plans, the funding status must be calculated separately for each. As a result, a company may report both a pension asset and a pension liability on its balance sheet for a single reporting date.

Okay, so how about other comprehensive income (OCI)? It has the word *income* in its name, so it must be reported on the income statement, right? You are partially correct. Depending on the preference of the particular company, the amount of OCI reported in the *current* period may appear as an addition to the traditional income statement, on a separate statement of comprehensive income, or on a statement of changes in stockholders' equity. Both current and previously recognized OCI that has not yet been reversed should be aggregated and reported in the stockholders' equity section of the balance sheet.

Retirement is complex in so many ways. Hopefully, after completing this chapter, you will have a clearer idea about defined benefit plans and the calculation of pension expense. In Chapter 15 we will move on to a different category of expenses—leases.

TABLE 14-8 BLP's Pension Plan and Partial Balance Sheet, December 31, 2010

	Plan X	Plan Y
FV of plan assets	$10,000,000	$8,000,000
PBO	7,500,000	12,000,000
Expected PBO payments in next 12 months	5,000,000	9,500,000
FV of plan assets	$10,000,000	$8,000,000
Less: PBO	7,500,000	12,000,000
Over(under)funded status	$2,500,000	($4,000,000)
Current asset:	$2,500,000	
Current liability:		
Expected PBO payments in next 12 months		$9,500,000
Less: FV of plan assets		8,000,000
Excess to be reported as current		$1,500,000
Noncurrent liability:		$2,500,000

BLP, Inc.
Partial Balance Sheet
December 31, 2010

Assets

Current assets:

Pension asset	$2,500,000

Liabilities

Current liabilities:

Pension liability	$1,500,000

Noncurrent liabilities:

Pension liability	$2,500,000

QUIZ

1. **Which of the following is *not* a component of pension expense?**
   A. Service cost
   B. Actual interest cost incurred on the beginning balance of the projected benefit obligation
   C. Actual interest earned on the beginning balance of plan assets
   D. Expected interest earned on the beginning balance of plan assets

2. **What amounts are credited to plan assets?**
   A. Actual interest earned on the beginning balance of plan assets
   B. Expected interest earned on the beginning balance of plan assets
   C. Amount funded
   D. Payments to retirees

3. **What amount is credited to projected benefit obligation?**
   A. Payments to retirees
   B. Amount funded
   C. Service cost
   D. Expected interest incurred on the beginning balance of projected benefit obligation

4. **When the pension plan is underfunded**
   A. the projected benefit obligation is greater than the fair value of the plan assets.
   B. the projected benefit obligation is less than the fair value of the plan assets.
   C. the projected benefit obligation equals the fair value of the plan assets.
   D. None of these answers are correct.

5. **The prepaid/accrued pension cost account may need an additional adjustment when**
   A. the pension plan is overfunded.
   B. the pension plan is underfunded.
   C. the service cost does not equal the amount funded.
   D. Both A and B are correct.

   Use the following information and the data in the table below to answer questions 6 to 10.

   Obligation payments expected to be paid to employees:

   2011 = $230,000

Cumulative net loss(gain):

2010 = $16,000
Prior service cost = $150,000

Assume total expected future years of service:
2010 = 10
2011 = 7
2012 = 3

Average remaining service life of employees for gain/loss recognition = 20 years

Balance of plan assets on December 31, 2009 = $100,000

Balance of PBO on December 31, 2009 = $125,000

	2010
Service cost	$150,000
Interest cost	10%
Actual interest earned	15%
Expected interest	13%
Amount funded	$100,000
Payments to retirees	$25,000

6. What is the amortization of the prior service cost, if any, for 2010?
   A. $15,000
   B. $150,000
   C. $75,000
   D. $7,500

7. What amount of loss (gain) should be reported as a part of interest expense for 2010?
   A. $175
   B. $1,750
   C. $300
   D. ($175)

8. What is the pension expense for 2010?
   A. $147,325
   B. $224,675
   C. $222,500
   D. $224,500

9. **What should be the adjusting journal entry to the prepaid/accrued account and OCI at the end of 2010?**

   A. Debit OCI and credit prepaid/accrued for $52,175.
   B. Debit prepaid/accrued and credit OCI for $72,500.
   C. Debit prepaid/accrued and credit OCI for $52,175.
   D. No adjusting entry is needed.

10. **How should the pension plan be reported on the balance sheet at the end of 2010?**

    A. As a current asset for the amount of $72,500
    B. As a noncurrent liability for the amount of $72,500
    C. As a current liability for the amount of $72,500
    D. As a current liability for the amount of $40,000 and a noncurrent liability for the amount of $32,500

chapter 15

Leases

CHAPTER OBJECTIVES

After completing this chapter, the student should

- Understand the financial statement presentation for leases
- Understand the difference between an operating lease and a capital lease
- Understand how to determine the classification of a capital lease
- Account for an operating lease from both the lessee's and the lessor's perspectives
- Account for a direct financing lease from both the lessee's and the lessor's perspectives
- Account for a sales-type lease from both the lessee's and the lessor's perspectives
- Understand bargain purchase options
- Understand guaranteed/unguaranteed residual value
- Understand initial direct costs of the lessor
- Understand sale leasebacks
- Understand the required disclosures for leases

Overview

Have you ever wanted something but only needed to use it for a short while? Maybe it was a hammer or a karaoke machine. You may have decided that it was worth purchasing the item rather than asking all your friends if they had one that you could borrow. With any luck, you actually might use the product again, and it wasn't that expensive. How about a boat, though, for those two years you lived by the ocean. You knew that you were going to live there only for a short while and afterward would move somewhere inland and would barely have time to do the things you needed to do, let alone anything fun. You just couldn't justify spending thousands of dollars for something that would be used for such a short time. Lucky for you, there is something known as a *lease*.

Leases are obtained as opposed to purchasing for a variety of reasons. Sometimes the potential buyer is worried about the item soon becoming obsolete, and a lease is a way to hedge the risk. Often any claims against the party obtaining the asset can be exercised only against the leased asset itself rather than all the party's possessions. Leases also allow one to pull one over on Uncle Sam because the entire amount of the leased asset can be written off and usually more quickly than under a purchase arrangement. In some cases, as you will soon see, an asset and corresponding liability even may be kept off the books. Yes, that is what you would call legal off-balance-sheet financing. Ah, the power of leases! So let's hit the waves—oh, wait a second, we mean leases.

Financial Statement Presentation

Two new accounts will be covered in this chapter. The first account, *leased equipment under capital lease*, can be thought of as a new asset and can be treated in a manner similar to that of a purchased asset. The account is reported on the balance sheet and is classified as an asset, usually in the property, plant, and equipment section. The second new account, *obligation under capital leases*, is treated as a liability on the balance sheet. Therefore, like other liabilities, the obligation under capital lease is separated into appropriate current and non-current amounts.

General Information

A lease enables use of an asset, usually for an extended period of time, without an actual purchase. One of the primary business advantages to leasing an asset versus purchasing that same asset is that the full amount of the lease payment is deductible on a tax return. When a purchase is made, only part of the cost of the asset can be written off on the tax return as depreciation expense each year.

There are two types of leases for generally accepted accounting principles (GAAP) purposes—operating and capital. An *operating lease* has the characteristics of what most people normally would dub a lease. With each payment, the lessee (individual or organization desiring use of the asset) records lease expense, and the lessor (the individual or organization that owns the asset and is willing to loan it out to others for a fee) records lease revenue. A *capital lease* is a bit more complex. You can think of it as a virtual sale and purchase of the leased asset. The rights and benefits of ownership are transferred to the lessee, and the lessee virtually "owns" the asset. After briefly presenting the accounting treatment for an operating lease, we will spend the majority of this chapter describing capital leases.

Classification of Leases

As we have already mentioned, leases may be either operating or capital. How, though, can you tell the difference? To help you with the determination and proper accounting treatment for leases, there is a set of if-then rules that must be followed. Some identifying criteria as well as the rules are listed below. Whether one, some, all, or none of the criteria presented below are present for a particular lease must be determined first.

1. The lessee obtains ownership of the property by the end of the lease term.
2. There is a bargain purchase option attached to the lease. In other words, the lessee takes ownership of the asset by the end of the lease term by paying a relatively small amount of money.
3. The lease term is equal to 75 percent or more of the life of the leased property.
4. The present value (PV) of the minimum lease payments (MLP) is equal to 90 percent or more of the fair market value (FMV) of the leased property.

To be considered a capital lease, the lease first must meet one of the preceding four criteria. If none of the criteria are met, the lease is immediately deemed an operating lease.

If a lease meets the first-round qualifications for capital treatment, then another set of criteria are considered. The second-round capital treatment qualifications are a bit stricter; two criteria (rather than one or the other) must be satisfied for the lease to be recorded in a capital fashion. Those criteria are listed below.

1. The lessor is reasonably assured to collect the MLP.
2. There are no uncertainties from the lessor's standpoint regarding any additional costs to be incurred by the lessor.

Making comparisons based on the preceding process successfully allows for the proper classification of a lease into the operating or capital category from both the lessee's and lessor's viewpoints. A lessor makes even more precise categorizations, but we will discuss those in a bit.

Operating Leases—Lessee's Perspective

From the lessee's perspective, the journal entries needed to record an operating lease on the books are quite simple. No asset is reported on the books. However, a disclosure stating the future minimum lease payments must be included with the financial statements. The only item actually recorded is the rent expense paid. Thus the journal entry at the time of payment would be as follows:

Rent expense

Cash

If some of the rent expense paid for the leased asset is for the asset's use in a future period, the unexpired portion of the expense should be reported on the balance sheet as prepaid rent.

Operating Leases—Lessor's Perspective

From the lessor's perspective, the asset being leased is owned property, plant, or equipment of the company and is recorded as such on the company's balance sheet. As a result, all depreciation charges at the end of a reporting period on the leased equipment must be recorded and charged to the lessor's books. For all operating leases, the leased asset is depreciated over the economic life of the asset. Additionally, because the lessor normally is responsible for any executory costs that may be incurred related to the leased asset, such expenses also must be recognized by the lessor. Of course, since another party is paying the lessor for use of the equipment, the rental payments are recorded as revenue upon their realization. The possible lessor journal entries should seem familiar and are as follows:

To record the purchase of equipment to be leased:

Equipment leased to others

Cash

To record the depreciation on the leased equipment:

Depreciation expense—Equipment leased to others

Accumulated depreciation—Equipment leased to others

To record insurance on the equipment, an executory cost:

Insurance expense

        Cash

To record rental payments received:

Cash

        Rental revenue

Capital Leases

From the standpoint of the lessor, if a lease is a capital lease, it can be either a direct-financing lease or a sales-type lease. The distinguishing characteristic is a profit component. A *direct-financing lease* does not have a profit component, whereas a *sales-type lease* does.

Another factor that must be considered with capital leases is whether the payments are paid at the *end* of a period (ordinary annuity) or at the *beginning* of a period (annuity due). As annuities, both types of payments must be equal in amount, the length of time between payments must be equal, the interest rate must be constant, and the interest must be compounded according to ordinary annuity or annuity due treatment.

We have two final comments regarding capital leases. If either ownership is transferred or a bargain purchase option exists, the lessee depreciates the asset over its economic life. However, if neither of those characteristics is present, the lease is depreciated over the lease term. Additionally, the present value of the minimum lease payments is determined using the lower of the lessee's incremental borrowing rate or the lessor's interest rate that is implicit in the lease if it is either known or easily obtainable.

Okay, now that you have some background information, let's look at some examples for capital leases.

Direct Financing—Ordinary Annuity

Recall that to be a direct financing lease, the lease first must meet the criteria for a capital lease, and a profit component cannot be included. Additionally, recall that to qualify for ordinary annuity status, the payments must be made at the end of the period.

 EXAMPLE 15-1

BLP, Inc., leased an asset to another company on January 1, 2010. The lease is for four years. The asset has an estimated life of five years. BLP paid $50,000 for the asset when the company purchased it on December 20, 2009.

TABLE 15-1 Decision Chart (Example 15-1)

1	Transfer of ownership	Yes
2	Bargain purchase option	No
3	Life of lease = 75% or more of life of asset (4/5 = 0.8 → 80%)	Yes
4	PV MLP: 90% or more FMV of leased asset $15,774 × 3.169865 = $50,001.45 →MLP = 100% of FMV	Yes
1	Collectibility reasonably assured	Yes
2	No important uncertainties	Yes
Decision:	Capital lease for both lessee and lessor	

The lessee will pay BLP $15,774 each December 31 for four years. After the fourth payment, title will transfer to the lessee. The lessee's incremental borrowing rate is 10 percent, and the interest rate implicit in the lease is also 10 percent. From BLP's perspective, the collectibility is reasonably assured, and there are no important uncertainties. The lessee has agreed to pay insurance of $1,000 and taxes of $500 annually on December 31 of each year. Refer to Table 15-1 for the decision chart to determine whether or not this is a capital lease.

We highly recommend always completing an amortization schedule prior to making any journal entries. Refer to Table 15-2 for the amortization schedule related to this example.

Now you are ready for the journal entries. Refer to Table 15-3 for the journal entries for both the lessee and the lessor. Notice that the lessee depreciates the asset over the asset's life of five years and not the life of the lease (four years) because of the transfer of ownership.

TABLE 15-2 Amortization Schedule (Example 15-1)

Date	Payment	10% Interest	Principle	Book Value
1/1/10				50,000
12/31/10	15,774	5,000	10,774	39,226
12/31/11	15,774	3,923	11,851	27,375
12/31/12	15,774	2,737	13,037	14,338
12/31/13	15,774	1,436	14,338	(0)

TABLE 15-3 Journal Entries (Example 15-1)

Lessee

Date	Account		Debit	Credit
	Initial recording			
1/1/10	Leased equipment under capital lease		50,000	
	Obligation under capital lease			50,000
	Record payment of principle and interest			
12/31/10	Obligation under capital lease		10,774	
	Interest expense		5,000	
	Cash			15,774
	Record depreciation expense			
12/31/10	Depreciation expense	50,000/5	10,000	
	Accumulated depreciation			10,000
	Record executory costs			
12/31/10	Insurance expense		1,000	
	Taxes		500	
	Cash			1,500

Lessor

Date	Account	Debit	Credit
	Initial recording		
1/1/10	Minimum lease payments receivable	63,096	
	Asset		50,000
	Unearned interest revenue		13,096
	Record receipt of principle and interest		
12/31/10	Cash	15,774	
	Minimum lease payments receivable		15,774
	Unearned interest revenue	5,000	
	Interest revenue		5,000

TABLE 15-3 *(Continued)*

Lessee			Lessor		
Record payment of principle and interest			**Record receipt of principle and interest**		
12/31/11 Obligation under capital lease	11,851		12/31/11 Cash	15,774	
Interest expense	3,923		Minimum lease payments receivable		15,774
Cash		15,774	Unearned interest revenue	3,923	
			Interest revenue		3,923
Record depreciation expense					
12/31/11 Depreciation expense	50,000/5 10,000				
Accumulated depreciation		10,000			
Record executory costs					
12/31/11 Insurance expense	1,000				
Taxes	500				
Cash		1,500			
Record payment of principle and interest			**Record receipt of principle and interest**		
12/31/12 Obligation under capital lease	13,037		12/31/12 Cash	15,774	
Interest expense	2,737		Minimum lease payments receivable		15,774
Cash		15,774	Unearned interest revenue	2,737	
			Interest revenue		2,737
Record depreciation expense					
12/31/12 Depreciation expense	50,000/5 10,000				
Accumulated depreciation		10,000			

Record executory costs

Date	Account		
12/31/12	Insurance expense	1,000	
	Taxes	500	
	Cash		1,500

Record payment of principle and interest

Date	Account		
12/31/13	Obligation under capital lease	14,338	
	Interest expense	1,436	
	Cash		15,774

Record depreciation expense

Date	Account		
12/31/13	Depreciation expense	50,000/5	10,000	
	Accumulated depreciation		10,000

Record executory costs

Date	Account		
12/31/13	Insurance expense	1,000	
	Taxes	500	
	Cash		1,500

Record depreciation expense

Date	Account		
12/31/14	Depreciation expense	50,000/5	10,000	
	Accumulated depreciation		10,000

Record receipt of principle and interest

Date	Account		
12/31/13	Cash	15,774	
	Minimum lease payments receivable		15,774
	Unearned interest revenue	1,436	
	Interest revenue		1,436

Direct Financing—Annuity Due

Recall that to be a direct financing lease, the lease first must meet the criteria for a capital lease, and a profit component cannot be included. Additionally, recall that to qualify for annuity due status, the payments must be made at the beginning of the period.

EXAMPLE 15-2

BLP, Inc., leased an asset to another company on January 1, 2010. The lease is for four years. The asset has an estimated life of five years. BLP paid $34,869 for the asset when the company purchased it on December 20, 2009. The lessee will pay BLP $10,000 each January 1 for four years beginning immediately. After the fourth payment, title will transfer to the lessee. The lessee's incremental borrowing rate is 10 percent, and the interest rate implicit in the lease is 12 percent. From BLP's perspective, the collectibility is reasonably assured, and there are no important uncertainties. The lessee has agreed to pay insurance of $1,000 and taxes of $500 annually on December 31 of each year. Refer to Table 15-4 for the decision chart to determine whether or not this is a capital lease.

We highly recommend always completing an amortization schedule prior to making any journal entries. Refer to Table 15-5 for the amortization schedule related to this example. Note that the interest rate used is the lessee's 10 percent incremental borrowing rate because it is less than the 12 percent rate implicit in the lease. Before proceeding, make sure that you understand the process. Because the payments are made at the beginning of the period, unlike with an ordinary annuity, the entire amount of the payment is immediately subtracted from the balance (book value) on

TABLE 15-4 Decision Chart (Example 15-2)		
1	Transfer of ownership	Yes
2	Bargain purchase option	No
3	Life of lease = 75% or more of life of asset (4/5 = 0.8 → 80%)	Yes
4	PV MLP: 90% or more FMV of leased asset $10,000 × 3.486852 = $34,869 →MLP = 100% of FMV	Yes
1	Collectibility reasonably assured	Yes
2	No important uncertainties	Yes
Decision:	Capital lease for both lessee and lessor	

TABLE 15-5	Amortization Schedule (Example 15-2)			
Date	**Payment**	**10% Interest**	**Principle**	**Book Value**
1/1/10				34,869
1/1/10	10,000		10,000	24,869
12/31/10		2,487		27,356
1/1/11	10,000		10,000	17,356
12/31/11		1,736		19,091
1/1/12	10,000		10,000	9,091
12/31/12		908		10,000
1/1/13	10,000		10,000	(0)

January 1 of each year. On December 31 of each year, when the interest has accrued, it is added back to the balance (book value) to recognize that some of the beginning payment was intended to pay interest. The amount of that interest, however, is determined based on the full amount of the beginning-of-period payment being subtracted from the book value.

Now you are ready for the journal entries. Refer to Table 15-6 for the journal entries for both the lessee and the lessor. Notice that the lessee depreciates the asset over the asset's life of five years and not the life of the lease (four years) because there is a transfer of ownership at the end of the lease.

Sales Type—Ordinary Annuity

Recall that to be a sales type lease, the lease first must meet the criteria for a capital lease, and then a profit element must be included. Additionally, recall that to qualify for ordinary annuity status, payments must be made at the end of the period.

EXAMPLE 15-3

BLP, Inc., leased an asset to another company on January 1, 2010. The lease is for four years. The asset has an estimated life of five years. BLP paid $50,000 for the asset when the company purchased it on December 20, 2009. The FMV of the asset as of January 1, 2010, is $70,000. The lessee will pay BLP $20,000 each January 1 for four years beginning December 31, 2010. After the fourth payment, the asset will revert back to BLP. The lessee's incremental borrowing rate is 13 percent, and the interest rate implicit in the lease is 10 percent. From BLP's perspective, the collectibility is

TABLE 15-6 Journal Entries (Example 15-2)

Lessee

Initial recording

Date	Account	Debit	Credit
1/1/10	Leased equipment under capital lease	34,869	
	Obligation under capital lease		34,869

Record payment of principle and interest

Date	Account	Debit	Credit
1/1/10	Obligation under capital lease	10,000	
	Cash		10,000

Accrue interest at year end

Date	Account	Debit	Credit
12/31/10	Interest expense	2,487	
	Obligation under capital lease		2,487

Record depreciation expense

Date	Account	Debit	Credit
12/31/10	Depreciation expense 34,869/5	6,974	
	Accumulated depreciation		6,974

Record executory costs

Date	Account	Debit	Credit
12/31/10	Insurance expense	1,000	
	Taxes	500	
	Cash		1,500

Record payment of principle and interest

Date	Account	Debit	Credit
1/1/11	Obligation under capital lease	10,000	
	Cash		10,000

Accrue interest at year end

Date	Account	Debit	Credit
12/31/11	Interest expense	1,736	
	Obligation under capital lease		1,736

Lessor

Initial recording

Date	Account	Debit	Credit
1/1/10	Minimum lease payments receivable	40,000	
	Asset		34,869
	Unearned interest revenue		5,131

Record receipt of principle and interest

Date	Account	Debit	Credit
1/1/10	Cash	10,000	
	Minimum lease payments receivable		10,000

Accrue interest at year end

Date	Account	Debit	Credit
12/31/10	Unearned interest revenue	2,487	
	Interest revenue		2,487

Record receipt of principle and interest

Date	Account	Debit	Credit
1/1/11	Cash	10,000	
	Minimum lease payments receivable		10,000

Accrue interest at year end

Date	Account	Debit	Credit
12/31/11	Unearned interest revenue	1,736	
	Interest revenue		1,736

Record depreciation expense

Date	Account	Debit	Credit
12/31/11	Depreciation expense 34,869/5	6,974	
	Accumulated depreciation		6,974

Record executory costs

Date	Account	Debit	Credit
12/31/11	Insurance expense	1,000	
	Taxes	500	
	Cash		1,500

Record payment of principle and interest

Date	Account	Debit	Credit
1/1/12	Obligation under capital lease	10,000	
	Cash		10,000

Accrue interest at year end

Date	Account	Debit	Credit
12/31/12	Interest expense	908	
	Obligation under capital lease		908

Record depreciation expense

Date	Account	Debit	Credit
12/31/12	Depreciation expense 34,869/5	6,974	
	Accumulated depreciation		6,974

Record executory costs

Date	Account	Debit	Credit
12/31/12	Insurance expense	1,000	
	Taxes	500	
	Cash		1,500

Record payment of principle and interest

Date	Account	Debit	Credit
1/1/13	Obligation under capital lease	10,000	
	Cash		10,000

Record receipt of principle and interest

Date	Account	Debit	Credit
1/1/12	Cash	10,000	
	Minimum lease payments receivable		10,000

Accrue interest at year end

Date	Account	Debit	Credit
12/31/12	Unearned interest revenue	908	
	Interest revenue		908

Record receipt of principle and interest

Date	Account	Debit	Credit
1/1/13	Cash	10,000	
	Minimum lease payments receivable		10,000

TABLE 15-6 (*Continued*)

		Lessee		Lessor
	Record depreciation expense			
12/31/13	Depreciation expense	34,869/5	6,974	
	Accumulated depreciation			6,974
	Record executory costs			
12/31/13	Insurance expense		1,000	
	Taxes		500	
	Cash			1,500
	Record depreciation expense			
12/31/14	Depreciation expense	34,869/5	6,974	
	Accumulated depreciation			6,974

TABLE 15-7	Decision Chart (Example 15-3)	
1	Transfer of ownership	No
2	Bargain purchase option	No
3	Life of lease = 75% or more of life of asset (4/5 = 0.8 → 80%)	Yes
4	PV MLP: 90% or more FMV of leased asset $20,000 × 3.169865 = $63,397 $63,397/$70,000 = 0.9056 →MLP = 91% of FMV	Yes
1	Collectibility reasonably assured	Yes
2	No important uncertainties	Yes
Decision:	Capital lease for both lessee and lessor	

reasonably assured, and there are no important uncertainties. The lessee has agreed to pay insurance of $1,000 and taxes of $500 annually on December 31 of each year. Refer to Table 15-7 for the decision chart to determine whether or not this is a capital lease.

We highly recommend always completing an amortization schedule prior to making any journal entries. Refer to Table 15-8 for the amortization schedule related to this example. Note that the interest rate used is the 10 percent rate implicit in the lease because it is less than the 13 percent incremental borrowing rate of the lessee. The calculations for the amortization table for ordinary annuity sales type leases are the same as those for the amortization of ordinary annuity direct financing leases.

Now you are ready for the journal entries. Refer to Table 15-9 for the journal entries for both the lessee and the lessor. Notice that the lessee depreciates the asset over the period of the lease (four years) because there is not a transfer of ownership or a bargain purchase option at the end of the lease. Notice that the entries for the lessee are identical to those for

TABLE 15-8	Amortization Schedule (Example 15-3)			
Date	Payment	10% Interest	Principle	Book Value
1/1/10				63,397
12/31/10	20,000	6,340	13,660	49,737
12/31/11	20,000	4,974	15,026	34,710
12/31/12	20,000	3,471	16,529	18,181
12/31/13	20,000	1,818	18,182	(0)

TABLE 15-9 Journal Entries (Example 15-3)

Lessee

Initial recording

Date	Account	Debit	Credit
1/1/10	Leased equipment under capital lease	63,397	
	Obligation under capital lease		63,397

Record payment of principle and interest

Date	Account	Debit	Credit
12/31/10	Obligation under capital lease	13,660	
	Interest expense	6,340	
	Cash		20,000

Record depreciation expense

Date	Account	Debit	Credit
12/31/10	Depreciation expense 63,397/4	15,849	
	Accumulated depreciation		15,849

Record executory costs

Date	Account	Debit	Credit
12/31/10	Insurance expense	1,000	
	Taxes	500	
	Cash		1,500

Lessor

Initial recording

Date	Account	Debit	Credit
1/1/10	Minimum lease payments receivable	80,000	
	Sales revenue		63,397
	Unearned interest revenue		16,603
1/1/10	COGS	50,000	
	Asset		50,000

Record receipt of principle and interest

Date	Account	Debit	Credit
12/31/10	Cash	20,000	
	Minimum lease payments receivable		20,000
	Unearned interest revenue	6,340	
	Interest revenue		6,340

Record payment of principle and interest

12/31/11	Obligation under capital lease	15,026	
	Interest expense	4,974	
	Cash		20,000

Record depreciation expense

12/31/11	Depreciation expense	63,397/4	15,849	
	Accumulated depreciation		15,849

Record executory costs

12/31/11	Insurance expense	1,000	
	Taxes	500	
	Cash		1,500

Record payment of principle and interest

12/31/12	Obligation under capital lease	16,529	
	Interest expense	3,471	
	Cash		20,000

Record depreciation expense

12/31/12	Depreciation expense	63,397/4	15,849	
	Accumulated depreciation		15,849

Record receipt of principle and interest

12/31/11	Cash	20,000	
	Minimum lease payments receivable		20,000
	Unearned interest revenue	4,974	
	Interest revenue		4,974

Record receipt of principle and interest

12/31/12	Cash	20,000	
	Minimum lease payments receivable		20,000
	Unearned interest revenue	3,471	
	Interest revenue		3,471

TABLE 15-9 (Continued)

Lessee

Record executory costs

		Debit	Credit
12/31/12	Insurance expense	1,000	
	Taxes	500	
	Cash		1,500

Record payment of principle and interest

		Debit	Credit
12/31/13	Obligation under capital lease	18,182	
	Interest expense	1,818	
	Cash		20,000

Record depreciation expense

		Debit	Credit
12/31/13	Depreciation expense 63,397/4	15,849	
	Accumulated depreciation		15,849

Record executory costs

		Debit	Credit
12/31/13	Insurance expense	1,000	
	Taxes	500	
	Cash		1,500

Lessor

Record receipt of principle and interest

		Debit	Credit
12/31/13	Cash	20,000	
	Minimum lease payments receivable		20,000
	Unearned interest revenue	1,818	
	Interest revenue		1,818

a direct financing lease. Those for the lessor, however, differ. The asset is still taken off the lessor's books, but rather than doing so as part of the minimum lease payment receivable entry, the asset is removed with a simultaneous debit to cost of goods sold (COGS). Therefore, the additional credit that accompanies the unearned interest revenue to balance the debit to minimum lease payments receivable must be to sales revenue. As a result, the difference between the sales revenue and COGS represents the profit element included in the lease. The entries for the subsequent years do not differ from those made for a direct financing lease.

NOTE *The journal entries to take the leased asset off the lessee's books and again place the asset on the lessor's records at the end of the lease's term are not reflected in this example.*

Sales Type—Annuity Due

Recall that to be a sales type lease, the lease first must meet the criteria for a capital lease, and then a profit element must be included. Additionally, recall that to qualify for annuity due status, the payments must be made at the beginning of the period.

EXAMPLE 15-4

BLP, Inc., leased an asset to another company on January 1, 2010. The lease is for four years. The asset has an estimated life of five years. BLP paid $50,000 for the asset when the company purchased it on December 20, 2009. The FMV of the asset as of January 1, 2010, is $75,000. The lessee will pay BLP $20,000 each January 1 for four years beginning immediately. After the fourth payment, title will transfer to the lessee. The lessee's incremental borrowing rate is 10 percent, and the interest rate implicit in the lease is also 10 percent. From BLP's perspective, the collectibility is reasonably assured, and there are no important uncertainties. The lessee has agreed to pay insurance of $1,000 and taxes of $500 annually on December 31 of each year. Refer to Table 15-10 for the decision chart to determine whether or not this is a capital lease.

We highly recommend always completing an amortization schedule prior to making any journal entries. Refer to Table 15-11 for the amortization schedule related to this example. Notice that the amortization calculations for an annuity due sales type lease are the same as those for an annuity due direct financing lease.

TABLE 15-10 Decision Chart (Example 15-4)

1	Transfer of ownership	Yes
2	Bargain purchase option	No
3	Life of lease = 75% or more of life of asset (4/5 = 0.8 → 80%)	Yes
4	PV MLP: 90% or more FMV of leased asset $20,000 × 3.486852 = $69,737 $69,737/$75,000 = 0.9298 →MLP = 93% of FMV	Yes
1	Collectibility reasonably assured	Yes
2	No important uncertainties	Yes
Decision:	Capital lease for both lessee and lessor	

Now you are ready for the journal entries. Refer to Table 15-12 for the journal entries for both the lessee and the lessor. Notice that the lessee depreciates the asset over the asset's life of five years and not the life of the lease (four years) because there is a transfer of ownership at the end of the lease. Notice that the general journal entry templates for the lessor are identical to those used by the lessor for an ordinary annuity sales type lease except for the dates when the entries are made.

TABLE 15-11 Amortization Schedule (Example 15-4)

Date	Payment	10% Interest	Principle	Book Value
1/1/10				69,734
1/1/10	20,000		20,000	49,734
12/31/10		4,973		54,707
1/1/11	20,000		20,000	34,707
12/31/11		3,471		38,178
1/1/12	20,000		20,000	18,178
12/31/12		1,822		20,000
1/1/13	20,000		20,000	(0)

TABLE 15-12 Journal Entries (Example 15-4)

Lessee

Initial Recording

Date	Account	Debit	Credit
1/1/10	Leased equipment under capital lease	69,734	
	Obligation under capital lease		69,734

Record payment of principle and interest

Date	Account	Debit	Credit
1/1/10	Obligation under capital lease	20,000	
	Cash		20,000

Accrue interest at year end

Date	Account	Debit	Credit
12/31/10	Interest expense	4,973	
	Obligation under capital lease		4,973

Record depreciation expense

Date	Account	Debit	Credit
12/31/10	Depreciation expense 69,734/5	13,947	
	Accumulated depreciation		13,947

Record executory costs

Date	Account	Debit	Credit
12/31/10	Insurance expense	1,000	
	Taxes	500	
	Cash		1,500

Lessor

Initial Recording

Date	Account	Debit	Credit
1/1/10	Minimum lease payments receivable	80,000	
	Sales revenue		69,734
	Unearned interest revenue		10,266
1/1/10	COGS	50,000	
	Asset		50,000

Record receipt of principle and interest

Date	Account	Debit	Credit
1/1/10	Cash	20,000	
	Minimum lease payments receivable		20,000

Accrue interest at year end

Date	Account	Debit	Credit
12/31/10	Unearned interest revenue	4,973	
	Interest revenue		4,973

TABLE 15-12 (Continued)

	Lessee				Lessor		
Record payment of principle and interest				**Record receipt of principle and interest**			
1/1/11	Obligation under capital lease	20,000		1/1/11	Cash	20,000	
	Cash		20,000		Minimum lease payments receivable		20,000
Accrue interest at year end				**Accrue interest at year end**			
12/31/11	Interest expense	3,471		12/31/11	Unearned interest revenue	3,471	
	Obligation under capital lease		3,471		Interest revenue		3,471
Record depreciation expense							
12/31/11	Depreciation expense 69,734/5	13,947					
	Accumulated depreciation		13,947				
Record executory costs							
12/31/11	Insurance expense	1,000					
	Taxes	500					
	Cash		1,500				
Record payment of principle and interest				**Record receipt of principle and interest**			
1/1/12	Obligation under capital lease	20,000		1/1/12	Cash	20,000	
	Cash		20,000		Minimum lease payments receivable		20,000
Accrue interest at year end				**Accrue interest at year end**			
12/31/12	Interest expense	1,822		12/31/12	Unearned interest revenue	1,822	
	Obligation under capital lease		1,822		Interest revenue		1,822
Record depreciation expense							
12/31/12	Depreciation expense 69,734/5	13,947					
	Accumulated depreciation		13,947				

Record executory costs

		Debit	Credit
12/31/12	Insurance expense	1,000	
	Taxes	500	
	Cash		1,500

Record payment of principle and interest

		Debit	Credit
1/1/13	Obligation under capital lease	20,000	
	Cash		20,000

Record depreciation expense

			Debit	Credit
12/31/13	Depreciation expense	69,734/5	13,947	
	Accumulated depreciation			13,947

Record executory costs

		Debit	Credit
12/31/13	Insurance expense	1,000	
	Taxes	500	
	Cash		1,500

Record depreciation expense

			Debit	Credit
12/31/14	Depreciation expense	69,734/5	13,947	
	Accumulated depreciation			13,947

Record receipt of principle and interest

		Debit	Credit
1/1/13	Cash	20,000	
	Minimum lease payments receivable		20,000

Bargain Purchase Options

A *bargain purchase option* exists when the contract allows for the lessee to purchase the asset for a price that is so much lower than the fair market value (FMV) of the asset at the end of the lease term that the lessee is reasonably assured to accept the option.

From the lessee's standpoint, when a bargain purchase option is part of a lease, the present value of the bargain purchase amount is added to the present value of the annual payments to determine the present value of the minimum lease payments and the amount at which to record the leased equipment and capital lease obligation on the lessee's books. All other entries and calculations remain the same. Note, however, that at the end of the lease's term, the capital lease obligation will remain on the books for a value equal to that of the bargain purchase amount.

From the lessor's standpoint, for both direct financing and sales types leases, the debit to minimum lease payments receivable is the normal amount plus the nondiscounted value of the bargain purchase option, whereas the asset account under direct financing leases and the sales revenue account under sales type leases are credited for the present value of the annual payments plus the present value of the bargain purchase option. Unearned interest is credited subsequently for the difference. Let's try an example.

EXAMPLE 15-5

BLP, Inc., leased an asset to another company on January 1, 2010. The lease is for three years. The asset has an estimated life of five years. BLP paid $100,000 for the asset when it was originally purchased. The FMV of the asset as of January 1, 2010, is $125,000. The lessee will pay BLP $40,000 each December 31 for three years. The lessee's incremental borrowing rate is 8 percent, and the interest rate implicit in the lease is 10 percent. From BLP's perspective, the collectibility is reasonably assured, and there are no important uncertainties. The lessee may purchase the asset for $500 at the end of the lease's term, when the FMV of the asset is expected to be $75,000. Refer to Table 15-13 for the decision chart to determine whether or not this is a capital lease.

As we have repeated five times now, we highly recommend always completing an amortization schedule prior to making any journal entries. Refer to Table 15-14 for the amortization schedule related to this example. Notice that the present value of the bargain purchase option is added to the present value of the annual payments to determine the present value of the minimum lease payments. Additionally, the book value of the lease obligation that remains on December 31, 2012, is $500, the amount of the bargain purchase option.

TABLE 15-13 Decision Chart (Example 15-5)

1	Transfer of ownership	No
2	Bargain purchase option	Yes
3	Life of lease = 75% or more of life of asset (3/5 = 0.6 → 60%)	No
4	PV MLP: 90% or more FMV of leased asset $40,000 × 2.577097 = $103,084 $500 × 0.793832 = $397 PV MLP = $103,084 + $397 = $103,481 $103,085/$125,000 = 0.8247 → MLP = 82% of FMV	No
1	Collectibility reasonably assured	Yes
2	No important uncertainties	Yes
Decision:	Capital lease for both lessee and lessor	

Now, once again, you are ready for the journal entries. Refer to Table 15-15 for the journal entries for both the lessee and the lessor. Notice that the lessee depreciates the asset over the asset's life of five years and not the life of the lease (three years) because a bargain purchase option is present. Notice that the remaining $500 in the lessee's obligation under capital lease account is eliminated by paying the lessor the money to purchase the asset, and likewise, the lessor records receipt of the $500 to eliminate its minimum lease payments receivable. All other entries remain the same.

TABLE 15-14 Amortization Schedule (Example 15-5)

Date	Payment	8% Interest	Principle	Book Value
1/1/10				103,481
12/31/10	40,000	8,278	31,722	71,759
12/31/11	40,000	5,741	34,259	37,500
12/31/12	40,000	3,000	37,000	500

TABLE 15-15 Journal Entries (Example 15-5)

Lessee

	Account	Debit	Credit
Initial recording			
1/1/10	Leased equipment under capital lease	103,481	
	Obligation under capital lease		103,481
Record payment of principle and interest			
12/31/10	Obligation under capital lease	31,722	
	Interest expense	8,278	
	Cash		40,000
Record depreciation expense			
12/31/10	Depreciation expense	103,481/5	20,696
	Accumulated depreciation		20,696
Record payment of principle and interest			
12/31/11	Obligation under capital lease	34,259	
	Interest expense	5,741	
	Cash		40,000
Record depreciation expense			
12/31/11	Depreciation expense	103,481/5	20,696
	Accumulated depreciation		20,696

Lessor

	Account	Debit	Credit
Initial recording			
1/1/10	Minimum lease payments receivable	120,500	
	Asset		103,481
	Unearned interest revenue		17,019
Record receipt of principle and interest			
12/31/10	Cash	40,000	
	Minimum lease payments receivable		40,000
	Unearned interest revenue	8,278	
	Interest revenue		8,278
Record receipt of principle and interest			
12/31/11	Cash	40,000	
	Minimum lease payments receivable		40,000
	Unearned interest revenue	5,741	
	Interest revenue		5,741

Record payment of principle and interest

12/31/12	Obligation under capital lease	37,000	
	Interest expense	3,000	
	Cash		40,000

Record depreciation expense

12/31/12	Depreciation expense	103,481/5	20,696	
	Accumulated depreciation			20,696

Record payment of bargain purchase option

12/31/12	Obligation under capital lease	500	
	Cash		500

Record depreciation expense

12/31/13	Depreciation expense	103,481/5	20,696	
	Accumulated depreciation			20,696

Record depreciation expense

12/31/14	Depreciation expense	103,481/5	20,696	
	Accumulated depreciation			20,696

Record receipt of principle and interest

12/31/12	Cash	40,000	
	Minimum lease payments receivable		40,000
	Unearned interest revenue	3,000	
	Interest revenue		3,000

Record receipt of bargain purchase option payment

12/31/12	Cash	500	
	Minimum lease payments receivable		500

Guaranteed/Unguaranteed Residual Values

Sometimes lease contracts also contain provisions for guaranteed residual values. A *guaranteed residual value* is an assurance made by the lessee that the leased asset will be worth a certain amount at the end of the lease period. It essentially shifts some of the risk of the lessor inherent in any lease contract to the lessee. The accounting treatment of a guaranteed residual value is the same as that of a bargain purchase option. Therefore, its present value is added to the present value of the minimum lease payments to determine the capital lease obligation amount. Likewise, implications to the lessor are the same as a bargain purchase option. The only difference between a guaranteed residual value and a bargain purchase option is the removal from the books at the end of the lease, which is governed by both the asset's condition and the lease's provisions. If the fair value of the leased asset is less than the guaranteed residual value, the asset likely is returned, and the difference between the fair market value and the guaranteed residual value is paid in cash to the lessor with a corresponding loss on disposal recognized on the books. If the fair value of the leased asset is greater than the guaranteed residual value, the asset is likely to be returned with no gain or loss recognition. While these are two common scenarios, remember that the contract provisions prevail and may require payment of the guaranteed residual value by the lessee regardless of the asset's condition or may direct the accounting treatment otherwise.

An unguaranteed residual value as part of a sales type capital lease is treated a bit differently. The present value of the unguaranteed residual value is subtracted from the cost of the asset, and the amount is also excluded from sales revenue.

Because the treatment of guaranteed and unguaranteed residual values is so similar to that of bargain purchase options, we will omit an example.

Initial Direct Costs of Lessor

The treatment of the initial direct costs incurred by a lessor in conjunction with a lease differs depending on the type of lease. For an operating lease, the costs are capitalized and expensed in proportion to the amount of rental payments received. For a direct financing capital lease, the initial direct costs are recorded as a debit to unearned interest and a credit to cash or some payable account. Essentially, the costs are deferred, and the book value of the lease is increased. However, because the future cash flows do not change, a lower implicit rate of interest results, and interest revenue is reduced. For a sales type capital lease, the initial direct costs are expensed as incurred either as part of cost of goods sold or as a separate selling expense item.

Sale Leaseback

A *sale leaseback* involves the trading of roles of the lessee and lessor. In other words, the original lessee becomes the lessor, and the original lessor becomes the lessee. Such a tradeoff occurs instantly at the time of the transaction, with usually no visible sign of a difference in the use of the leased asset. Two factors must be considered in determining the proper accounting treatment for a sale leaseback. Those factors are the type of lease involved (operating versus capital) and the percentage of rights that will be retained by the original lessor.

For both operating and capital leases, a tentative gain and an excess gain are calculated. Under both types of leases, the tentative gain is calculated as the selling price minus the net book value of the asset. In regard to the excess gain, for an operating lease, the present value of the minimum lease payments is always subtracted from the tentative gain, whereas for a capital lease, the lesser of the present value of the minimum lease payments or the fair value of the leased asset is subtracted.

In regard to the rights retained, three categories exist for the original lessor (party that becomes the lessee).

First Category

The first category includes leases in which the present value of the payments is equal to or greater than 90 percent of the asset's fair value and thus are normally deemed capital leases. Gains are all deferred and amortized over the leaseback period. To determine the amount of recognized loss or deferred loss, we have developed a two-step process:

> *Step 1:* Compute the loss as sales price minus book value (BV) of the asset.
>
> *Step 2a:* The loss calculated in step 1 is recognized immediately *if* the FMV < BV.
>
> *Step 2b:* The loss calculated in step 1 is deferred and amortized over the life of the leaseback *if* FMV > sales price.

EXAMPLE 15-6

CATEGORY 1: GAIN
On January 1, 2010, BLP, Inc., sold a piece of equipment to another company and simultaneously leased it back for three years. The equipment's sale price and fair value were $40,000. It was currently being carried on BLP's books for $25,000 and had an estimated remaining useful life of four

TABLE 15-16	Decision Chart (Example 15-6)	
1	Transfer of ownership	No
2	Bargain purchase option	No
3	Life of lease = 75% or more of life of asset (3/4 = 0.3 → 75%)	Yes
4	PV MLP: 90% or more FMV of leased asset $15,000 × 2.486852 = $37,303 $37,303/$40,000 = 0.9326 →MLP = 93% of FMV	Yes
Decision:	Capital lease	

years. The annual payment was $15,000. The appropriate interest rate was 10 percent. The equipment will not revert to the lessee at the end of the lease. See Table 15-16 to determine if this is a capital or operating lease. In Table 15-17 we present the calculations for determining the amount of gain or loss to be recognized, if any.

EXAMPLE 15-7

CATEGORY 1 LOSS

On January 1, 2010, BLP, Inc., sold a piece of equipment to another company and simultaneously leased it back for three years. The equipment's sales price was $20,000, and its fair market value was $40,000. It was currently being carried on BLP's books for $25,000 and had an estimated remaining useful life of four years. The annual payment was $15,000. The

TABLE 15-17	Calculations (Example 15-6)	
90% of FV of equipment → $40,000 × 0.9 =		36,000 < 37,303
Category 1 Sale Leaseback		
	Sales price	$40,000
	− Equipment NBV	(25,000)
	Tentative gain	$15,000
Gain of $15,000 is deferred and amortized over leaseback period		
December 31, 2010: Recognized gain (1/3 of $15,000)		$5,000
December 31, 2011: Recognized gain (1/3 of $15,000)		$5,000
December 31, 2012: Recognized gain (1/3 of $15,000)		$5,000

TABLE 15-18	Decision Chart (Example 15-7)	
1	Transfer of ownership	No
2	Bargain purchase option	No
3	Life of lease = 75% or more of life of asset (3/4 = 0.3 → .75%)	Yes
4	PV MLP: 90% or more FMV of leased asset $15,000 × 2.486852 = $37,303 $37,303/$40,000 = 0.9326 →MLP = 93% of FMV	Yes
Decision:	Capital lease	

appropriate interest rate was 10 percent. The equipment will not revert to the lessee at the end of the lease. See Table 15-18 to determine if this is a capital or operating lease. In Table 15-19 we present the calculations for determining the amount of gain or loss to be recognized, if any.

Second Category

The second category includes leases in which the present value of the payments is between 10 and 90 percent of the asset's fair value and may be either operating or capital leases.

Part of the gains will be recognized immediately, and part of the gains will be deferred. The deferred gain will be equal to the PV of the MLP, and these gains will be amortized over the life of the leaseback period. The difference between the tentative gain and the PV of the MLP is called the *excess gain*, and this amount of gain is recognized immediately.

TABLE 15-19	Calculations (Example 15-7)	
90% of FV of equipment → $40,000 × 0.9 =		36,000 < 37,303
Category 1 Sale Leaseback		
	Sales price	$20,000
	− Equipment NBV	(25,000)
	Tentative loss	$5,000
Because FMV ($40,000) is > sales price ($20,000):		
Entire loss deferred and amortized over life of lease		

To determine the amount of recognized loss or deferred loss, we have developed a two-step process:

Step 1: Compute the loss as sales price minus book value of the asset.

Step 2a: The loss calculated in step 1 is recognized immediately *if* FMV < BV.

Step 2b: The loss calculated in step 1 is deferred and amortized over the life of the leaseback *if* FMV > sales price.

EXAMPLE 15-8

CATEGORY 2 GAIN

On January 1, 2010, BLP, Inc., sold a piece of equipment to another company and simultaneously leased it back for three years. The equipment's sale price and fair value were $100,000. It was currently being carried on BLP's books for $65,000 and had an estimated remaining useful life of 10 years. The annual payment was $5,000. The appropriate interest rate was 10 percent. The equipment will not revert to the lessee at the end of the lease. See Table 15-20 to determine if this is a capital or operating lease. In Table 15-21 we present the calculations for determining the amount of gain or loss to be recognized, if any.

Notice that the $35,000 gain is deferred up to the amount of the present value of the minimum lease payments, $12,434, and the remaining gain of $22,566 is recognized immediately.

Third Category

The third category includes leases in which the present value of the payments is 10 percent or less and that thus are normally identified as operating leases. Gains and losses are recognized immediately.

TABLE 15-20	Decision Chart (Example 15-8)	
1	Transfer of ownership	No
2	Bargain purchase option	No
3	Life of lease = 75% or more of life of asset $(3/10 = 0.3 \rightarrow 30\%)$	No
4	PV MLP: 90% or more FMV of leased asset $\$5,000 \times 2.486852 = \$12,434$ $\$12,434/\$100,000 = 0.1243$ $\rightarrow$ MLP = 12% of FMV	No
Decision:	Operating lease	

TABLE 15-21 Calculations (Example 15-8)

10% of FV of equipment → $100,000 x 0.1 =	10,000 < 12,434
90% of FV of equipment → $100,000 x 0.9 =	90,000 > 12,434
Category 2 Sale Leaseback	

Sales price	$100,000	
− Equipment NBV	(65,000)	
Tentative gain	$35,000	
−PV minimum lease payments	(12,434)	**Deferred Gain**
Excess gain	$22,566	**Gain Recognized Immediately**
January 1, 2010: Recognized gain	$22,566	
December 31, 2010: Recognized gain (1/3 of $12,434)	$4,145	
December 31, 2011: Recognized gain (1/3 of $12,434)	$4,145	
December 31, 2012: Recognized gain (1/3 of $12,434)	$4,145	

 **EXAMPLE 15-9**

CATEGORY 3 GAIN

On January 1, 2010, BLP, Inc., sold a piece of equipment to another company and simultaneously leased it back for three years. The equipment's sale price and fair value were $130,000. It was currently being carried on BLP's books for $65,000 and had an estimated remaining useful life of 10 years. The annual payment was $5,000. The appropriate interest rate was 10 percent. The equipment will not revert to the lessee at the end of the lease. See Table 15-22 to determine if this is a capital or operating lease.

TABLE 15-22 Decision Chart (Example 15-9)

1	Transfer of ownership	No
2	Bargain purchase option	No
3	Life of lease = 75% or more of life of asset (3/10 = 0.3 → 30%)	No
4	PV MLP: 90% or more FMV of leased asset $5,000 × 2.486852 = $12,434 $12,434/$130,000 = 0.0956 →MLP = 9.6% of FMV	No
Decision:	Operating lease	

TABLE 15-23 Calculations (Example 15-8)		
10% of FV of equipment → $130,000 × 0.1 =	13,000 > 12,434	
Category 3 Sale Leaseback		
Sales price	$130,000	
− Equipment NBV	(65,000)	**Entire amount recognized**
Tentative gain	$65,000	**immediately**

In Table 15-23 we present the calculations for determining the amount of gain or loss to be recognized, if any.

Required Disclosures

GAAP mandates that certain disclosures be made in reference to leases. As you might suspect, the rules differ depending on the type of lease (i.e., operating versus capital). For operating leases, the main disclosure items are the future minimum rental payments for each of the next five years in total and the rental expense for each period. The disclosures for capital leases are a bit more detailed and include the gross amount of assets recorded as capital leases by major classes according to function and the future minimum lease payments for the next five years in total with specific separations for executory and imputed interest costs. There are other disclosures specific to these two types of leases, but these are the most important. In addition, both types of leases should note any restrictions or attached renewal or purchase options.

Other Topics

We have introduced basic information regarding leases in this chapter. There are many other issues that make the subject more complex and are beyond the scope of this text. The subject of leveraged leases is one such topic that falls into this category.

Wow! That was a lot for one chapter—operating and capital leases, direct-financing and sale-type leases as seen through the lessor's eyes, bargain purchase options, guaranteed and unguaranteed residual values, initial direct costs, sale leasebacks, and disclosures. With this, we conclude our discussion of the income statement and move on to a statement that honors the heartbeat of any business, a king if you will. What are we talking about? The statement of cash flows, of course!

QUIZ

1. **Which of the following accounts will a lessee use under an operating lease?**

   A. Leased equipment to others
   B. Rent expense
   C. Obligation under capital lease
   D. Leased equipment under capital lease

   Use the following information to answer questions 2 through 4.

   GBW, Inc, leased a kayak to LJ Enterprises on January 1, 2010, when the fair market value of the boat was $850. The term of the lease was three years, and the kayak was expected to have an economic life of six years. At the end of the lease, the kayak would be given back to GBW, Inc., with no option for LJ Enterprises to purchase the vessel. LJ Enterprises was to pay GBW $300 at the end of each year. LJ Enterprises' incremental borrowing rate is 7 percent, whereas the rate implicit in the lease is 8 percent. GBW is reasonably assured to collect the minimum lease payments and has no uncertainties as to any additional costs to be incurred.

2. **Which of the following makes this lease a capital lease?**

   A. A bargain purchase option is attached to the lease.
   B. The life of the lease is 75 percent or more of the life of the kayak.
   C. The present value of the minimum lease payments is 90 percent or more of the fair value of the kayak.
   D. This lease is not a capital lease; it is an operating lease.

3. **What amount should be recorded by LJ Enterprises as a credit to obligation under capital lease on December 31, 2010?**

   A. $900
   B. $787
   C. $850
   D. $0

4. **What should be included in the journal entry made by LJ Enterprises on December 31, 2012?**

   A. A credit to cash of $280
   B. A credit to interest expense of $20
   C. A debit to obligation under capital lease of $300
   D. A debit to obligation under capital lease of $280

   Use the following information to answer questions 5 through 8.

   LRC Unlimited leased an entertainment system to PJC, Inc., on January 1, 2009. LRC had paid $20,000 for the system when it purchased it in January 2007. The fair market value of the system immediately before the signing of the lease was $30,000. The term of the lease was two years, and the expected economic life of the system was three years. PJC was to pay LRC $16,000 annually on January 1 starting this year. PJC was granted the option to buy the system at the end of the lease for $500. PJC's incremental borrowing rate was 9 percent, whereas the rate implicit in the lease was 10 percent. LRC is reasonably assured to collect the minimum lease payments and has no uncertainties as to any additional costs to be incurred.

5. What amount should the lessor record as sales revenue on January 1, 2009, in regard to the lease?
   A. $31,100
   B. $30,679
   C. $32,500
   D. $32,000

6. As a sales type lease, what is the gross profit that should be recognized on signing of this lease by LRC Unlimited?
   A. $12,500
   B. $1,100
   C. $11,100
   D. $12,000

7. What is the value of the obligation under capital lease on PJC's books on December 31, 2009, just after accounting for any interest?
   A. $16,000
   B. $16,459
   C. $15,100
   D. $459

8. PJC would depreciate the entertainment equipment using a life of
   A. five years.
   B. two years.
   C. three years.
   D. zero years—PJC would not depreciate the equipment; LRC would.

9. Under a sale leaseback, when the present value of the lease payments is greater than 10 percent but less than 90 percent of the fair value of the property at the signing of the lease and the sale price of the asset is greater than the asset's net book value, which of the following is part of the accounting treatment?
   A. A gain is deferred up to the present value of the leaseback, and any remaining gain is recognized immediately.
   B. A gain is deferred for the full amount of the sale price minus the net book value.
   C. A loss is recognized immediately.
   D. A gain is recognized immediately for the full amount of the sale price minus the net book value.

10. **Disclosures to the financial statements in regard to leases include**

   A. for operating leases, the future minimum rental payments for the next 10 years separated by year and in total.

   B. for capital leases, the future minimum lease payments for the next 10 years separated by year and in total.

   C. for operating leases, the gross amount of assets recorded as capital leases by major classes according to function.

   D. for capital leases, the future minimum lease payments for the next five years separated by year and in total.

Part V

The Statement of Cash Flows—Where's the Cash?

chapter 16

Cash Flow Statement

CHAPTER OBJECTIVES

After completing this chapter, the student should

- Understand the financial statement presentation for the cash flow statement
- Understand what is included in operating activities, investing activities, and financing activities
- Understand and compute the direct method cash flow statement
- Understand and compute the indirect method cash flow statement

Overview

Cash, as we mentioned in Chapter 15, is the lifeblood of any business. Can you imagine operating a business without funds to make purchases and carry on the day to day activities that are essential to being successful? Well, we hope your answer to that question was "No." Heck, even as a person, survival is nearly impossible without some form of cash, whether it be dollar bills, a check, or a credit card, so what would make you think that a business is any different? We guess that it is like everyone always says—money really does make the world go round.

Do you remember those cash and accrual basis accounting designations? Here is where thinking about that will especially come in handy. What most people do not realize is that profit, net income, earnings, or whatever else that someone may want to call that bottom line figure is not, we repeat not, the same as cash in hand. We cannot begin to count the number of times that a business—whether intentionally for fraudulent purposes or simply because owners or managers are ignorant themselves—has communicated its earnings as the cash available in the bank. A company may have outstanding income that tops the charts for its industry, but that does not matter at all if cash is not available to support the business. Hence this is where a lot of companies get in trouble. They can manipulate earnings, but they cannot manipulate their cash positions to match those gross overstatements in income. Thus no company's financial story is complete without a cash flow statement to accompany the other financials.

Yep, here comes Mr. Cash Flow, that two-faced character who is indirect yet direct at the same time. He has a complicated personality, that's for sure! Who cares about his personality, though, as long as there is a positive number at the end of his autobiography (aka *the cash flow statement*), his friends will never trail far behind.

Financial Statement Presentation

The *statement of cash flows* is one of the major financial statements included in a company's annual report. Recall that one of the objectives of financial accounting is to provide useful information about a company's cash flows. Therefore, this objective is met by this statement. You will see that the statement of cash flows provides information about both a company's cash receipts and cash payments for an accounting period.

Financial accounting is accrual basis, right? Yes, except for the statement of cash flows. With this statement we are actually doing the opposite—going from an accrual basis accounting system to a cash basis system. Generally accepted accounting principles (GAAP) dictate that the income statement must show how much revenue was earned and how much expense was incurred. This is great for reporting purposes, but the owner's real interest is in knowing how much cash came in and how much cash left the business.

A statement of cash flows can be prepared with a little help from two of the other major financial statements—an income statement for the current year and comparative balance sheets for the current and prior year. By the time that changes in every balance sheet account are "accounted for" and a little bit of extra information is considered, the statement of cash flows is complete.

There are three sections in the statement of cash flows—operating activities, investing activities, and financing activities. In the following sections we will discuss what is included within each category. We also will include a discussion of other relevant topics.

Operating Activities

As we mentioned, there are two formats for preparing a statement of cash flows—the direct method and the indirect method. The two approaches differ only in their operating activities sections. Regardless of method, though, the same amount will be obtained for cash provided for or obtained from operating activities. Both presentations will be shown in this chapter. First, though, let's discuss the two methods' requirements in a bit more detail. The "preferred" method is the direct method. By *preferred*, we mean that GAAP, under the directive of the Financial Accounting Standards Board (FASB), encourages its use. However, if the direct method is presented, the indirect method also must be included in a footnote. Election of the direct method thus requires double the work. Can you guess what method companies prefer? Yep, you got it! The indirect method is used by well over the majority of companies, and that choice is perfectly acceptable. However, the indirect method does require a disclosure for the interest and taxes that actually were paid in cash.

Direct Method

The premise behind the direct method is that cash collected and paid in operating a business is calculated "directly." The direct method can be worked by following a series of nine steps. Refer to Table 16-1 for those steps. Right now, you only need to look at the words. The numbers in Table 16-1 relate to the full example presented at the end of this chapter. We have included two approaches using simple addition and subtraction. If these don't help you to understand this complex topic, there is yet another method that may be useful. In the first approach, the beginning and ending balances are used directly in the calculation rather than determining the increases and decreases beforehand. In the second approach, a process similar to the indirect method is followed. An income statement item (e.g., sales revenue) is the first item included, followed by any increases or decreases in related accounts, as noted in Table 16-1. *For any collections*, as you will see in a minute, you follow the same rules as the indirect method to determine whether or not increases or decreases are added or subtracted, (i.e., subtract an increase in assets, add a decrease in assets, subtract a decrease in liabilities, add an increase in liabilities—liabilities are treated in the same direction as they have changed, and changes in assets are treated in the opposite direction). *For any payments*, you follow the opposite rules as the indirect method to determine whether or not increases or decreases are added or subtracted, (i.e., add an increase in assets, subtract a decrease in assets, add a decrease in liabilities, subtract an increase in liabilities—assets are now treated in the same direction as they have changed, and changes in liabilities are treated in the opposite direction).

TABLE 16-1 Direct Method: Step-by-Step Process

		Method 1		Method 2	
Step 1:	**Collections from customers**				
	Sales revenue		500,000	Sales revenue	500,000
	+ Beg AR	Collected this year	45,000	+ Decrease in AR	15,000
	− End AR	Not collected yet	(30,000)		515,000
	Collections from customers		515,000		
Step 2:	**Interest and dividends collected**				
	Interest and dividend revenue			N/A in this problem	
	+ Beg interest receivable	Collected this year			
	− End interest receivable	Not collected yet			
	+ Beg dividend receivable	Collected this year			
	− End dividend receivable	Not collected yet			
	Interest and dividends collected		0		
Step 3:	**Other operating receipts**		0	N/A in this problem	
	Do not include gains and losses on sales of assets and liabilities because they are listed separately on I/S				
Step 4:	**Payments to suppliers**				
	COGS		350,000	COGS	350,000
	− Beg inventory	Paid for this year	(75,000)	+ Increase in inventory	10,000
	+ End inventory	Not paid for yet	85,000	+ Decrease in AP	25,000
	+ Beg AP	Paid for this year	25,000		385,000
	− End AP	Not paid for yet	0		
	Payments to suppliers		385,000		
Step 5:	**Payments to employees**				
	Salary expense		80,000	Salaries expense	80,000
	+ Beg salary payable	Paid this year	7,000	−Increase in salaries payable	(815)
	− End salary payable	Not paid for yet	(7,815)		79,185
	Payments to employees		79,185		

Step 6: **Payments of interest**

Interest expense		4,950	Interest expense	4,950
+ Beg interest payable		0	−Increase in interest payable	(750)
− End interest payable	Not paid for yet	(750)	−Amortization of bond discount	(200)
− Amortization of bond discount	Not cash payment	(200)		4,000
+ Amortization of bond premium	Not cash payment	0		
Interest paid		4,000		

Step 7: **Other operating payments**

Other operating expense		5,000	Other operating expense	5,000
− Beg prepaid	Paid last year	(3,000)	−Decrease in prepaid insurance	(1,000)
+ End prepaid	Paid this year	2,000		4,000
Other operating payments		4,000		

Step 8: **Payment of income taxes**

Income tax expense		9,615	Income tax expense	9,615
+ Beg income tax payable	Paid this year	10,000	+Decrease income tax payable	2,000
− End income tax payable	Not paid for yet	(8,000)		11,615
+ Beg deferred tax payable	Paid this year	0		
− End deferred tax payable	Not paid for yet	0		
Income taxes paid		11,615		

Step 9: Summary

Collections from customers	515,000
Interest and dividends collected	0
Other operating receipts	0
Payments to suppliers	(385,000)
Payments to employees	(79,185)
Payments of interest	(4,000)
Other operating payments	(4,000)
Payment of income taxes	(11,615)
Cash provided by operating activities	31,200

Another way to determine the proper figures needed for the direct method is to rely on journal entries. In the case of collections, the revenue account is credited for the related income statement amount, whereas any adjustments are debited or credited as they increase or decrease. The plug is to cash, and the cash entry signifies the actual cash figure to be used in the statement of cash flows. With this method, all you need to remember is normal account balances (debit versus credit) and the way to increase or decrease each type of account (debit or credit). This is something that you should already know, so this should be fairly painless. See Table 16-2 for the entries that would be used for the information provided in Table 16-1. Notice that your entry to cash in each case matches the result obtained in Table 16-1.

TABLE 16-2 Direct Method: Journal Entry Approach

Collections from customers:	Cash	**515,000**	
	Accounts receivable		15,000
	Sales revenue		500,000
Payments to suppliers:	Cost of goods sold	350,000	
	Inventory	10,000	
	Accounts payable	25,000	
	Cash		**385,000**
Payments to employees:	Salaries expense	80,000	
	Salaries payable		815
	Cash		**79,185**
Payment of interest:	Interest expense	4,950	
	Interest payable		750
	Discount on bonds payable		200
	Cash		**4,000**
Other operating payments:	Other operating expenses	5,000	
	Prepaid insurance		1,000
	Cash		**4,000**
Payment of income taxes:	Income tax expense	9,615	
	Income tax payable	2,000	
	Cash		**11,615**

Indirect Method

The starting point for the indirect method is net income, which is obtained from the income statement. Because net income is an accrual basis number, we must change it to a "cash" amount. Therefore, we must subtract all the noncash revenue and add all the noncash expenses. The most common noncash expense is depreciation. Think about the journal entry made when depreciation expense is recorded: Debit depreciation expense and credit accumulated depreciation. Cash is not part of the entry at all!

Once net income has been adjusted for all the noncash items that were on the income statement, it is time to "account" for all the changes in the current assets and current liabilities. Ultimately, every increase or decrease in the current assets and current liabilities is added or subtracted. A way to remember whether to add or subtract is using the mnemonic *SIL*—a *s*ource of cash (addition) is an *i*ncrease in a *l*iability. Thus, if a current liability increased from one year to the next, you would add the change to the adjusted net income to compute the cash flow from operating activities. Likewise, if a current liability decreased from one year to the next, you would subtract the change from the adjusted net income to compute the cash flow from operating activities. Recall that liabilities have normal credit balances, and assets are just the opposite—with normal debit balances. It is logical, then, that an increase in a current asset is subtracted and a decrease in a current asset is added. For a visual representation of this process, see the following chart:

Liabilities ↑	+ (add)	Assets ↓
Liabilities ↓	– (subtract)	Assets ↑

EXAMPLE 16-1

BLP, Inc., reported net income in 2010 of $100,000. The income statement reflected depreciation expense of $10,000. The balance sheets for 2009 and 2010 reflected the following changes: a decrease in accounts receivable of $500, an increase in inventory of $4,000, an increase in accounts payable of $1,000, and a decrease in salaries payable of $2,000. What is the amount of cash flows from operating activities? The answer is shown in Table 16-3.

TABLE 16-3 Cash Flows from Operating Activities (Example 16-1)	
Net income	100,000
Add: Depreciation expense	10,000
Add: Increase in accounts payable	1,000
Add: Decrease in accounts receivable	500
Less: Decrease in salaries payable	(2,000)
Less: Increase in inventories	(4,000)
Cash flows from operating activities	105,500

Investing Activities

The investing activities section "accounts" for the changes in long-term assets (the items that the company has "invested" in). These changes can be tricky, especially if you have purchased or sold some depreciable assets during the year. The easiest way to determine all the changes in the accounts is to recreate the journal entries that caused the account to change. Problems usually give you enough information to determine if any assets have been purchased or sold. If they have been sold, look for the gain or loss to be disclosed on the income statement. Also look for the depreciation expense that usually appears on the income statement.

The presentation of the investing activities section is the same for both the direct and the indirect methods.

EXAMPLE 16-2

During 2010, BLP, Inc., purchased a building for $200,000. The company also sold a building that had a cost of $170,000 and a book value of $50,000 for a gain of $10,000. The balance sheets for 2009 and 2010 reflected a net $30,000 increase in the building account. What is the amount of cash flows from investing activities?

The best way to approach the process of determining the net cash flows from investing activities is to recreate the journal entries that generated the net change in the building account. From these journal entries, whatever happened in the cash account is what is reflected on the cash flow statement in the investing activities section. The solution to this problem is shown in Table 16-4.

TABLE 16-4 Amount of Cash Flows from Investing (Example 16-2)

Building		200,000	
Cash			200,000
Cash	Plug—investing	60,000	
Accumulated depreciation—building	170,000 – 50,000	120,000	
Building	Given		170,000
Gain on sale of building	Given – operating		10,000
Cash flows from investing activities			
Purchased building		(200,000)	
Sold building		60,000	
Cash used in investing activities		(140,000)	

Financing Activities

The financing activities section "accounts" for changes in the long-term debt and equity sections of the balance sheet (the items that the company uses to "finance" its business). Items usually included here would be borrowings or repayments of debt, issuing additional stock, or paying dividends (only the amount that actually has been paid out in cash is included, which may or may not be the same amount as declared). Like the investing activities section, the presentation of the financing activities section is the same for both the direct and indirect methods.

 **EXAMPLE 16-3**

During 2010, BLP, Inc., sold 1,000 shares of $10 par common stock for $25 each. The balance sheets for 2009 and 2010 reflected a net $125,000 decrease in the notes payable account, a net increase in the common stock account of $10,000, and a net increase in the PIC—CS account of $15,000. There was no additional information related to the notes payable account. What is the amount of cash flows from financing activities?

Again, the best way to approach determining the net cash flows from financing activities is to recreate the journal entries that generated the net change in the respective accounts. The solution can be found in Table 16-5.

Other Relevant Topics

A reconciliation of the cash balance is essential. The statement includes the sum of the cash flows from operating, investing, and financing activities. This sum *must equal* the change in cash reported on the comparative balance sheets.

TABLE 16-5 Amount of Cash Flows from Financing (Example 16-3)			
Cash	1,000 × $25	25,000	
Common stock	1,000 × $10		10,000
PIC—CS	1,000 × $15		15,000
Notes payable		125,000	
Cash			125,000
Cash flows from financing activities			
Sold stock		25,000	
Repaid debt		(125,000)	
Cash used in financing activities		(100,000)	

The change then is combined with the beginning cash balance to equal the ending cash balance.

Sometimes investing and financing transactions will take place simultaneously with no effect on cash (e.g., a company purchases a building with a note payable or through an issuance of common stock). Even though they do not affect cash, a schedule of such activities must be presented on the face of the statement of cash flows. As we said, sometimes a company will purchase an asset by issuing a note payable. No cash changes hands initially, so the transaction is not reported on the statement. However, the transaction is important to the company and will require cash payments in the future. Therefore, it must be disclosed to the reader.

EXAMPLE 16-4

Now that you have a road map, let's try a *big* cash-flow problem. You will need to have at least three pieces of paper and a calculator handy for working this out. It will take some time, but take it from two people who have pulled their hair out trying to do it other ways, this process is well worth the effort! If you follow these guidelines, preparing this statement should be a cinch. The comparative balance sheets are presented in Table 16-6. The income statement is presented in Table 16-7.

Step 1: Compute the changes in all the balance sheet accounts. Next, set up T-accounts with the changes noted. For instance, if cash increased by 10,000, show the cash T-account with a 10,000 debit balance. Use one complete sheet of paper for the cash T-account. Place all the other T-accounts on another sheet of paper. When this process is complete, the cash T-account will be the rough draft of the cash-flow statement.

Step 2: Recreate the journal entries for net income and any dividends that were paid, and post those entries to the respective T-accounts.

Step 3: Recreate the journal entries for the additional information that was disclosed with the income statement and balance sheets, and post those entries to the respective T-accounts as well. The additional information related to this example is as follows:

1. BLP, Inc., paid dividends of $5,000.

2. BLP, Inc., sold 1,000 shares of $10 par common stock for $35 per share.

3. BLP, Inc., purchased equipment of $15,000 by issuing a 10 percent note payable on July 1, 2010.

4. BLP, Inc., sold equipment costing $10,000 (book value of $2,000) for $5,000.

Step 4: Go through any remaining T-accounts that have not been completely "accounted for," and recreate the entries that likely would cause the changes in the accounts, and again, post those entries to the respective T-accounts.

TABLE 16-6 Comparative Balance Sheets (Example 16-4)

	2010	2009
Assets		
Current assets		
Cash	$96,200	$30,000
Accounts receivable	30,000	45,000
Prepaid insurance	2,000	3,000
Inventory	85,000	75,000
Noncurrent assets		
Building	100,000	100,000
Accumulated depreciation—building	(30,000)	(25,000)
Equipment	80,000	75,000
Accumulated depreciation—equipment	(46,000)	(30,000)
Land	200,000	200,000
Intangible	18,000	20,000
Total assets	$535,200	$493,000
Liabilities		
Current liabilities		
Accounts payable	$0	$25,000
Salaries payable	7,815	7,000
Interest payable	750	0
Income tax payable	8,000	10,000
Noncurrent liabilities		
Notes payable	15,000	0
Bonds payable	50,000	50,000
Discount on bonds payable	(800)	(1,000)
Total liabilities	80,765	91,000
Stockholders' equity		
Common Stock	$110,000	$100,000
Paid–in capital—common stock	225,000	200,000
Retained earnings	119,435	102,000
Total stockholders' equity	454,435	402,000
Total liabilities and stockholders' equity	$535,200	$493,000

TABLE 16-7 Income Statement (Example 16-4)		
Sales		$500,000
Cost of goods sold		(350,000)
Gross profit		150,000
Operating expenses		
Salaries expense	$80,000	
Depreciation expense	29,000	
Amortization expense	2,000	
Other operating expenses	5,000	(116,000)
Operating income		34,000
Other items		
Interest expense	(4,950)	
Gain on sale of equipment	3,000	(1,950)
Pretax income from continuing operations		32,050
Income tax expense		(9,615)
Net income		$22,435

All the journal entries are presented in Table 16-8. After the journal entries are recreated, you must post them to the appropriate T-accounts. When posting "cash," make certain that you post to the operating, investing, or financing activities sections appropriately. The completed T-accounts are presented in Table 16-9.

We have worked this example using the indirect method, but the numbers for the direct method are included in Table 16-1.

Well, we are almost to the end! Now you know more about cash inflows and outflows than you ever thought possible. You can verify changes in the cash account from both a direct and indirect perspective and can classify cash flows properly as operating, investing, or financing activities. Unfortunately, even we accountants do not always get the numbers perfect for cash flows, as well as for many other areas of financial statements. Other times, assumptions change, and corrections need to be made. In Chapter 17 we will show you how to deal with such changes and errors.

TABLE 16-8 Journal Entries (Example 16-4)

1	Cash	Operating	22,435	
	Retained earnings			22,435
2	Retained earnings		5,000	
	Cash	Financing		5,000
3	Cash	Financing	35,000	
	Common stock	1,000 × 10		10,000
	PIC—CS	1,000 × 25		25,000
4	Equipment	Investing/financing	15,000	
	Notes payable	Investing/financing		15,000
5	Cash	Investing	5,000	
	Accumulated depreciation—equipment		8,000	
	Equipment			10,000
	Gain on sale of equipment	Operating		3,000
6	Cash	Operating	15,000	
	Accounts receivable			15,000
7	Inventory	Operating	10,000	
	Cash			10,000
8	Cash	Operating	1,000	
	Prepaid insurance			1,000
9	Depreciation expense	Operating	29,000	
	Accumulated depreciation—building			5,000
	Accumulated depreciation—equipment			24,000
10	Amortization expense	Operating	2,000	
	Intangibles			2,000
11	Accounts payable	Operating	25,000	
	Cash			25,000
12	Income taxes payable	Operating	2,000	
	Cash			2,000
13	Cash	Operating	815	
	Salaries payable			815
14	Cash	Operating	750	
	Interest payable			750
15	Interest expense	Operating	200	
	Discount on bonds payable			200

TABLE 16-9 Completed T-Accounts (Example 16-4)

Cash	
	66,200
Operating activities:	
1) Net income	22,435
9) Add: Depreciation expense	29,000
10) Add: Amortization expense	2,000
15) Add: Amortization of discount on bonds payable	200
6) Add: Decrease in accounts receivable	15,000
8) Add: Decrease in prepaid insurance	1,000
13) Add: Increase in salaries payable	815
14) Add: Increase in interest payable	750
5) Less: Gain on sale of equipment	(3,000)
7) Less: Increase in inventory	(10,000)
11) Less: Decrease in accounts payable	(25,000)
12) Less: Decrease in income taxes payable	(2,000)
Net cash provided by operating activities:	31,200
Investing activities:	
5) Sold equipment	5,000
Net cash provided by investing activities:	5,000
Financing activities:	
2) Paid dividend	(5,000)
3) Sold common stock	35,000
Net cash provided by financing activities:	30,000

Cash reconciliation:

Net increase (decrease) in cash	66,200
Add: Beginning cash balance	30,000
Equals: Ending cash balance	96,200

Investing and financing not affecting cash:

Purchased equipment	(15,000)
Issued notes payable	15,000

Accounts receivable

15,000	
6) 15,000	

Inventory

10,000	
7) 10,000	

Prepaid insurance

1,000	
	8) 1,000

Building

No change

Accum. depr. building

	5,000
9) 5,000	

Equipment

5,000	
4) 15,000	5) 10,000

Accum. depr. equipment

	16,000
5) 8,000	9) 24,000

Land

No change

Intangibles

2,000	
10) 2,000	

TABLE 16-9 (Continued)

Accounts payable

	25,000
11) 25,000	

Income taxes payable

	2,000
12) 2,000	

Salaries payable

	815
13) 815	

Interest payable

	750
14) 750	

Notes payable

	15,000
4) 15,000	

Bonds payable

No change

Discount on BP

200	
15) 200	

Common stock

	10,000
3) 10,000	

PIC–CS

	25,000
3) 25,000	

Retained earnings

	17,435
2) 5,000	1) 22,435

QUIZ

1. **The purpose of a statement of cash flows is to**
   A. reconcile a cash basis balance sheet with an accrual basis income statement.
   B. reconcile an accrual basis balance sheet with a cash basis income statement.
   C. reconcile a cash basis balance sheet and income statement to determine the cash inflows and outflows.
   D. reconcile an accrual basis balance sheet and income statement to determine the cash inflows and outflows.

2. **Which of the following is *not* reported in the cash flows from operating activities section on a statement of cash flows?**
   A. A decrease in accounts receivable
   B. An increase in accounts payable
   C. The sale of additional common stock
   D. Depreciation expense

3. **Which of the following is reported in the cash flows from investing activities section on a statement of cash flows?**
   A. The payment of dividends
   B. A sale of equipment
   C. The sale of additional shares of preferred stock
   D. An increase in accumulated depreciation—equipment

4. **Which of the following is *not* reported in the cash flows from financing activities section on a statement of cash flows?**
   A. A decrease in dividends payable
   B. An issuance of bonds
   C. An additional sale of stock
   D. Payment of dividends

5. **PBW, Inc., reported net income of $200,000 in 2010. Also reported on the income statement was a depreciation expense of $50,000. The company's comparative balance sheet reported a decrease in accounts receivable of $5,000, an increase in inventory of $7,000, and an increase in accounts payable of $10,000. PBW paid $15,000 in dividends during 2010. What is the cash provided from operating activities?**
   A. $137,000
   B. $158,000
   C. $238,000
   D. $258,000

   Use the following information to answer questions 6 through 10.

   BLP, Inc., had the following activity in 2010:

   - **The company purchased a building for $250,000. A note payable was written for $100,000 of the purchase price, and the balance was paid in cash.**

- During the year, the company sold one of its current buildings for $165,000. The building originally had cost $220,000, and at the time of sale, it was being carried on the books for $175,000.
- The company purchased a piece of equipment for $50,000 and wrote a note payable for the full purchase price.
- On February 25, the company purchased a $15,000 patent in exchange for 1,500 shares of $10 par common stock of BLP.
- During the year, a current patent carried on the books at $11,500 was sold for $13,000.
- The company has a policy of amortizing all intangibles directly to the related intangible account.
- On January 1, the company issued 22 bonds with a face value of $1,000 each and received $24,400 in return.
- On November 15, the company declared dividends in the amount of $5,000. On December 31, half those dividends were distributed.
- Part of the premium on bonds payable was amortized in the amount of $400 for the year.
- On January 1, the company purchased fifty $1,000 ABC Company bonds at a price of $47,949. The bonds had a stated interest rate of 6 percent payable annually and a 7 percent effective interest rate. BLP elected to use the effective interest method for amortization purposes.
- During the year, the company issued 500 shares of $10 par value common stock for $60 per share.
- During the year, the company issued 1,000 shares of $25 par value preferred stock for $45.
- The company repaid $125,000 of its outstanding notes payable.

2010 Income Statement:

Sales		$750,000
Cost of goods sold		(525,000)
Gross profit		225,000
Operating expenses		
Salaries expense	$8,500	
Depreciation expense	70,000	
Amortization expense	2,000	
Other operating expenses	4,000	(84,500)
Operating income		140,500
Other items		
Interest expense	(600)	
Loss on sale of building	(10,000)	
Gain on sale of equipment	1,500	
Interest revenue	8,356	(744)
Pretax income from continuing operations		$139,756
Income tax expense		(34,939)
Net income		$104,817

Comparative Balance Sheets:

	2010	2009
Assets		
Current assets		
Cash	$184,251	$25,000
Accounts receivable	50,000	30,000
Interest receivable	2,000	0
Prepaid rent	3,500	2,500
Inventory	76,000	100,000
Noncurrent assets		
Investment in securities	48,305	0
Building	150,000	120,000
Accumulated depreciation—building	(20,000)	(15,000)
Equipment	200,000	150,000
Accumulated depreciation—equipment	(50,000)	(30,000)
Patents	16,500	15,000
Total assets	$660,556	$397,500
Liabilities		
Current liabilities		
Accounts payable	$30,000	$10,000
Salaries payable	9,100	8,300
Interest payable	500	1,000
Income tax payable	3,189	1,900
Deferred tax liability	500	350
Dividends payable	2,500	0
Noncurrent liabilities		
Notes payable	65,000	40,000
Bonds payable	42,000	20,000
Premium on bonds payable	5,000	3,000
Total liabilities	157,789	84,550
Stockholders' equity		
Common stock	$100,000	$80,000
Paid–in–capital common stock	175,000	150,000
Preferred stock	45,000	20,000
Paid–in–capital preferred stock	25,000	5,000
Retained earnings	157,767	57,950
Total stockholders' equity	502,767	312,950
Total liabilities and stockholders' equity	$660,556	$397,500

6. Using the indirect method for preparing the statement of cash flows, what is the net cash provided (used) by operating activities?

   A. $207,300
   B. $2,334
   C. $63,300
   D. $159,251

7. What is the net cash provided (used) by investing activities?

   A. ($28,100)
   B. ($49,949)
   C. ($19,949)
   D. ($22,000)

8. What is the net cash provided (used) by financing activities?

   A. $221,900
   B. ($28,100)
   C. ($226,900)
   D. ($23,100)

9. Using the direct method to prepare the operating activities section of the statement of cash flows, what should be the cash collections from interest?

   A. $6,000
   B. $8,356
   C. $10,000
   D. $10,356

10. Using the direct method to prepare the operating activities section of the statement of cash flows, what should be the cash payments to suppliers?

    A. $501,000
    B. $529,000
    C. $481,000
    D. $505,000

chapter 17

Accounting Changes

CHAPTER OBJECTIVES

After completing this chapter, the student should

- Understand the financial statement presentation for accounting changes
- Understand and account for a change in accounting principle
- Understand and account for a change in accounting estimate
- Understand and account for a change in reporting entity
- Understand how to correct an error

Overview

Everyone changes his or her mind, makes mistakes, and finds better ways of doing things. What would make you think that accountants and the business world are any different? You're right, they aren't!

It isn't that accountants are wishy-washy, although some might like to believe this statement. Sometimes it isn't even their fault! Generally accepted accounting principles (GAAP) and the other policymaking bodies are hard at work day after day trying to determine the most appropriate ways to account for all the transactions and events that may occur within a business setting. Therefore, it isn't surprising that revisions to Financial Accounting Standards Board (FASB) rules occur so frequently. When such changes occur, users need to follow.

Just like when you were a kid and didn't want to be placed in timeout, no accountant wants to defy GAAP rules and face the consequences.

Of course, contrary to popular belief, not everything in accounting is black and white; there are definitely some gray areas that provide some leeway in proper reporting without any new recommendation on the part of GAAP. There are simply times when financial conditions change for a specific company, and certain business practices become more common and new accounting methods appear to be more practical.

So how about errors? Well, accountants definitely have a reputation for being "detail oriented people." Unfortunately, everyone is human and makes mistakes. Maybe the error is a result of spending too many hours in the office looking at a computer screen or having a bit too much on one's mind. The reasoning doesn't matter. The only important thing to remember is that those errors, as well as the various changes, including others that we will discuss throughout this chapter, have to be accounted for in a certain way.

Financial Statement Presentation

Four different accounting changes exist that must be accounted for. They are a change in accounting principle, a change in accounting estimate, a change in reporting entity, and correction of errors:

A change in accounting principle is accounted for as a retrospective application of the new principle. Therefore, all prior period financial statements are presented as previously reported, and the current year's assets and liabilities are adjusted as necessary, along with an adjustment to the beginning balance of retained earnings.

A change in accounting estimate is accounted for as a prospective change. The company uses the new estimate in the current year and in future years with no changes to prior statements.

A change in reporting entity is accounted for as a retrospective restatement (prior period restatement). The financial statements are presented as if the current operating form had been in effect previously.

A correction of an error is accounted for as a prior-period adjustment. The change is recorded as an adjustment to the beginning balance of retained earnings and is shown net of tax.

Change in Accounting Principle

A *change in accounting principle* is a change from one generally accepted accounting principle to another. For example, a change in accounting principle could result from a change in inventory costing methods (FIFO to weighted average or LIFO to FIFO) or a change in depreciation methods (from double-declining balance to straight-line). It could even be the result of FASB adopting a new accounting principle. The first two situations represent changes made voluntarily by the company, whereas the last situation is a mandatory change required by the FASB.

So that you do not become confused, what is *not* a change in accounting principle? Neither the initial adoption of GAAP nor the change from non-GAAP to GAAP (this is a correction of an error) is considered to be a change in accounting principle. If a company is currently depreciating assets using the double-declining balance method and purchases new assets, choosing to depreciate them using the sum of the years' digits method, a change in accounting principle has not occurred. Instead, the company is simply opting to use a different generally accepted principle for accounting for assets that are different in substance from the assets that are currently being depreciated using the double declining balance method.

In addition to the financial statement presentation previously discussed, some additional disclosures are required. The reason for the change, a description of the prior period information that has been adjusted, the effect of the change on any line item that was affected, net income, earnings per share (EPS), and the cumulative effect of the change on retained earnings at the beginning of the earliest period presented must be included within the notes to the financial statements.

EXAMPLE 17-1

BLP, Inc., started investing in oil and gas wells in 2009. The company decided to adopt the successful efforts method of reporting the wells. (If you don't remember or know, the successful efforts method capitalizes only the costs associated with the drilling of wells in which oil and gas is found and expenses any costs associated with unsuccessful wells.) For a variety of reasons, the company decided to switch from the successful efforts method to the full costing method of accounting for oil and gas wells as of January 1, 2010. The full costing method capitalizes the costs of all the wells, both successful and unsuccessful, and expenses none of the costs of exploration.

If $100,000 was spent on successful wells and $50,000 was spent on unsuccessful wells in 2009, the adjustment to the beginning balance of retained earnings as of January 1, 2010, would be an increase of $50,000 net of taxes (the $50,000 from the unsuccessful well was expensed previously under the successful efforts method, but it would not have been under the full costing method). Additionally, the assets on the 2010 balance sheet would need to be increased by $50,000.

Before we continue on to the next accounting change, we need to mention that sometimes it is impracticable to apply accounting changes retrospectively. For instance, a change *to* last in, first out (LIFO) requires that the various cost indexes and any liquidations be known. Because this would be difficult to determine after the fact, when inventory costing methods are converted to LIFO, the change is accounted for prospectively from the first moment practicable. There are other items that are treated similarly, but the LIFO exception is the most common.

An additional exception is that sometimes it may be difficult to distinguish a change in principle from a change in estimate. The main item that falls in this category is a change in depreciation methods. A depreciation method is usually selected because it provides a rational allocation of expenses that reflects a matching of expenses with the related revenues. Therefore, even though changing from straight-line to sum of the years' digits may appear to be a change in principle in form, in substance, it is actually a change in estimate. The change is treated prospectively, as will be discussed in the next section, and is deemed a change in accounting estimate effected by a change in accounting principle.

Change in Accounting Estimate

Accounting for a *change in accounting estimate* is one of the easiest changes for which to account. Since there are so many numbers on the financial statements that are based on estimates, the simplicity is especially appreciated! Estimates are, as you would assume, always changing. As new information becomes available, a better estimate usually can be determined. Think about the financial statements for a minute. Try to name some of the accounts that rely on estimates: allowance for bad debts, inventory that has become obsolete, useful lives of property, plant, and equipment (PPE), residual values for PPE, recoverable mineral reserves, warranty liabilities, and pension costs. These represent just a handful of the guessing games that businesses and their accountants play.

A company properly accounts for a change in estimate prospectively and thus uses the new estimate for the current and future years. However, it ignores any effect that the change may have had in the past. Therefore, none of the numbers on past financial statements are altered. Let's look at an example of a change in estimate.

 **EXAMPLE 17-2**

BLP, Inc., has an oil well listed on its books at a cost of $25 million and a salvage value of $1 million. The company has been depleting the oil well based on an estimate of 1 million barrels of oil. Depletion of $10 million has been recorded since the oil well was purchased five years ago. This year a new estimate was prepared by the petroleum engineers, and it was determined that approximately 1,750,000 barrels of oil remain to be removed. The new depletion rate of $8 per barrel should be used for the current and future years. The $8 is computed as follows: depletable cost ($25 million – $10 million) minus salvage value ($1 million) divided by the remaining barrels of oil (1,750,000). If 80,000 barrels of oil are removed and sold during 2010, the depletion expense would be $640,000 (80,000 × $8) rather than the original $1,920,000 (80,000 × $24) that would have been recorded under the old estimate.

Change in Reporting Entity

A *change in reporting entity* occurs when the companies included in the financial statements have changed form. Such changes could be the result of a sole proprietorship becoming a partnership or corporation, two companies merging during the year, a company creating a subsidiary, or even the acquisition of a new company or two. The end result of any of these situations is that the companies included in previous years' financial statements are different from the companies included in the current year's financial statements. Everyone looking at the financial statements is curious as to why the companies are different and likely want to know what the previous years' financial statements would have looked like had the new companies been in existence or combined last year. As a result, GAAP requires that the accounting for a change in reporting entity be a retrospective restatement (prior period restatement). Thus all financial statements presented should reflect the entities in existence in the current year.

The company also must present a footnote including a description of the change and why the change occurred. Additionally, the note should state the effect of the change on income before extraordinary items, the effect of the change on net income, and the effect of the change on the EPS numbers for all the periods presented.

This is all the information that we will cover here regarding a change in reporting entity. Such changes are more appropriately classified as advanced accounting topics instead of intermediate accounting ones.

Correction of an Error

An *error* is an unintentional mistake that could arise from a number of different situations. For instance, a materially incorrect computation in a past period that was discovered in the current period would be considered an error. Other examples of errors are use of a non-GAAP accounting rule, use of an estimate not made in good faith, or incorrect mathematical calculations. Finally, an error also could arise from the omission of a deferral or an accrual.

As we stated at the beginning of this chapter, corrections of errors are presented on a company's financial statements as adjustments to the beginning balance of retained earnings. Think about this for a minute. Retained earnings represent an after tax number. Therefore, when we include the prior-period adjustment, it also must be included as an after tax number.

When you make a mistake in life, everyone wants to know all the details, especially when it personally affects them! The same is true with financial statements. Therefore, in the footnotes, the cause of the error, its effect on income before extraordinary items, and its effect on net income and EPS numbers must be included for all the periods presented.

So enough about what errors are. Let's move on to the fun of figuring out how to correct those errors. There are two approaches that can be taken with error correction. The first approach involves using a base set of numbers and then comparing them with another set of numbers that includes the error. This is an excellent way to determine the effect of the error on the various components of the financial statements.

EXAMPLE 17-3

In the current year, BLP, Inc., purchased some equipment for $1,000. The $1,000 should have been capitalized to the asset equipment account but instead was expensed to the repair and maintenance account. Remember that net income is closed to the retained earnings account at the end of each year and thus is reported with stockholders' equity on the balance sheet. See Table 17-1 for the effects on the income statement and balance sheet.

Notice the effect of the error on the following accounts: Expenses are overstated, which makes net income understated. Because the net income is understated, the retained earnings also will be understated. The assets are understated, and there is no effect on the liabilities.

The second approach that can be taken involves actually making the journal entries. Probably the easiest way to see how to make a correcting journal entry is to recreate the entry that was made and then make the entry that should have been made. After those two entries are examined, it is usually much easier to make a correcting journal entry.

EXAMPLE 17-4

Let's continue with the preceding example. The actual entry that was made was

| Repair and maintenance expense | 1,000 | |
| Cash | | 1,000 |

TABLE 17-1 Errors (Example 17-3)					
	Base	With Error		Base	With Error
Assets	100,000	99,000	Revenue	20,000	20,000
Liabilities	25,000	25,000	Expenses	(16,000)	(17,000)
Equity	75,000	74,000	Net income	4,000	3,000

The entry that should have been made is

Equipment	1,000	
Cash		1,000

The entry to correct the error would be

Equipment	1,000	
Repair and maintenance expense		1,000

Another approach to correcting journal entries is to reverse the original incorrect entry and make the correct one. Either method will provide the same end result. One additional item that must be considered is if the error affected any other accounts. For example, if bonuses were paid based on net income, the bonuses may have been affected. You also may have inventory errors that affect two different years. There are many complex situations involving errors. Our best advice is to think through each set of circumstances very carefully. Then make the actual journal entries and the entries that should have been made. Using this advice, you should be able to analyze any situation involving errors.

Before moving on to discussing the impact of errors on multiple years, we wish to make one additional note. The approaches that we have listed previously are mathematical and visual methods of determining the effect of errors on a company's books. While a lot of people need to follow one of these approaches, there are some who can easily eyeball the effect of the error. To do so, the basic accounting equation and the interconnectivity between financial statements must be remembered. Try it; you may be one of those lucky few. If not, there are always the other two approaches.

So far we have shown how to correct an error made and found in the current year. How do we correct the error that was made in a prior year? This is where the prior-period adjustment comes in.

EXAMPLE 17-5

Last year, BLP, Inc., inadvertently recorded a purchase of equipment of $1,000 to repair and maintenance expense. The error was not discovered until the current year, when a new entry level accountant noticed that a piece of equipment was not included in the depreciation calculation on which she was working. She referred back to the general ledger for the previous year and discovered that the cost of the equipment had been expensed. After discussing the situation with the controller, the two decided that it was a material error and should be disclosed on the statement of retained earnings. See Table 17-2 for the statement of retained earnings assuming that the company has $10,000 in net income, $2,000 in dividends for the current year, and a 30 percent tax rate for the previous year.

TABLE 17-2 Prior-Period Adjustment (Example 17-5)	
Retained earnings, 1/1/10	74,000
Add: Prior-period adjustment, net of $300 tax	700
Retained earnings, adjusted beginning balance	74,700
Add: Net income	10,000
Less: Dividends	(2,000)
Retained earnings, 12/31/10	82,700

Well, we are almost there! We have admitted our mistakes (errors), told you we used faulty assumptions (changes in estimates), altered our focus and adopted new techniques (changes in accounting principle), and even changed our businesses (changes in reporting entity), all while using proper accounting. Every single one of you who have read each chapter of this book should be an accounting pro by now! Okay, so maybe not. Not even we are accounting pros by any means! Things are changing every day, and no one really has a handle on everything there is to know. The biggest change right now to hit the accounting world is the International Financial Reporting Standards (IFRS). In Chapter 18 we will briefly discuss this accounting revolution as it pertains to the United States.

QUIZ

1. **Which of the following changes is accounted for as a retrospective application of the new accounting principle?**

   A. A change from LIFO to FIFO inventory valuation methods
   B. A change from declining balance to straight-line depreciation methods
   C. A change from partnership status to corporate status
   D. A change from a non-GAAP method to a GAAP method

2. **How is a change from units-of-output depreciation method to straight-line depreciation method accounted for?**

   A. A retrospective application of a new accounting principle
   B. A prospective adjustment
   C. A restatement of prior financial statements
   D. A prior-period adjustment

3. **BLP, Inc., has equipment costing $110,000. This equipment was purchased in January 2005. It has been depreciated by the straight-line method using a salvage value of $10,000 and a 10-year life. At the beginning of 2010, it was determined that the remaining life would be only four more years. What is the depreciation expense for 2010?**

   A. $11,111
   B. $12,222
   C. $12,500
   D. $15,000

4. **Which of the following would be considered a change in a reporting entity?**

   A. A partnership incorporated during the current year.
   B. BLP merged with ABC during the current year.
   C. BLP purchased DEF during the current year.
   D. All the above are considered a change in a reporting entity.

5. **BLP, Inc., forgot to accrue $500 of interest revenue in 2009. The error was discovered in 2010 when the company received the interest. Which of the following is a *true* statement?**

   A. Assets in 2009 are overstated.
   B. Assets in 2010 are understated.
   C. Net income in 2009 is understated.
   D. Net income in 2010 is overstated.

6. **Which of the following would be considered an error and should be accounted for as a prior-period adjustment?**

   A. Changing from the LIFO to the FIFO inventory method
   B. Changing from the FIFO to the LIFO inventory method
   C. Changing from a non-GAAP inventory method to FIFO
   D. Changing from the weighted-average to the LIFO inventory method

7. On December 31, 2009, BLP, Inc., reported a retained earnings balance of $50,000. Early in 2010, though, one of the company's astute accountants identified that an inventory purchase totaling $16,000 had been omitted from the 2009 financial statements. If BLP has a 25 percent tax rate, what adjustment should be made to the financial statements presented in 2010?

   A. A decrease to the beginning retained earnings balance of $12,000
   B. A decrease to the beginning retained earnings balance of $16,000
   C. An increase to the beginning retained earnings balance of $12,000
   D. A decrease in the current year's net income of $16,000

8. Jones Company was incorporated on January 1, 2007. At that time, the company decided to use the FIFO inventory costing method. During 2009, $25,000 of inventory was recorded at year end. In 2010, the company's financial officers decided that the weighted-average method would be more appropriate. The officials determined that had inventory been recorded under the weighted-average method in 2009, it would have totaled $34,000. If the tax rate was 30 percent in 2009, what should be the adjustment to retained earnings in 2010?

   A. A decrease of $6,300
   B. An increase of $6,300
   C. An increase of $9,000
   D. A decrease of $9,000

9. LJC Unlimited had capital assets listed on its books at a cost of $50,000 that were being depreciated using the straight-line method, a life of 10 years, and a residual value of $5,000. Two years after their purchase, the company decided to switch to the double-declining balance method for the assets' remaining life. What should be the adjustment to the beginning balance of retained earnings not considering any tax effects?

   A. $9,000
   B. $10,000
   C. $10,250
   D. $0

10. Failing to record a purchase of inventory in a particular year affects what financial statements?

   A. The balance sheet only
   B. The income statement only
   C. The balance sheet and income statement
   D. No financial statement is affected.

International Financial Reporting Standards

CHAPTER OBJECTIVE

After completing this chapter, the student should

- Understand where to find additional information on international financial reporting standards

Overview

Accounting is a language based on numbers and journal entries rather than letters, words, and sentences. Just as languages may include a number of different dialects, generally accepted accounting principles (GAAP) constitute just one accounting dialect. While GAAP has been the primary principle system used in the United States, initiatives are in place to replace GAAP with a different dialect—the International Financial Reporting Standards (IFRS). Why is such a change desired? Well, have you ever traveled to a foreign country or even to a large city in the United States? Just looking around you, you tend to assume that everyone speaks the same language, right? Unfortunately, though, mouths open, and something unrecognizable comes out. You feel left out and have this crazy feeling that everyone is talking about you or, at the very least, trying to hide something from you. No one likes to feel left out of the loop, and that is exactly what IFRS is trying to prevent. If everyone uses the same accounting system throughout the world, all users will understand exactly what the financial statements are speaking about regardless of whether they are looking at statements from a company based in Ireland, Italy, or the United States.

So here we are at the last chapter of this book. Throughout this book, you have learned *a lot* about U.S. GAAP! However, there is still the realization that there is so much more to learn, not only about U.S. GAAP but also about international accounting standards as well.

Current Status

With the economies of all nations becoming more and more dependent on one another, especially over the last few decades, it should not be surprising that a need for a common set of accounting standards has emerged. In fact, there have been organizations working toward a uniform set of international accounting standards for at least 30 years now. From the standpoint of the United States, the Securities and Exchange Commission (SEC), the American Institute of Certified Public Accountants (AICPA), and the Financial Accounting Standards Board (FASB) all have been hard at work aligning U.S. GAAP with international accounting rules.

So what organization is responsible for issuing such international standards? The responsible party is the International Accounting Standards Board (IASB), and its representatives are in charge of issuing what are known as International Financial Reporting Standards (IFRS). The IASB has agreed to work with the SEC to align U.S. GAAP with IFRS, and both groups hope to have the process completed by 2014 at the earliest or 2016 at the latest. What about CPA candidates? How will they be affected by this accounting revolution? Plans are under way to make IFRS questions eligible for testing on the Uniform CPA Exam beginning in 2011.

Because this area of accounting is currently ever-changing, we have chosen simply to note its existence and provide you with the opportunity to research it further on your own. Our best advice is to visit the Web sites of some or all of the organizations mentioned above to learn more about the present status of convergence.

Our look into intermediate accounting is finally complete. We hope that you have enjoyed the journey and, as we mentioned at the beginning of this book, maybe even have made some new friends along the way (accounts as well as other accounting aficionados). We have definitely enjoyed and have had some fun compiling this book; we hope that you have had fun as well. Whether you disliked accounting before and just needed some extra material to help you trudge through a class or maybe even your job or liked accounting so much that you simply wanted to get your hands on as much related information as you could, we believe that this book likely has served its purpose. Remember, there is a lot more to accounting than you will find in this or any other book. Despite its reputation, accounting really is an intriguing subject!

Final Exam

1. Mulligan, Inc., established a petty cash account on February 10, 2010, in the amount of $150. During the remainder of the month, the following small expenditures were made by the company: office supplies, $25; break room refreshments, $15; and postage, $45. At the end of the month, $63 remained in the petty cash drawer. Based on that information, the cash short and over account will have which of the following balances?

   A. $2 credit balance

   B. $2 debit balance

   C. $20 debit balance

   D. A cash short and over account is not needed.

2. Which of the following statements is *not correct* concerning the periodic and perpetual inventory systems?

   A. Under the perpetual system, COGS is a real account with a balance that is updated as each sale is made.

   B. Two entries are made to record a sale under the periodic inventory system.

   C. The inventory amount found on the balance sheet under the periodic system is the beginning balance, which is replaced with the physically counted amount at the end of the period.

   D. A physical count of inventory must be taken under the perpetual inventory system.

3. Amethyst, Inc., originally issued 2,000 shares of $15 par value common stock for $30 each on February 25, 2010. On August 31, 2010, the company reacquired 500 of those shares at a cost of $20 per share. On October 19, 2010, the company reissued 300 of those shares at a price of $22 per share. Two days later, on October 21, 2010, the company reissued 100 of the shares at a price of $18 per share. As a result of all these events, and assuming that these are the only events that affect PIC—TS, what should be the balance of PIC—TS on December 31, 2010, using the cost of treasury stock method?

A. $0

B. $400

C. $29,900

D. $30,400

4. Which of the following statements about current liabilities is *not true*?

A. Current liabilities have a normal credit balance and are presented on the balance sheet as a liability.

B. Current liabilities can be satisfied with either current assets or the creation of other current liabilities.

C. Current liabilities do not ever have to be paid.

D. Current liabilities are created by past transactions.

5. Long-term notes receivable are a _____ asset and have a normal _____ balance.

A. fixed, debit

B. long-term, debit

C. long-term, credit

D. fixed, credit

6. Which of the following types of investments cannot include equity securities?

A. Trading securities

B. Available-for-sale securities

C. Securities with the intent to sell in the near future

D. Held-to-maturity securities

7. Given the data below and the fact that the year-end cost on January 1, 2010, was $10,000, what would be the ending inventory under the dollar value LIFO inventory method on December 31, 2012?

Year	Year-End Cost	Index
2010	$12,000	1.05
2011	$11,500	1.10
2012	$13,000	1.15

A. $14,950

B. $11,477

C. $11,454

D. $11,500

8. Pearson Company prepared its bank reconciliation at the end of the period. Given the following information, and provided that the account is the only source of cash for the company, what amount should be recorded as cash on the balance sheet as of the period end?

Cash balance per the bank statement: $83,500

Deposits in transit: $1,600

Outstanding checks: $1,250

$100 bank service charge

$350 interest earned during the period

A. $84,100

B. $83,850

C. $83,500

D. $83,750

9. On May 14, 2010, Jeffres Company invested in 100 shares of A stock at $30 per share. The company also bought 200 debt securities in B company at $20 per security. The company intended to sell the securities in the near future. At the end of the year, the value per share of A was $35, and the value per security of B was $14. On December 31, 2010, the

balance sheet date, the investments would be recorded on the balance sheet at _____ and _____, respectively.

A. $3,500; $2,800

B. $3,000; $4,000

C. $2,800; $3,500

D. $500; $1,200

10. Based on the information in question 9, the journal entry to record the change to fair market value would include

A. a debit to trading securities A for $3,500 and a credit to trading securities B for $2,800.

B. a debit to trading securities A for $500 and a credit to trading securities B for $2,800.

C. a credit to trading securities B for $1,200 and a debit to unrealized loss on trading securities for $700.

D. a credit to trading securities B for $1,200 and a credit to unrealized gain on trading securities for $700.

11. BLP, Inc., has decided to issue 100 bonds at 102. The bonds will include 10 warrants with each bond. On the issue date, the FMV of each bond is 98, and the FMV of each warrant is $7. Each warrant allows the holder to purchase one share of $5 par stock for $25 per share. They will pay interest of 8 percent. At the date of issue, the journal entry will include a

A. debit to cash of $102,000.

B. a credit to cash of $100,000.

C. a credit to premium on bonds payable of $4,800.

D. a debit to common stock warrants of $6,800.

12. On January 1, 2010, LJ, Inc., sold $250,000 of clothing to GBW, Inc., in exchange for a five-year non-interest-bearing long-term note receivable. GBW's incremental borrowing rate is 7 percent. What will be the present value of the note receivable?

A. $250,000

B. $233,645

C. $178,247

D. $232,500

13. A fire destroyed part of the inventory of the McGuire Company. For the current year, the company had net sales of $120,000 and began the year with $40,000 in inventory, with $60,000 in additional purchases during the year. If gross profit is 25 percent of sales, what would be the company's ending inventory?

A. $90,000

B. $100,000

C. $30,000

D. $10,000

14. On April 5, 2010, LJ, Inc., purchased 500 equity securities in GBW, Inc., at $5 per share that it classified as available-for-sale. On December, 31, 2010, as it was preparing its financial statements, LJ, Inc., determined that the fair market value of the securities had increased to $15 per share. What would be the journal entry to adjust the value of the securities?

A. A debit to available-for-sale securities—GBW for $5,000 and a credit to unrealized gain for $5,000

B. A debit to unrealized increase/decrease—GBW for $7,500 and a credit to allowance to value AFS securities for $7,500

C. A debit to unrealized increase/decrease—GBW for $5,000 and a credit to allowance to value AFS securities—GBW for $5,000

D. A debit to allowance to value AFS securities—GBW for $5,000 and a credit to unrealized increase/decrease—GBW for $5,000

15. Discount on long-term notes receivable is a(n) _____ account to long-term notes receivable.

A. expense

B. complementary

C. contra

D. control

16. The purpose of a statement of cash flows is to

   A. reconcile a cash basis balance sheet with an accrual basis income statement.

   B. reconcile an accrual basis balance sheet with a cash basis income statement.

   C. reconcile a cash basis balance sheet and income statement to determine the cash inflows and outflows.

   D. reconcile an accrual basis balance sheet and income statement to determine the cash inflows and outflows.

17. Which of the following is a *false* statement?

   A. For noncumulative preferred stock, all dividends, whether declared or not, should be considered in the numerator change.

   B. For noncumulative preferred stock, only declared dividends should be considered in the numerator change.

   C. For cumulative preferred stock, all dividends, whether declared or not, should be considered in the numerator change.

   D. All the above statements are true.

18. Capitalizing an expenditure means

   A. the expenditure is debited to an asset account.

   B. the expenditure is debited to an expense account.

   C. the expenditure is credited to an expense account.

   D. the expenditure is credited to property, plant, and equipment.

19. BLP, Inc., purchased a piece of equipment on January 2, 2010, for $120,000. The company determined that it will have a useful life of five years and will be worth $20,000 at the end of that time. BLP decided to depreciate this asset using the sum of the years' digits method. (*Hint:* Prepare a complete depreciation schedule for this asset for each year of its life prior to answering the following questions. Make certain your schedule shows the date, depreciation expense, accumulated depreciation, and book value for each year of the asset's life.) The depreciation expense for 2012 will be

   A. $33,333.

   B. $26,667.

   C. $20,000.

   D. $13,333.

20. Based on the information in question 19, the book value as of December 31, 2014, will be

   A. $60,000.

   B. $40,000.

   C. $26,667.

   D. $20,000.

21. Under a sale leaseback, when the present value of the lease payments is greater than 10 percent but less than 90 percent of the fair value of the property at the signing of the lease and the sale price of the asset is greater than the asset's net book value, which of the following is part of the accounting treatment?

   A. A gain is deferred up to the present value of the leaseback, and any remaining gain is recognized immediately.

   B. A gain is deferred for the full amount of the sale price minus the net book value.

   C. A loss is recognized immediately.

   D. A gain is recognized immediately for the full amount of the sale price minus the net book value.

22. Which of the following is reported in the cash flows from the investing activities section on a statement of cash flows?

   A. The payment of dividends

   B. A sale of equipment

   C. The sale of additional shares of preferred stock

   D. An increase in accumulated depreciation—equipment

23. Which of the following statements regarding intangibles is *false*?

   A. Intangibles are presented on the financial statements as an asset.

   B. Intangibles are presented on the financial statements net of any amortization.

   C. Accumulated amortization for intangibles is presented on the face of the balance sheet.

   D. Intangibles are presented on the balance sheet.

24. BLP, Inc., agreed to construct a boathouse for a company at a price of $400,000. The costs incurred and estimated to complete the project are presented below:

	2009	2010	2011
Cost incurred each year	100,000	150,000	75,000
Cost incurred to date	100,000	250,000	325,000
Estimated cost to complete	225,000	75,000	0
Total estimated cost	325,000	325,000	325,000

How much revenue is recognized in 2009 under the percentage-of-completion method (round any percentages used to the nearest whole number)?

A. $24,000

B. $124,000

C. $184,000

D. $92,000

25. Net assets are

A. assets plus liabilities.

B. assets minus liabilities.

C. assets plus stockholders' equity.

D. assets minus revenues.

26. Goodwill

A. can be recorded only if it is developed internally.

B. can be amortized over five years.

C. has a definite life.

D. has an indefinite life.

27. Cuso, Inc., sold books valued at $45,000 to Nusch, Inc., in exchange for a long-term note receivable with a 5 percent interest rate. It was indeterminable what the value of the note would be in the marketplace, but another seller is willing to accept the note in exchange for $60,000 worth of goods. Payments of $5,000 along with accrued interest will be made semiannually. At what value should the long-term note receivable be recorded?

A. $45,000

B. $60,000

C. $47,250

D. $52,500

28. Which of the following is not reported in the cash flows from operating activities section on a statement of cash flows?

A. A decrease in accounts receivable

B. An increase in accounts payable

C. The sale of additional common stock

D. Depreciation expense

29. Burrs Company accounts for its bad debts using the allowance method. On December 31, the company had gross accounts receivable recorded on its books of $200,000. On that date, the allowance for bad debts account had a credit balance of $22,000. During the year, the company had $500,000 in sales. Bad debts are calculated as 5 percent of outstanding accounts receivable. What entry needs to be made to the allowance for bad debts account to record this information?

A. A credit entry for $10,000

B. A debit entry for $32,000

C. A credit entry for $25,000

D. A credit entry for $32,000

30. BLP, Inc., has decided to purchase JKL Company for $500,000. The book value of JKL Company's net assets is $349,500, and the fair market value of those same assets is $426,000. BLP should record goodwill at

A. $150,500.

B. $74,000.

C. $426,000.

D. $500,000.

31. Regarding internal controls over intangibles, which of the following statements is *false*?

A. Management is responsible for proper valuation of intangibles.

B. Computer systems and programs should not allow alterations of the value of intangibles.

C. There is no need for any independent internal verification of intangibles.

D. Documentation should be maintained on all intangible assets, including acquisition date, related costs, and descriptions of each intangible.

32. Which of the following statements is the *correct definition* of an accrued liability?

A. A liability that has been incurred but not yet paid nor recorded

B. A revenue that has been earned but not yet paid nor recorded

C. An expense that has been paid in advance

D. A revenue that has been paid in advance

33. BLP, Inc., has net income of $200,000 and a tax rate of 30 percent. The company decided to pay its president a 10 percent bonus on net income after deducting both the bonus and taxes. How much is the bonus the president will receive?

A. $14,433

B. $55,670

C. $56,075

D. $13,084

34. BLP, Inc., purchased land and a building for $100,000. The fair market value of the land was $25,000, and the fair market value of the building was $90,000. The book value on the seller's books of the land was $15,000, and the book value on the seller's books of the building was $82,000. The journal entry BLP will make to record the purchase will include

A. a debit to cash of $100,000.

B. a debit to land of $15,000.

C. a debit to building of $82,000.

D. a debit to land of $21,739.

35. BLP, Inc., has 20,000 shares of $10 par common stock issued and outstanding when the board of directors declares a 10 percent stock dividend. The FMV of the common stock on the declaration date is $15 per share. The journal entry to record this dividend will include

A. a debit to retained earnings of $30,000.

B. a credit to common stock of $60,000.

C. a credit to common stock of $30,000.

D. a debit to retained earnings of $60,000.

36. Which of the following contingencies must be both disclosed and recorded?

A. Probable gain contingency

B. Reasonably possible gain contingency

C. Remote loss contingency

D. Probable loss contingency

37. Which method of amortization of bond discounts and premiums is GAAP?

A. Straight-line method

B. Declining-balance method

C. Effective interest method

D. Sum of the years' digits method

38. BLP, Inc., decided to issue 100 bonds on January 2, 2010. The life of the bonds will be three years. The stated rate of interest will be 8 percent, and interest will be paid annually on December 31 of each year. These bonds were issued at $95,027, which reflects an effective interest rate of 10 percent. (*Hint:* Prepare an amortization table and journal entries prior to answering the questions.) The journal entry to issue the bonds includes a

A. debit to cash of $100,000.

B. debit to premium on bonds payable of $4,973.

C. credit to bonds payable of $95,027.

D. debit to discount on bonds payable of $4,973.

39. Based on the information in question 38, at the first interest payment date of December 31, 2010, the journal entry will include a

A. credit to discount on bonds payable of $1,503.

B. debit to premium on bonds payable of $1,503.

C. credit to interest expense of $9,503.

D. debit to cash of $8,000.

40. The account common stock warrants is reflected on the financial statements as

    A. an asset.

    B. a liability.

    C. an expense.

    D. additional paid-in capital.

41. At the end of the term of a long-term note receivable but before receiving payment, the present value or net value of the note is equal to

    A. the amount of the original discount on long-term notes receivable.

    B. the face value of the note.

    C. $0.

    D. the same net amount as at establishment of the note.

42. BLP, Inc., sold 500 shares of $10 par common stock along with 100 shares of $5 par preferred stock for a total of $23,000. At the time of sale, the FMV of the common stock was $40 per share, and the FMV of the preferred stock was $50 per share. Which of the following would be included in the journal entry to record this sale?

    A. A credit to common stock for $18,400

    B. A credit to preferred stock for $4,600

    C. A credit to PIC—CS for $13,400

    D. A credit to cash for $23,000

43. BLP, Inc., sold 500 shares of 7 percent, $10 par preferred stock with 500 common stock warrants (CSW) attached for $60,000. Each warrant allows the holder to purchase one share of common stock for $30. On the date of sale, the FMV of the PS was $100 per share, and the FMV of the CSW was $40 each. Which of the following would be included in the journal entry to record this sale?

    A. A debit to preferred stock for $5,000

    B. A credit to cash for $60,000

    C. A debit to PIC—PS for $37,857

    D. A credit to CSW for $17,143

44. Which of the following cost flow assumptions will produce the highest net income assuming a period of rising prices?

    A. LIFO periodic

    B. Average cost perpetual

    C. FIFO perpetual

    D. LIFO perpetual

45. On January 1, 2012, LC Enterprises adopted a compensatory stock option plan for its key employees. The plan enabled eligible employees to purchase 10 shares of $5 par common stock for each option granted to them. The exercise price would be $10. The number of eligible employees totaled 20, and each of those employees was granted 20 options. On the grant date, the FMV of the options was determined to be $15. The options will fully vest at the end of four years, on December 31, 2015. What amount should be recorded as compensation expense on December 31, 2012?

    A. $15,000

    B. $60,000

    C. $750

    D. $10,000

46. Which of the following is *true* of treasury stock recorded under the par value method but not under the cost method?

    A. The initial journal entry consists of a debit to cash for the total proceeds amount and a credit to common stock, with any additional amount of proceeds over par being credited to PIC—CS.

    B. The reacquisition of shares is recorded at cost, with a debit to treasury stock and a credit to cash for the repurchase price.

    C. A reissuance above cost is recorded as a debit to cash for the reissuance price, along with a credit to treasury stock for the reacquisition cost and a credit to PIC—TS for the portion of the reissuance price that exceeds the reacquisition cost.

    D. A reissuance above cost is recorded as a debit to cash for the reissuance price, along with a credit to treasury stock for the par value of the common stock and a credit to PIC—CS for the portion of the reissuance price that exceeds the par value.

47. The account discount on bonds payable is presented on the financial statements

    A. on the income statement as an addition to revenues.

    B. on the balance sheet as a deduction from bonds payable.

    C. on the income statement as an addition to expenses.

    D. on the balance sheet as an addition to bonds payable.

48. The date of declaration is the

    A. date the board of directors determines that a dividend will be paid.

    B. date the stock stops selling with the dividend attached.

    C. same as the date of record.

    D. date the dividend is paid.

49. Which of the following is a *false* statement?

    A. Cumulative preferred stock does not share an equal percentage of par value with common stock when dividends are paid.

    B. Fully participating preferred stock shares an equal percentage of par value with common stock when dividends are paid.

    C. Partially participating preferred stock shares an equal percentage of par value with common stock when dividends are paid.

    D. Cumulative preferred stock is entitled to dividends in arrears.

50. GBW, Inc., has decided to issue a garage to a shareholder as a property dividend. When the board of directors declared the dividend, the garage was listed on the books at $30,000, whereas the fair market value was $50,000. The dividend will be paid before the end of the year. Based on this information, which of the following entries will be made to record the declaration?

    A. A credit to garage for $20,000

    B. A debit to property dividend payable for $50,000

    C. A credit to gain on disposal of garage of $20,000

    D. A debit to loss on disposal of garage of $20,000

51. On the balance sheet, assets are listed

    A. in order of increasing magnitude.

    B. in order of liquidity.

C. in order of decreasing magnitude.

D. alphabetically.

52. **Which of the following is *not* a true statement?**

    A. Common stock must have a par value.

    B. Common stock can be authorized with or without a par value.

    C. Preferred stock can be authorized with a stated value.

    D. Common stock can be issued in exchange for property.

53. **Which of the following is *not* a characteristic of a small stock dividend?**

    A. The percentage of the dividend distribution is 20 to 25 percent of the currently outstanding shares of stock.

    B. The dividend distribution is recorded at the FMV of the stock on the date of the dividend declaration.

    C. The entry to record the dividend declaration may include a credit to PIC—CS or PIC—PS.

    D. The dividend distribution is recorded at the FMV of the stock on the date of the dividend payment.

54. **Property, plant, and equipment accounts should be presented in the financial statements**

    A. net of accumulated amortization.

    B. net of accumulated depletion.

    C. net of accumulated depreciation.

    D. as expenses.

55. **BLP, Inc., has $300,000 of 10 percent bonds payable that were issued at a discount in 2007. These bonds mature in 2027. The discount is amortized at $1,000 per year. Each $1,000 bond is convertible into 40 shares of common stock. The tax rate is 30 percent. What is the change in the numerator for these convertible securities?**

    A. $12,000

    B. $20,300

    C. $21,700

    D. $31,000

56. Which is a *true statement* regarding stock options and warrants?

   A. Stock options and warrants are always ranked last.

   B. Stock options and warrants never use the treasury stock method.

   C. Stock options and warrants always use the treasury stock method.

   D. Stock options and warrants do not affect EPS.

57. In 2010, GBW, Inc., had net income of $250,000. The company had 10,000 shares of $1 par value, 10 percent cumulative preferred stock outstanding but had not declared a dividend as of the end of the year. On January 1, 2010, GBW had 5,000 shares of common stock outstanding. On June 1, the company's board of directors declared a two-for-one stock split. Additionally, on August 31, the company repurchased 2,000 shares. For purposes of a basic EPS calculation, what is the weighted-average number of shares outstanding for 2010?

   A. 5,000

   B. 10,000

   C. 8,667

   D. 9,334

58. Using the same facts as in question 57, what is GBW's basic EPS for 2010?

   A. $26.68

   B. $26.78

   C. $24.90

   D. $25.10

59. Which of the following statements is *false* regarding convertible preferred stock as it pertains to diluted EPS computations?

   A. The amount of preferred dividends is subtracted from net income to determine the basic EPS numerator.

   B. The number of new shares of common stock that the preferred stock would be converted into is added to the basic EPS denominator.

   C. The amount of preferred dividends is multiplied by the reciprocal of the tax rate before being added back to the basic EPS numerator.

   D. No tax effects are taken into consideration.

60. **Which of the following statements is *true*?**

    A. Construction in progress under the completed contract method includes both the construction costs and the gross profit.

    B. Construction in progress under the percentage-of-completion method includes both the construction costs and the gross profit.

    C. Construction in progress is not an inventory account.

    D. None of these statements are true.

61. **Under the direct write-off method of accounting for accounts receivable, which of the following represents the journal entry that would be made to write off an account that is not expected to be repaid?**

    A. Debit bad debt expense and credit allowance for bad debts

    B. Debit accounts receivable and credit bad debt expense

    C. Debit bad debt expense and credit accounts receivable

    D. Debit allowance for bad debt expense and credit accounts receivable

62. **The formula to compute double-declining balance depreciation is**

    A. cost minus salvage value divided by life.

    B. cost minus salvage value times (remaining life at the beginning of the year divided by the sum of the years' digits).

    C. cost minus salvage value times double the straight-line rate.

    D. book value times double the straight-line rate.

63. **Which of the following statements is *true*?**

    A. The installment method for accounts receivable is always used when a customer agrees to pay the total bill in predetermined portions.

    B. The cost recovery method for accounts receivable uses a partial billings account.

    C. The installment method for accounts receivable is used when collection is not reasonably assured.

    D. The cost recovery method for accounts receivable is used when collection is absolutely assured.

64. **When is revenue recognized under the completed contract method?**

    A. At the point of sale

    B. Incrementally over the life of the project

C. When the project is completed

D. The year after the project is completed

65. **Which of the following is an example of a future taxable item?**

A. Warranty expense when book expense is more than the tax deduction

B. Contingent liability when book expense is more than the tax deduction

C. Prepaid rent when book income is less than taxable income

D. Depreciation expense when book expense is less than the tax deduction

66. **BLP, Inc., determined that the enacted tax rates are 30, 35, and 40 percent for 2009, 2010, and 2011, respectively. The taxable income for 2009 is $120,000. The book and tax depreciation for each year is shown in the following table:**

	2009	2010	2011
Book depreciation	100,000	150,000	75,000
Tax depreciation	75,000	125,000	55,000

In 2009, the deferred tax asset account should be

A. credited for $7,500.

B. debited for $8,000.

C. debited for $8,750.

D. debited for $24,250.

67. **On its December 31, 2009, balance sheet, LJC, Inc., reported a deferred tax asset of $5,000. For 2010, financial income before taxes of $120,000 was reported. As part of that income, the company had included municipal bond interest of $15,000. Additionally, the company had straight-line depreciation of $10,000 for the year recorded on its books, whereas MACRS tax depreciation totaled $25,000 for the year. No other temporary or permanent differences existed on December 31, 2010. LJC's enacted tax rate for the current and future years is 20 percent. What is LJC's taxable income for 2010?**

A. $90,000

B. $105,000

C. $120,000

D. $95,000

68. Using the information in question 67, LJC's 2010 current year tax obligation is

A. $19,000.

B. $18,000.

C. $24,000.

D. $21,000.

69. On December 31, 2010, PJB, Inc., had the following deferred tax items:

A deferred tax asset of $16,000 related to prepaid rent

A deferred tax liability of $10,000 related to long-term construction contracts

A deferred tax liability of $5,000 related to installment sales for 2011

Which of the following should be reported on PJB's balance sheet for 2010?

A. A noncurrent deferred liability of $1,000

B. A current deferred asset of $16,000 and a current deferred liability of $15,000

C. A current deferred asset of $11,000 and a noncurrent deferred liability of $10,000

D. A noncurrent deferred asset of $16,000 and a noncurrent deferred liability of $15,000

70. Which of the following methods for accounting for warranties is the theoretically best choice for the financial statements?

A. Expense warranty accrual method

B. Sales warranty accrual method

C. Modified cash basis method

D. Both expense warranty accrual method and modified cash basis method

71. A three-year non-interest-bearing long-term note receivable is received in exchange for some goods held by LR, Inc. The company has an incremental borrowing rate of 6 percent. Interest revenue from the note will accrue annually. In order to properly value the long-term note receivable on the company's books at the date of inception, which of the following time value of money factors would need to be used?

A. The present value of an ordinary annuity at three periods and a 6 percent rate

B. The present value of a single sum at six periods and a 3 percent rate

C. The present value of a single sum at three periods and a 6 percent rate

D. The present value of an annuity due at three periods and a 6 percent rate

72. Which of the following is *not* a component of pension expense?

A. Service cost

B. Actual interest cost incurred on beginning balance of projected benefit obligation

C. Actual interest earned on beginning balance of plan assets

D. Expected interest earned on beginning balance of plan assets

73. When the pension plan is underfunded

A. the projected benefit obligation > fair value of the plan assets.

B. the projected benefit obligation < fair value of the plan assets.

C. the projected benefit obligation = fair value of the plan assets.

D. None of these answers are correct.

Use the following information and the data in the following table to answer questions 74 through 76.

Obligation payments expected to be paid to employees:
2011 = $230,000

Cumulative net loss (gain):
2010 = $16,000
Prior service cost = $150,000

Assume total expected future years of service:

2010 = 10

2011 = 7

2012 = 3

Average remaining service life of employees for gain/loss recognition = 20 years

Balance of plan assets on December 31, 2009 = $100,000

Balance of PBO on December 31, 2009 = $125,000

	2010
Service cost	$150,000
Interest cost	10%
Actual interest earned	15%
Expected interest	13%
Amount funded	$100,000
Payments to retirees	$25,000

74. What is the pension expense for 2010?

    A. $147,325

    B. $224,675

    C. $222,500

    D. $224,500

75. Using the information from question 74, what should be the adjusting journal entry to the prepaid/accrued account and OCI at the end of 2010?

    A. Debit OCI and credit prepaid/accrued for $52,175

    B. Debit prepaid/accrued and credit OCI for 72,500

    C. Debit prepaid/accrued and credit OCI for $52,175

    D. No adjusting entry is needed.

76. How should the pension plan be reported on the balance sheet at the end of 2010?

    A. As a current asset for the amount of $72,500

    B. As a noncurrent liability for the amount of $72,500

C. As a current liability for the amount of $72,500

D. As a current liability for the amount of $40,000 and a noncurrent liability for the amount of $32,500

77. Which of the following accounts will a lessee use under an operating lease?

A. Leased equipment to others

B. Rent expense

C. Obligation under capital lease

D. Leased equipment under capital lease

78. GBW, Inc, leased a kayak to LJ Enterprises on January 1, 2010, when the fair market value of the boat was $850. The term of the lease was three years, and the kayak was expected to have an economic life of six years. At the end of the lease, the kayak would be given back to GBW, Inc., with no option for LJ Enterprises to purchase the vessel. LJ Enterprises was to pay GBW $300 at the end of each year. LJ Enterprises' incremental borrowing rate is 7 percent, whereas the rate implicit in the lease is 8 percent. GBW is reasonably assured to collect the minimum lease payments and has no uncertainties as to any additional costs to be incurred. Which of the following makes this lease a capital lease?

A. A bargain purchase option is attached to the lease.

B. The life of the lease is 75 percent or more of the life of the kayak.

C. The present value of the minimum lease payments is 90 percent or more of the fair value of the kayak.

D. This lease is not a capital lease; it is an operating lease.

79. Using the information in question 78, what amount should be recorded by LJ Enterprises as a credit to obligation under capital lease on December 31, 2010?

A. $900

B. $787

C. $850

D. $0

80. LRC Unlimited leased an entertainment system to PJC, Inc., on January 1, 2009. LRC had paid $20,000 for the system when it purchased it in January 2007. The fair market value of the system immediately before the signing of the lease was $30,000. The term of the lease was two years, and the expected economic life of the system was three years. PJC was to pay LRC $16,000 annually on January 1 starting this year. PJC was granted the option to buy the system at the end of the lease for $500. PJC's incremental borrowing rate was 9 percent, whereas the rate implicit in the lease was 10 percent. LRC is reasonably assured to collect the minimum lease payments and has no uncertainties as to any additional costs to be incurred. As a sales type lease, what is the gross profit that should be recognized on signing of this lease by LRC Unlimited?

   A. $12,500

   B. $1,100

   C. $11,100

   D. $12,000

81. Using the information from question 80, PJC would depreciate the entertainment equipment using a life of

   A. five years.

   B. two years.

   C. three years.

   D. zero years—PJC would not depreciate the equipment; LRC would.

82. On January 3, 2010, GBW, Inc., purchased bonds from LJ, Inc., that it intends to hold to their maturity date of January 1, 2015. GBW paid $91,889.09 for the $100,000 face value bonds. The bonds carry a stated interest rate of 6 percent and have an effective rate of 8 percent. The interest on the bonds is to be paid semiannually. What is the amount of interest revenue that should be recorded on December 31, 2010, under the effective interest method?

   A. $2,188.91

   B. $702.59

   C. $3,000.00

   D. $3,702.59

83. The prepaid/accrued pension cost account may need an additional adjustment when

    A. the pension plan is overfunded.

    B. the pension plan is underfunded.

    C. the service cost does not equal the amount funded.

    D. Both a and b are correct.

84. Using the information in the following table, what would the cost of goods sold be under the LIFO perpetual system?

	Units	Cost
Beginning inventory	75	$5
Purchase 2/3/10	100	$7
Purchase 2/16/10	25	$6
Sold 2/1/10	50	
Sold 2/20/10	75	

    A. $825

    B. $850

    C. $725

    D. $750

85. The general rule for recording amortization on intangibles is

    A. only intangibles with an indefinite life should be amortized.

    B. only the double-declining balance method of amortization is allowed.

    C. never amortize over more than three years.

    D. amortize over the lesser of useful life, legal life, or 40 years.

86. The two types of securities that are recorded on the balance sheet at fair market value are

    A. trading and debt held to maturity.

    B. available-for-sale and debt held to maturity.

    C. trading and available-for-sale.

    D. none of the above.

87. PBW, Inc., reported net income of $200,000 in 2010. Also reported on the income statement was depreciation expense of $50,000. The company's comparative balance sheet reported a decrease in accounts receivable of $5,000, an increase in inventory of $7,000, and an increase in accounts payable of $10,000. PBW paid $15,000 in dividends during 2010. What is the cash provided from operating activities?

    A. $137,000

    B. $158,000

    C. $238,000

    D. $258,000

88. Which of the following is *not* reported in the cash flows from financing activities section on a statement of cash flows?

    A. A decrease in dividends payable

    B. An issuance of bonds

    C. An additional sale of stock

    D. Payment of dividends

89. An employee is responsible for paying all but

    A. the employee's share of FICA.

    B. the employer's share of FICA.

    C. federal income tax on the employee's earnings.

    D. medical insurance authorized by the employee to be taken out of earnings.

90. Which of the following changes is accounted for as a retrospective application of the new accounting principle?

    A. A change from LIFO to FIFO inventory valuation methods

    B. A change from declining balance to straight-line depreciation methods

    C. A change from partnership status to corporate status

    D. A change from a non-GAAP method to a GAAP method

91. BLP, Inc., has equipment costing $110,000. This equipment was purchased in January 2005. It has been depreciated by the straight-line method using a salvage value of $10,000 and a 10-year life. At the beginning of 2010, it was determined that the remaining life would only be four more years. What is the depreciation expense for 2010?

    A. $11,111

    B. $12,222

    C. $12,500

    D. $15,000

92. BLP, Inc., forgot to accrue $500 of interest revenue in 2009. The error was discovered in 2010 when the company received the interest. Which of the following is a *true* statement?

    A. Assets in 2009 are overstated.

    B. Assets in 2010 are understated.

    C. Net income in 2009 is understated.

    D. Net income in 2010 is overstated.

93. Accounts receivable has a normal _____ balance, and you can decrease the account by _____ it.

    A. credit; crediting

    B. credit; debiting

    C. debit; crediting

    D. debit; debiting

94. J Unlimited had book income of $200,000 in 2010. Included within that income was $26,000 related to life insurance proceeds on its key officers. Additionally, the company had incurred $12,000 in fines related to illegal gambling activities. Rent on one of the company's buildings had been collected in the amount of $20,000, which constituted the outstanding rent payments for 2010. Based on this information, how many temporary differences must J Unlimited account for at the end of 2010?

    A. One

    B. Two

    C. Three

    D. Zero

95. On December 31, 2009, BLP, Inc., reported a retained earnings balance of $50,000. Early in 2010, though, one of the company's astute accountants identified that an inventory purchase totaling $16,000 had been omitted from 2009's financial statements. If BLP has a 25 percent tax rate, what adjustment should be made to the financial statements presented in 2010?

A. A decrease to the beginning retained earnings balance of $12,000

B. A decrease to the beginning retained earnings balance of $16,000

C. An increase to the beginning retained earnings balance of $12,000

D. A decrease in the current year's net income of $16,000

96. LJC Unlimited had capital assets listed on its books at a cost of $50,000 that were being depreciated using the straight-line method, a life of 10 years, and a residual value of $5,000. Two years after their purchase, the company decided to switch to the double-declining balance method for the assets' remaining life. What should be the adjustment to the beginning balance of retained earnings not considering any tax effects?

A. $9,000

B. $10,000

C. $10,250

D. $0

97. On October 2, 2010, Corr's Autobody purchased some radiators at a total purchase price of $300,000 from the company's supplier on account with terms of 2/15, n/30. The company uses a periodic inventory system and has a policy of not recording discounts until taken. Corr's paid off the payable on October 13, 2010. Based on that information, what amount should be credited to cash to record the transaction?

A. $300,000

B. $6,000

C. $294,000

D. $255,000

98. BLP, Inc., has been retaining cash for the past couple of years. The last year that the company paid a dividend was 2007. BLP has decided that this year it will pay a dividend. The total amount declared for 2010 is $150,000. The company has issued and has outstanding 30,000 shares of $10 par common stock. BLP also has issued and outstanding 10,000 shares of 5 percent, $20 par cumulative preferred stock. The preferred stock fully participates with the common stock. What amount of dividends will the preferred stock receive in 2010?

   A. $30,000

   B. $90,000

   C. $60,000

   D. $72,000

The following table represents the information for GBW, Inc., for 2009. Use the information to answer questions 99 and 100.

Total credit sales	$200,000
Total COGS	$160,000
Installment sales	$100,000
Installment COGS	$ 70,000
Cash receipts on installment sales—2009	$ 60,000
Cash receipts on other credit sales	$ 80,000

99. What is the gross profit rate on installment sales for 2009?

   A. 70 percent

   B. 30 percent

   C. 40 percent

   D. 80 percent

100. What total amount of gross profit should be presented on GBW's income statement for 2009?

   A. $10,000

   B. $58,000

   C. $70,000

   D. $28,000

Answer Key

Chapter 1	Chapter 3	Chapter 5	Chapter 7
1. C	1. B	1. C	1. C
2. D	2. A	2. A	2. A
3. B	3. B	3. D	3. B
4. C	4. C	4. C	4. D
5. B	5. A	5. B	5. B
6. C	6. B	6. C	6. D
7. A	7. C	7. B	7. B
8. B	8. B	8. D	8. A
9. D	9. C	9. D	9. D
10. B	10. C	10. A	10. C

Chapter 2	Chapter 4	Chapter 6	Chapter 8
1. B	1. D	1. C	1. B
2. A	2. C	2. A	2. B
3. C	3. A	3. D	3. C
4. D	4. C	4. A	4. D
5. C	5. D	5. B	5. A
6. D	6. D	6. B	6. C
7. A	7. A	7. D	7. B
8. A	8. D	8. A	8. D
9. C	9. D	9. B	9. A
10. B	10. A	10. C	10. B
11. D			

Chapter 9
1. A
2. B
3. C
4. D
5. A
6. C
7. A
8. D
9. B
10. C

Chapter 10
1. A
2. B
3. C
4. D
5. D
6. C
7. D
8. C
9. A
10. B

Chapter 11
1. A
2. C
3. C
4. C
5. B

6. D
7. B
8. A
9. B
10. C

Chapter 12
1. B
2. C
3. A
4. B
5. B
6. C
7. B
8. A
9. D
10. B

Chapter 13
1. D
2. C
3. D
4. C
5. A
6. A
7. B
8. A
9. C
10. D

Chapter 14
1. C
2. D
3. C
4. A
5. D
6. C
7. A
8. B
9. C
10. D

Chapter 15
1. B
2. C
3. B
4. D
5. A
6. C
7. B
8. C
9. A
10. D

Chapter 16
1. D
2. C
3. B
4. A
5. D

6. A
7. C
8. B
9. A
10. C

Chapter 17
1. A
2. B
3. C
4. D
5. C
6. C
7. A
8. B
9. D
10. C

Final Exam

1. B	21. A	41. B	61. C	81. C
2. B	22. B	42. C	62. D	82. D
3. B	23. C	43. D	63. C	83. D
4. C	24. B	44. C	64. C	84. D
5. B	25. B	45. A	65. D	85. D
6. D	26. D	46. D	66. D	86. C
7. C	27. A	47. B	67. A	87. D
8. B	28. C	48. A	68. B	88. A
9. A	29. B	49. C	69. C	89. B
10. C	30. B	50. C	70. A	90. A
11. A	31. C	51. B	71. C	91. C
12. C	32. A	52. A	72. C	92. C
13. D	33. D	53. D	73. A	93. C
14. D	34. D	54. C	74. B	94. D
15. C	35. A	55. C	75. C	95. A
16. D	36. D	56. C	76. D	96. D
17. A	37. C	57. D	77. B	97. C
18. A	38. D	58. A	78. C	98. D
19. C	39. A	59. C	79. B	99. B
20. D	40. D	60. B	80. C	100. D

appendix A

Chapter	Account	Financial Statement	Classification	Normal Balance	To Increase	To Decrease
1	Cash	Balance sheet	Current assets	debit	debit	credit
1	Accounts receivable	Balance sheet	Current assets	debit	debit	credit
1	Allowance for bad debts	Balance sheet	Current assets	credit	credit	debit
1	Bad debt expense	Income statement	Operating expense	debit	debit	credit
1	Sales	Income statement	Revenue	credit	credit	debit
2	Inventory	Balance sheet	Current assets	debit	debit	credit
2	Cost of goods sold	Income statement	Expense	debit	debit	credit
2	Purchases	Income statement	COGS	debit	debit	credit
2	Purchase discounts	Income statement	COGS	credit	credit	debit
2	Purchase returns	Income statement	COGS	credit	credit	debit
2	Freight-in	Income statement	COGS	debit	debit	credit
2	Freight-out	Income statement	Operating expense	debit	debit	credit
2	Sales discounts	Income statement	Revenue	debit	debit	credit
2	Sales returns	Income statement	Revenue	debit	debit	credit
3	Long-term note receivable	Balance sheet	Long-term assets	debit	debit	credit
3	Discount on LTNR	Balance sheet	Long-term assets	credit	credit	debit
4	Trading securities	Balance sheet	Current assets	debit	debit	credit
4	Available-for-sale securities	Balance sheet	Long-term assets	debit	debit	credit
4	Debt held to maturity	Balance sheet	Long-term assets	debit	debit	credit
4	Unrealized gains and losses—trading securities	Balance sheet	Stockholders' equity	N/A	N/A	N/A
4	Realized gain on sale of trading securities	Income statement	Revenue	credit	credit	debit
4	Dividend revenue	Income statement	Revenue	credit	credit	debit
4	Interest revenue	Income statement	Revenue	credit	credit	debit
4	Unrealized increase/decrease—available-for-sale securities	Balance sheet	Stockholders' equity	N/A	N/A	N/A
4	Realized gain on sale of available-for-sale securities	Income statement	Revenue	credit	credit	debit
4	Allowance to value available-for-sale securities	Balance sheet	Stockholders' equity	N/A	N/A	N/A
4	Investment in debt—HM	Balance sheet	Long-term assets	debit	debit	credit
5	Property, plant, and equipment	Balance sheet	Long-term assets	debit	debit	credit
5	Accumulated depreciation	Balance sheet	Long-term assets	credit	credit	debit
5	Depreciation expense	Income statement	Expense	debit	debit	credit
5	Discount on notes payable	Balance sheet	Liabilities	debit	debit	credit
6	Intangibles	Balance sheet	Intangibles	debit	debit	credit
6	Goodwill	Balance sheet	Intangibles	debit	debit	credit
6	Patent	Balance sheet	Intangibles	debit	debit	credit

No.	Account	Statement	Category			
6	Franchise	Balance sheet	Intangibles	debit	debit	credit
6	Copyright	Balance sheet	Intangibles	debit	debit	credit
6	Computer software costs	Balance sheet	Intangibles	debit	debit	credit
6	Trademarks	Balance sheet	Intangibles	debit	debit	credit
6	Trade names	Balance sheet	Intangibles	debit	debit	credit
7	Accounts Payable	Balance sheet	Liabilities	credit	credit	debit
7	Interest payable	Balance sheet	Liabilities	credit	credit	debit
7	Short-term notes payable	Balance sheet	Liabilities	credit	credit	debit
7	Salaries payable	Balance sheet	Liabilities	credit	credit	debit
7	Taxes payable	Balance sheet	Liabilities	credit	credit	debit
7	Discount on STNP	Balance sheet	Liabilities	debit	debit	credit
7	Unearned warranty revenue	Balance sheet	Liabilities	credit	credit	debit
7	Warranty revenue	Income statement	Revenue	credit	credit	debit
8	Long-term notes payable	Balance sheet	Long-term liabilities	credit	credit	debit
8	Bonds payable	Balance sheet	Long-term liabilities	credit	credit	debit
8	Discount on bonds payable	Balance sheet	Long-term liabilities	debit	debit	credit
8	Premium on bonds payable	Balance sheet	Long-term liabilities	credit	credit	debit
8	Common stock warrants	Balance sheet	Stockholders' equity	credit	credit	debit
9	Common stock	Balance sheet	Stockholders' equity	credit	credit	debit
9	Preferred stock	Balance sheet	Stockholders' equity	credit	credit	debit
9	Additional paid-in capital on common stock	Balance sheet	Stockholders' equity	credit	credit	debit
9	Additional paid-in capital on preferred stock	Balance sheet	Stockholders' equity	credit	credit	debit
9	Additional paid-in capital from other sources	Balance sheet	Stockholders' equity	credit	credit	debit
9	Common stock option warrants	Balance sheet	Stockholders' equity	credit	credit	debit
9	Treasury stock	Balance sheet	Stockholders' equity	debit	debit	credit
10	Retained earnings	Balance sheet	Stockholders' equity	credit	credit	debit
10	Dividends payable	Balance sheet	Liabilities	credit	credit	debit
12	Construction in progress	Balance sheet	Assets	debit	debit	credit
12	Partial billings	Balance sheet	Contra-asset	credit	credit	debit
12	Construction expense	Income statement	Expense	debit	debit	credit
12	Construction revenue	Income statement	Revenue	credit	credit	debit
12	Deferred gross profit	Balance sheet	Contra-asset	credit	credit	debit
12	Gross profit realized on installment sales	Income statement	Revenue	credit	credit	debit
12	Gross profit realized on cost-recovery transactions	Income statement	Revenue	credit	credit	debit

Chapter	Account	Financial Statement	Classification	Normal Balance	To Increase	To Decrease
13	Deferred tax asset	Balance sheet	Assets	debit	debit	credit
13	Deferred tax liability	Balance sheet	Liabilities	credit	credit	debit
13	Allowance to reduce deferred tax asset to net realizable value	Balance sheet	Contra-asset	credit	credit	debit
14	Other comprehensive income	Income statement		credit	credit	debit
14	Plan assets	Balance sheet	Assets	debit	debit	credit
14	Projected benefit obligation	Balance sheet	Liabilities	credit	credit	debit
14	Prepaid pension cost	Balance sheet	Assets	debit	debit	credit
14	Accrued pension cost	Balance sheet	Liabilities	credit	credit	debit
15	Leased equipment under capital lease	Balance sheet	Assets	debit	debit	credit
15	Obligation under capital lease	Balance sheet	Liabilities	credit	credit	debit

appendix **B**

Present Value of Single Sum
Table of Factors
Interest Rates (i)

Periods (n)	1.50%	2.00%	2.50%	3.00%	3.50%	4.00%	4.50%	5.00%	5.50%	6.00%	6.50%	7.00%
1	0.985222	0.980392	0.975610	0.970874	0.966184	0.961538	0.956938	0.952381	0.947867	0.943396	0.938967	0.934579
2	0.970662	0.961169	0.951814	0.942596	0.933511	0.924556	0.915730	0.907029	0.898452	0.889996	0.881659	0.873439
3	0.956317	0.942322	0.928599	0.915142	0.901943	0.888996	0.876297	0.863838	0.851614	0.839619	0.827849	0.816298
4	0.942184	0.923845	0.905951	0.888487	0.871442	0.854804	0.838561	0.822702	0.807217	0.792094	0.777323	0.762895
5	0.928260	0.905731	0.883854	0.862609	0.841973	0.821927	0.802451	0.783526	0.765134	0.747258	0.729881	0.712986
6	0.914542	0.887971	0.862297	0.837484	0.813501	0.790315	0.767896	0.746215	0.725246	0.704961	0.685334	0.666342
7	0.901027	0.870560	0.841265	0.813092	0.785991	0.759918	0.734828	0.710681	0.687437	0.665057	0.643506	0.622750
8	0.887711	0.853490	0.820747	0.789409	0.759412	0.730690	0.703185	0.676839	0.651599	0.627412	0.604231	0.582009
9	0.874592	0.836755	0.800728	0.766417	0.733731	0.702587	0.672904	0.644609	0.617629	0.591898	0.567353	0.543934
10	0.861667	0.820348	0.781198	0.744094	0.708919	0.675564	0.643928	0.613913	0.585431	0.558395	0.532726	0.508349
11	0.848933	0.804263	0.762145	0.722421	0.684946	0.649581	0.616199	0.584679	0.554911	0.526788	0.500212	0.475093
12	0.836387	0.788493	0.743556	0.701380	0.661783	0.624597	0.589664	0.556837	0.525982	0.496969	0.469683	0.444012
13	0.824027	0.773033	0.725420	0.680951	0.639404	0.600574	0.564272	0.530321	0.498561	0.468839	0.441017	0.414964
14	0.811849	0.757875	0.707727	0.661118	0.617782	0.577475	0.539973	0.505068	0.472569	0.442301	0.414100	0.387817
15	0.799852	0.743015	0.690466	0.641862	0.596891	0.555265	0.516720	0.481017	0.447933	0.417265	0.388827	0.362446
16	0.788031	0.728446	0.673625	0.623167	0.576706	0.533908	0.494469	0.458112	0.424581	0.393646	0.365095	0.338735
17	0.776385	0.714163	0.657195	0.605016	0.557204	0.513373	0.473176	0.436297	0.402447	0.371364	0.342813	0.316574
18	0.764912	0.700159	0.641166	0.587395	0.538361	0.493628	0.452800	0.415521	0.381466	0.350344	0.321890	0.295864
19	0.753607	0.686431	0.625528	0.570286	0.520156	0.474642	0.433302	0.395734	0.361579	0.330513	0.302244	0.276508
20	0.742470	0.672971	0.610271	0.553676	0.502566	0.456387	0.414643	0.376889	0.342729	0.311805	0.283797	0.258419
21	0.731498	0.659776	0.595386	0.537549	0.485571	0.438834	0.396787	0.358942	0.324862	0.294155	0.266476	0.241513
22	0.720688	0.646839	0.580865	0.521893	0.469151	0.421955	0.379701	0.341850	0.307926	0.277505	0.250212	0.225713
23	0.710037	0.634156	0.566697	0.506692	0.453286	0.405726	0.363350	0.325571	0.291873	0.261797	0.234941	0.210947
24	0.699544	0.621721	0.552875	0.491934	0.437957	0.390121	0.347703	0.310068	0.276657	0.246979	0.220602	0.197147
25	0.689206	0.609531	0.539391	0.477606	0.423147	0.375117	0.332731	0.295303	0.262234	0.232999	0.207138	0.184249
26	0.679021	0.597579	0.526235	0.463695	0.408838	0.360689	0.318402	0.281241	0.248563	0.219810	0.194496	0.172195
27	0.668986	0.585862	0.513400	0.450189	0.395012	0.346817	0.304691	0.267848	0.235605	0.207368	0.182625	0.160930
28	0.659099	0.574375	0.500878	0.437077	0.381654	0.333477	0.291571	0.255094	0.223322	0.195630	0.171479	0.150402
29	0.649359	0.563112	0.488661	0.424346	0.368748	0.320651	0.279015	0.242946	0.211679	0.184557	0.161013	0.140563
30	0.639762	0.552071	0.476743	0.411987	0.356278	0.308319	0.267000	0.231377	0.200644	0.174110	0.151186	0.131367

Present Value of Single Sum
Table of Factors
Interest Rates (*i*)

Periods (*n*)	7.50%	8.00%	8.50%	9.00%	9.50%	10.00%	10.50%	11.00%	11.50%	12.00%	12.50%	13.00%
1	0.930233	0.925926	0.921659	0.917431	0.913242	0.909091	0.904977	0.900901	0.896861	0.892857	0.888889	0.884956
2	0.865333	0.857339	0.849455	0.841680	0.834011	0.826446	0.818984	0.811622	0.804360	0.797194	0.790123	0.783147
3	0.804961	0.793832	0.782908	0.772183	0.761654	0.751315	0.741162	0.731191	0.721399	0.711780	0.702332	0.693050
4	0.748801	0.735030	0.721574	0.708425	0.695574	0.683013	0.670735	0.658731	0.646994	0.635518	0.624295	0.613319
5	0.696559	0.680583	0.665045	0.649931	0.635228	0.620921	0.607000	0.593451	0.580264	0.567427	0.554929	0.542760
6	0.647962	0.630170	0.612945	0.596267	0.580117	0.564474	0.549321	0.534641	0.520416	0.506631	0.493270	0.480319
7	0.602755	0.583490	0.564926	0.547034	0.529787	0.513158	0.497123	0.481658	0.466741	0.452349	0.438462	0.425061
8	0.560702	0.540269	0.520669	0.501866	0.483824	0.466507	0.449885	0.433926	0.418602	0.403883	0.389744	0.376160
9	0.521583	0.500249	0.479880	0.460428	0.441848	0.424098	0.407136	0.390925	0.375428	0.360610	0.346439	0.332885
10	0.485194	0.463193	0.442285	0.422411	0.403514	0.385543	0.368449	0.352184	0.336706	0.321973	0.307946	0.294588
11	0.451343	0.428883	0.407636	0.387533	0.368506	0.350494	0.333438	0.317283	0.301979	0.287476	0.273730	0.260698
12	0.419854	0.397114	0.375702	0.355535	0.336535	0.318631	0.301754	0.285841	0.270833	0.256675	0.243315	0.230706
13	0.390562	0.367698	0.346269	0.326179	0.307338	0.289664	0.273080	0.257514	0.242900	0.229174	0.216280	0.204165
14	0.363313	0.340461	0.319142	0.299246	0.280674	0.263331	0.247132	0.231995	0.217847	0.204620	0.192249	0.180677
15	0.337966	0.315242	0.294140	0.274538	0.256323	0.239392	0.223648	0.209004	0.195379	0.182696	0.170888	0.159891
16	0.314387	0.291890	0.271097	0.251870	0.234085	0.217629	0.202397	0.188292	0.175227	0.163122	0.151901	0.141496
17	0.292453	0.270269	0.249859	0.231073	0.213777	0.197845	0.183164	0.169633	0.157155	0.145644	0.135023	0.125218
18	0.272049	0.250249	0.230285	0.211994	0.195230	0.179859	0.165760	0.152822	0.140946	0.130040	0.120020	0.110812
19	0.253069	0.231712	0.212244	0.194490	0.178292	0.163508	0.150009	0.137678	0.126409	0.116107	0.106685	0.098064
20	0.235413	0.214548	0.195616	0.178431	0.162824	0.148644	0.135755	0.124034	0.113371	0.103667	0.094831	0.086782
21	0.218989	0.198656	0.180292	0.163698	0.148697	0.135131	0.122855	0.111742	0.101678	0.092560	0.084294	0.076798
22	0.203711	0.183941	0.166167	0.150182	0.135797	0.122846	0.111181	0.100669	0.091191	0.082643	0.074928	0.067963
23	0.189498	0.170315	0.153150	0.137781	0.124015	0.111678	0.100616	0.090693	0.081786	0.073788	0.066603	0.060144
24	0.176277	0.157699	0.141152	0.126405	0.113256	0.101526	0.091055	0.081705	0.073351	0.065882	0.059202	0.053225
25	0.163979	0.146018	0.130094	0.115968	0.103430	0.092296	0.082403	0.073608	0.065785	0.058823	0.052624	0.047102
26	0.152539	0.135202	0.119902	0.106393	0.094457	0.083905	0.074573	0.066314	0.059000	0.052521	0.046777	0.041683
27	0.141896	0.125187	0.110509	0.097608	0.086262	0.076278	0.067487	0.059742	0.052915	0.046894	0.041580	0.036888
28	0.131997	0.115914	0.101851	0.089548	0.078749	0.069343	0.061074	0.053822	0.047457	0.041869	0.036960	0.032644
29	0.122788	0.107328	0.093872	0.082155	0.071943	0.063039	0.055271	0.048488	0.042563	0.037383	0.032853	0.028889
30	0.114221	0.099377	0.086518	0.075371	0.065702	0.057309	0.050019	0.043683	0.038173	0.033378	0.029203	0.025565

Present Value of Ordinary Annuity
Table of Factors
Interest Rates (i)

Periods (n)	1.50%	2.00%	2.50%	3.00%	3.50%	4.00%	4.50%	5.00%	5.50%	6.00%	6.50%	7.00%
1	0.985222	0.980392	0.975610	0.970874	0.966184	0.961538	0.956938	0.952381	0.947867	0.943396	0.938967	0.934579
2	1.955883	1.941561	1.927424	1.913470	1.899694	1.886095	1.872668	1.859410	1.846320	1.833393	1.820626	1.808018
3	2.912200	2.883883	2.856024	2.828611	2.801637	2.775091	2.748964	2.723248	2.697933	2.673012	2.648476	2.624316
4	3.854385	3.807729	3.761974	3.717098	3.673079	3.629895	3.587526	3.545951	3.505150	3.465106	3.425799	3.387211
5	4.782645	4.713460	4.645828	4.579707	4.515052	4.451822	4.389977	4.329477	4.270284	4.212364	4.155679	4.100197
6	5.697187	5.601431	5.508125	5.417191	5.328553	5.242137	5.157872	5.075692	4.995530	4.917324	4.841014	4.766540
7	6.598214	6.471991	6.349391	6.230283	6.114544	6.002055	5.892701	5.786373	5.682967	5.582381	5.484520	5.389289
8	7.485925	7.325481	7.170137	7.019692	6.873956	6.732745	6.595886	6.463213	6.334566	6.209794	6.088751	5.971299
9	8.360517	8.162237	7.970866	7.786109	7.607687	7.435332	7.268790	7.107822	6.952195	6.801692	6.656104	6.515232
10	9.222185	8.982585	8.752064	8.530203	8.316605	8.110896	7.912718	7.721735	7.537626	7.360087	7.188830	7.023582
11	10.071118	9.786848	9.514209	9.252624	9.001551	8.760477	8.528917	8.306414	8.092536	7.886875	7.689042	7.498674
12	10.907505	10.575341	10.257765	9.954004	9.663334	9.385074	9.118581	8.863252	8.618518	8.383844	8.158725	7.942686
13	11.731532	11.348374	10.983185	10.634955	10.302738	9.985648	9.682852	9.393573	9.117079	8.852683	8.599742	8.357651
14	12.543382	12.106249	11.690912	11.296073	10.920520	10.563123	10.222825	9.898641	9.589648	9.294984	9.013842	8.745468
15	13.343233	12.849264	12.381378	11.937935	11.517411	11.118387	10.739546	10.379658	10.037581	9.712249	9.402669	9.107914
16	14.131264	13.577709	13.055003	12.561102	12.094117	11.652296	11.234015	10.837770	10.462162	10.105895	9.767764	9.446649
17	14.907649	14.291872	13.712198	13.166118	12.651321	12.165669	11.707191	11.274066	10.864609	10.477260	10.110577	9.763223
18	15.672561	14.992031	14.353364	13.753513	13.189682	12.659297	12.159992	11.689587	11.246074	10.827603	10.432466	10.059087
19	16.426168	15.678462	14.978891	14.323799	13.709837	13.133939	12.593294	12.085321	11.607654	11.158116	10.734710	10.335595
20	17.168639	16.351433	15.589162	14.877475	14.212403	13.590326	13.007936	12.462210	11.950382	11.469921	11.018507	10.594014
21	17.900137	17.011209	16.184549	15.415024	14.697974	14.029160	13.404724	12.821153	12.275244	11.764077	11.284983	10.835527
22	18.620824	17.658048	16.765413	15.936917	15.167125	14.451115	13.784425	13.163003	12.583170	12.041582	11.535196	11.061240
23	19.330861	18.292204	17.332110	16.443608	15.620410	14.856842	14.147775	13.488574	12.875042	12.303379	11.770137	11.272187
24	20.030405	18.913926	17.884986	16.935542	16.058368	15.246963	14.495478	13.798642	13.151699	12.550358	11.990739	11.469334
25	20.719611	19.523456	18.424376	17.413148	16.481515	15.622080	14.828209	14.093945	13.413933	12.783356	12.197877	11.653583
26	21.398632	20.121036	18.950611	17.876842	16.890352	15.982769	15.146611	14.375185	13.662495	13.003166	12.392373	11.825779
27	22.067617	20.706898	19.464011	18.327031	17.285365	16.329586	15.451303	14.643034	13.898100	13.210534	12.574998	11.986709
28	22.726717	21.281272	19.964889	18.764108	17.667019	16.663063	15.742874	14.898127	14.121422	13.406164	12.746477	12.137111
29	23.376076	21.844385	20.453550	19.188455	18.035767	16.983715	16.021889	15.141074	14.333101	13.590721	12.907490	12.277674
30	24.015838	22.396456	20.930293	19.600441	18.392045	17.292033	16.288889	15.372451	14.533745	13.764831	13.058676	12.409041

Present Value of Ordinary Annuity
Table of Factors
Interest Rates (i)

Periods (n)	7.50%	8.00%	8.50%	9.00%	9.50%	10.00%	10.50%	11.00%	11.50%	12.00%	12.50%	13.00%
1	0.930233	0.925926	0.921659	0.917431	0.913242	0.909091	0.904977	0.900901	0.896861	0.892857	0.888889	0.884956
2	1.795565	1.783265	1.771114	1.759111	1.747253	1.735537	1.723961	1.712523	1.701221	1.690051	1.679012	1.666102
3	2.600526	2.577097	2.554022	2.531295	2.508907	2.486852	2.465123	2.443715	2.422619	2.401831	2.381344	2.361153
4	3.349326	3.312127	3.275597	3.239720	3.204481	3.169865	3.135858	3.102446	3.069614	3.037349	3.005639	2.974471
5	4.045885	3.992710	3.940642	3.889651	3.839709	3.790787	3.742858	3.695897	3.649878	3.604776	3.560568	3.517231
6	4.693846	4.622880	4.553587	4.485919	4.419825	4.355261	4.292179	4.230538	4.170294	4.111407	4.053839	3.997550
7	5.296601	5.206370	5.118514	5.032953	4.949612	4.868419	4.789303	4.712196	4.637035	4.563757	4.492301	4.422610
8	5.857304	5.746639	5.639183	5.534819	5.433436	5.334926	5.239188	5.146123	5.055637	4.967640	4.882045	4.798770
9	6.378887	6.246888	6.119063	5.995247	5.875284	5.759024	5.646324	5.537048	5.431064	5.328250	5.228485	5.131655
10	6.864081	6.710081	6.561348	6.417658	6.278798	6.144567	6.014773	5.889232	5.767771	5.650223	5.536431	5.426243
11	7.315424	7.138964	6.968984	6.805191	6.647304	6.495061	6.348211	6.206515	6.069750	5.937699	5.810161	5.686941
12	7.735278	7.536078	7.344686	7.160725	6.983839	6.813692	6.649964	6.492356	6.340583	6.194374	6.053476	5.917647
13	8.125840	7.903776	7.690955	7.486904	7.291178	7.103356	6.923045	6.749870	6.583482	6.423548	6.269757	6.121812
14	8.489154	8.244237	8.010097	7.786150	7.571852	7.366687	7.170176	6.981865	6.801329	6.628168	6.462006	6.302488
15	8.827120	8.559479	8.304237	8.060688	7.828175	7.606080	7.393825	7.190870	6.996708	6.810864	6.632894	6.462379
16	9.141507	8.851369	8.575333	8.312558	8.062260	7.823709	7.596221	7.379162	7.171935	6.973986	6.784795	6.603875
17	9.433960	9.121638	8.825192	8.543631	8.276037	8.021553	7.779386	7.548794	7.329090	7.119630	6.919818	6.729093
18	9.706009	9.371887	9.055476	8.755625	8.471266	8.201412	7.945146	7.701617	7.470036	7.249670	7.039838	6.839905
19	9.959078	9.603599	9.267720	8.950115	8.649558	8.364920	8.095154	7.839294	7.596445	7.365777	7.146523	6.937969
20	10.194491	9.818147	9.463337	9.128546	8.812382	8.513564	8.230909	7.963328	7.709816	7.469444	7.241353	7.024752
21	10.413480	10.016803	9.643628	9.292244	8.961080	8.648694	8.353764	8.075070	7.811494	7.562003	7.325647	7.101550
22	10.617191	10.200744	9.809796	9.442425	9.096876	8.771540	8.464945	8.175739	7.902685	7.644646	7.400575	7.169513
23	10.806689	10.371059	9.962945	9.580207	9.220892	8.883218	8.565561	8.266432	7.984471	7.718434	7.467178	7.229658
24	10.982967	10.528758	10.104097	9.706612	9.334148	8.984744	8.656616	8.348137	8.057822	7.784316	7.526381	7.282883
25	11.146946	10.674776	10.234191	9.822580	9.437578	9.077040	8.739019	8.421745	8.123607	7.843139	7.579005	7.329985
26	11.299485	10.809978	10.354093	9.928972	9.532034	9.160945	8.813592	8.488058	8.182607	7.895660	7.625782	7.371668
27	11.441381	10.935165	10.464602	10.026580	9.618296	9.237223	8.881079	8.547800	8.235522	7.942554	7.667362	7.408556
28	11.573378	11.051078	10.566453	10.116128	9.697074	9.306567	8.942153	8.601622	8.282979	7.984423	7.704322	7.441200
29	11.696165	11.158406	10.660326	10.198283	9.769018	9.369606	8.997423	8.650110	8.325542	8.021806	7.737175	7.470088
30	11.810386	11.257783	10.746844	10.273654	9.834719	9.426914	9.047442	8.693793	8.363715	8.055184	7.766378	0.930233

Present Value of Annuity Due
Table of Factors
Interest Rates (i)

Periods (n)	1.50%	2.00%	2.50%	3.00%	3.50%	4.00%	4.50%	5.00%	5.50%	6.00%	6.50%	7.00%
1	1.000000	1.000000	1.000000	1.000000	1.000000	1.000000	1.000000	1.000000	1.000000	1.000000	1.000000	1.000000
2	1.985222	1.980392	1.975610	1.970874	1.966184	1.961538	1.956938	1.952381	1.947867	1.943396	1.938967	1.934579
3	2.955883	2.941561	2.927424	2.913470	2.899694	2.886095	2.872668	2.859410	2.846320	2.833393	2.820626	2.808018
4	3.912200	3.883883	3.856024	3.828611	3.801637	3.775091	3.748964	3.723248	3.697933	3.673012	3.648476	3.624316
5	4.854385	4.807729	4.761974	4.717098	4.673079	4.629895	4.587526	4.545951	4.505150	4.465106	4.425799	4.387211
6	5.782645	5.713460	5.645828	5.579707	5.515052	5.451822	5.389977	5.329477	5.270284	5.212364	5.155679	5.100197
7	6.697187	6.601431	6.508125	6.417191	6.328553	6.242137	6.157872	6.075692	5.995530	5.917324	5.841014	5.766540
8	7.598214	7.471991	7.349391	7.230283	7.114544	7.002055	6.892701	6.786373	6.682967	6.582381	6.484520	6.389289
9	8.485925	8.325481	8.170137	8.019692	7.873956	7.732745	7.595886	7.463213	7.334566	7.209794	7.088751	6.971299
10	9.360517	9.162201	8.970866	8.786109	8.607687	8.435332	8.268790	8.107822	7.952195	7.801692	7.656104	7.515232
11	10.222185	9.982585	9.752064	9.530203	9.316605	9.110896	8.912718	8.721735	8.537626	8.360087	8.188830	8.023582
12	11.071118	10.786848	10.514209	10.252624	10.001551	9.760477	9.528917	9.306414	9.092536	8.886875	8.689042	8.498674
13	11.907505	11.575341	11.257765	10.954004	10.663334	10.385074	10.118581	9.863252	9.618518	9.383844	9.158725	8.942686
14	12.731532	12.348374	11.983185	11.634955	11.302738	10.985648	10.682852	10.393573	10.117079	9.852683	9.599742	9.357651
15	13.543382	13.106249	12.690912	12.296073	11.920520	11.563123	11.222825	10.898641	10.589648	10.294984	10.013842	9.745468
16	14.343233	13.849264	13.381378	12.937935	12.517411	12.118387	11.739546	11.379658	11.037581	10.712249	10.402669	10.107914
17	15.131264	14.577709	14.055003	13.561102	13.094117	12.652296	12.234015	11.837770	11.462162	11.105895	10.767764	10.446649
18	15.907649	15.291872	14.712198	14.166118	13.651321	13.165669	12.707191	12.274066	11.864609	11.477260	11.110577	10.763223
19	16.672561	15.992031	15.353364	14.753513	14.189682	13.659297	13.159992	12.689587	12.246074	11.827603	11.432466	11.059087
20	17.426168	16.678462	15.978891	15.323799	14.709837	14.133939	13.593294	13.085321	12.607654	12.158116	11.734710	11.335595
21	18.168639	17.351433	16.589162	15.877475	15.212403	14.590326	14.007936	13.462210	12.950382	12.469921	12.018507	11.594014
22	18.900137	18.011209	17.184549	16.415024	15.697974	15.029160	14.404724	13.821153	13.275244	12.764077	12.284983	11.835527
23	19.620824	18.658048	17.765413	16.936917	16.167125	15.451115	14.784425	14.163003	13.583170	13.041582	12.535196	12.061240
24	20.330861	19.292204	18.332110	17.443608	16.620410	15.856842	15.147775	14.488574	13.875042	13.303379	12.770137	12.272187
25	21.030405	19.913926	18.884986	17.935542	17.058368	16.246963	15.495478	14.798642	14.151699	13.550358	12.990739	12.469334
26	21.719611	20.523456	19.424376	18.413148	17.481515	16.622080	15.828209	15.093945	14.413933	13.783356	13.197877	12.653583
27	22.398632	21.121036	19.950611	18.876842	17.890352	16.982769	16.146611	15.375185	14.662495	14.003166	13.392373	12.825779
28	23.067617	21.706898	20.464011	19.327031	18.285365	17.329586	16.451303	15.643034	14.898100	14.210534	13.574998	12.986709
29	23.726717	22.281272	20.964889	19.764108	18.667019	17.663063	16.742874	15.898127	15.121422	14.406164	13.746477	13.137111
30	24.376076	22.844385	21.453550	20.188455	19.035767	17.983715	17.021889	16.141074	15.333101	14.590721	13.907490	13.277674

Present Value of Annuity Due
Table of Factors
Interest Rates (i)

Periods (n)	7.50%	8.00%	8.50%	9.00%	9.50%	10.00%	10.50%	11.00%	11.50%	12.00%	12.50%	13.00%
1	1.000000	1.000000	1.000000	1.000000	1.000000	1.000000	1.000000	1.000000	1.000000	1.000000	1.000000	1.000000
2	1.930233	1.925926	1.921659	1.917431	1.913242	1.909091	1.904977	1.900901	1.896861	1.892857	1.888889	1.884956
3	2.795565	2.783265	2.771114	2.759111	2.747253	2.735537	2.723961	2.712523	2.701221	2.690051	2.679012	2.668102
4	3.600526	3.577097	3.554022	3.531295	3.508907	3.486852	3.465123	3.443715	3.422619	3.401831	3.381344	3.361153
5	4.349326	4.312127	4.275597	4.239720	4.204481	4.169865	4.135858	4.102446	4.069614	4.037349	4.005639	3.974471
6	5.045885	4.992710	4.940642	4.889651	4.839709	4.790787	4.742858	4.695897	4.649878	4.604776	4.560568	4.517231
7	5.693846	5.622880	5.553587	5.485919	5.419825	5.355261	5.292179	5.230538	5.170294	5.111407	5.053839	4.997550
8	6.296601	6.206370	6.118514	6.032953	5.949612	5.868419	5.789303	5.712196	5.637035	5.563757	5.492301	5.422610
9	6.857304	6.746639	6.639183	6.534819	6.433436	6.334926	6.239188	6.146123	6.055637	5.967640	5.882045	5.798770
10	7.378887	7.246888	7.119063	6.995247	6.875284	6.759024	6.646324	6.537048	6.431064	6.328250	6.228485	6.131655
11	7.864081	7.710081	7.561348	7.417658	7.278798	7.144567	7.014773	6.889232	6.767771	6.650223	6.536431	6.426243
12	8.315424	8.138964	7.968984	7.805191	7.647304	7.495061	7.348211	7.206515	7.069750	6.937699	6.810161	6.686941
13	8.735278	8.536078	8.344686	8.160725	7.983839	7.813692	7.649964	7.492356	7.340583	7.194374	7.053476	6.917647
14	9.125840	8.903776	8.690955	8.486904	8.291178	8.103356	7.923045	7.749870	7.583482	7.423548	7.269757	7.121812
15	9.489154	9.244237	9.010097	8.786150	8.571852	8.366687	8.170176	7.981865	7.801329	7.628168	7.462006	7.302488
16	9.827120	9.559479	9.304237	9.060688	8.828175	8.606080	8.393825	8.190870	7.996708	7.810864	7.632894	7.462379
17	10.141507	9.851369	9.575333	9.312558	9.062260	8.823709	8.596221	8.379162	8.171935	7.973986	7.784795	7.603875
18	10.433960	10.121638	9.825192	9.543631	9.276037	9.021553	8.779386	8.548794	8.329090	8.119630	7.919818	7.729093
19	10.706009	10.371887	10.055476	9.755625	9.471266	9.201412	8.945146	8.701617	8.470036	8.249670	8.039838	7.839905
20	10.959078	10.603599	10.267720	9.950115	9.649558	9.364920	9.095154	8.839294	8.596445	8.365777	8.146523	7.937969
21	11.194491	10.818147	10.463337	10.128546	9.812382	9.513564	9.230909	8.963328	8.709816	8.469444	8.241353	8.024752
22	11.413480	11.016803	10.643628	10.292244	9.961080	9.648694	9.353764	9.075070	8.811494	8.562003	8.325647	8.101550
23	11.617191	11.200744	10.809796	10.442425	10.096876	9.771540	9.464945	9.175739	8.902685	8.644646	8.400575	8.169513
24	11.806689	11.371059	10.962945	10.580207	10.220892	9.883218	9.565561	9.266432	8.984471	8.718434	8.467178	8.229658
25	11.982967	11.528758	11.104097	10.706612	10.334148	9.984744	9.656616	9.348137	9.057822	8.784316	8.526381	8.282883
26	12.146946	11.674776	11.234191	10.822580	10.437578	10.077040	9.739019	9.421745	9.123607	8.843139	8.579005	8.329985
27	12.299485	11.809978	11.354093	10.928972	10.532034	10.160945	9.813592	9.488058	9.182607	8.895660	8.625782	8.371668
28	12.441381	11.935165	11.464602	11.026580	10.618296	10.237223	9.881079	9.547800	9.235522	8.942554	8.667362	8.408556
29	12.573378	12.051078	11.566453	11.116128	10.697074	10.306567	9.942153	9.601622	9.282979	8.984423	8.704322	8.441200
30	12.696165	12.158406	11.660326	11.198283	10.769018	10.369606	9.997423	9.650110	9.325542	9.021806	8.737175	8.470088

Index